Directors & Designers

Directors & Designers

Christine White

intellect Bristol, UK / Chicago, USA

First published in the UK in 2009 by
Intellect, The Mill, Parnall Road, Fishponds, Bristol, BS16 3JG, UK

First published in the USA in 2009 by
Intellect, The University of Chicago Press, 1427 E. 60th Street,
Chicago, IL 60637, USA

A catalogue record for this book is available from the
British Library.

Cover designer: Holly Rose
Copy-editor: Heather Owen
Typesetting: Mac Style, Beverley, E. Yorkshire

ISBN 978-1-84150-289-2

Printed and bound by Gutenberg Press, Malta.

Contents

PART I: SETTING THE SCENE   7

Chapter 1:   Back and Forth to Russia: Scenography as an Academic Study from
Moscow 1994–St Petersburg 2004   9
Christine White

PART II: PERFORMING PARTNERS   19

Chapter 2:   Hand in Glove: The Designer as Director as Designer   21
Charles Erven

Chapter 3:   Political Performing Partners: Director Lee Strasberg, Scene Designer
Mordecai Gorelik, Playwright John Howard Lawson and the Group
Theatre   35
Anne Fletcher

Chapter 4:   The Director, the Designer and the Ghost/Creative Team in Site-Specific
Performance Practice   53
Kathleen Irwin

Chapter 5:   Director Petr Lébl and Designer William Nowák: To a Man   71
Věra Velemanová

Chapter 6:   The Organics of the Rehearsal Room: Contemporary Directing Practice
and the Director–Designer Relationship   87
Alison Oddey

Chapter 7:   Collaborative Models: Mielziner, Williams and Kazan   101
Julia Listengarten

Chapter 8:   Problematics of Theatrical Negotiations: Directing, Scenography and
State Ideology   119
Julia Listengarten

Chapter 9:   Methodological Practices for Directing and Designing   135
Christine White

Chapter 10: The Digital Platform as a Communication Tool   149
Adele Keeley

PART III: METAPHORS, METATHEATRE & METHODOLOGIES   161

Chapter 11: The Seductive Scene or Reclaiming Spectacle   165
Christine White

Chapter 12: Metatheatre: A Discourse on Contemporary Staging   179
Ewa Wąchocka

Chapter 13: A Metaphorical Mise-en-Scène: Elia Kazan and Max Gorelik at The
             Group Theatre   189
Scott Dahl

Chapter 14: Ideational Conflict and Resolution in the Design Process: Positive
             Outcomes from Negative Relationships   209
Harry Feiner

Chapter 15: Design as Action: Jean Cocteau and the Ballets Russes   231
Gregory Sporton

PART IV: POSTSCRIPT TO THE DIRECTOR   241

Chapter 16: From *Hamlet* with Love: A Letter to the Other   243
Lilja Blumenfeld

Bibliography   257

Notes on Contributors   261

Index   265

Part I

Setting the Scene

Chapter 1

Back and Forth to Russia: Scenography as an Academic Study from Moscow 1994–St Petersburg 2004

Christine White

This book is a collection of essays from international contributors who are researchers, scholars, practitioners and teachers, and charts some of the work of the International Federation for Theatre Research working group. In this respect the essays give contexts for the discussion and study of scenography as it has developed from the research beginning in Moscow 1995 under the guidance of Eric Alexander. The chapters focus on the relationships that make scenography, the way that scenography describes designed space and ideas of what scenography is. The quest for dramatic time and space is interrogated in the nature of describing these moments of the visual intersection of the ordinary, with the imaginative. This book is original in its combination of documenting practice, discussing theory and describing processes of making performances through such interactions. The need for imagination in both creation and reception is discussed in a variety of countries, making 'seeing' believing, and the creative relationships of Directors & Designers. Where there is cross-over of subject in respect of some of the essays, they have been included to provide insights from differing perspectives both in relation to personalities and the politics of productions, their contexts and differing ways of working.

In the summer of 1994 I joined another 11 concerned academics and practitioners in a dark and very hot room in Moscow at the World Congress of the International Federation for Theatre Research[1] to discuss what scenography was, why anyone would want to research it, and what should be included in such a study of it. At that time it was clear that Scenography was the word used in Europe to describe the designed space and one of the semantic challenges for the group was to describe what design for the theatre was, and how that then became scenography.[2] For example, we had a long discussion about the nature of sound as a scenographic element.

In addition to grappling with ideas amongst the 12 of those present, we discussed what we were involved with and concerned to address in the theatres and function rooms, which were part of the conference experience. Eric Alexander was instrumental to the development of such a research group and without him the study of scenography in the context of the International Federation for Theatre Research would not have been founded. By 1996, we had 80 members who were practising and researching scenography and through Dr Eva Sormova, a quadrennial meeting on scenography was developed to occur concurrently with the Quadrennial World Competition for Scenography in Prague.[3]

The research group set out to emphasize that scenography research was not simply to be regarded as a sub-group of Theatre History, but that there was a need to develop a separate identity for this research topic. The objectives were to promote an investigation of the history, theory, politics and practice of scenography, as defined as: stage setting, costume, lighting and sound design, and all other visual aspects of stage performance, including masks and puppets. It was important to the initial membership of the research group to develop a new vocabulary, by which we could construct an understood aesthetics and politics of scenography. This was also important as by this means we hoped to recognize the diversity of disciplines deployed by scenographers and 'their' varied understanding of responses from spectators to designed work.

My own concerns were rooted in my dual role as an academic and design practitioner. It was becoming necessary for practice to be taken seriously within an academic context and this was most important as universities struggled in the UK with their identity in the mid–1990s. As the *fin de siècle* was taking hold of previously stable places of vocational study and philosophical debate, I, along with my students wanted to both do the work and talk about it and its impact. It is interesting to me, and also disturbing, that there even needed to be a special research group that had to be formed to give status to scenography. However, scenography has now become de rigeur within academic establishments, where everyone is concerned suddenly with art, image and the visual; where performance is described as a visual medium and the nature of the text has been re-investigated to produce an agitated state with many academics producing debates in their work about the visual nature of performance, theatre and/or drama. In fact, it is interesting to note that many forms of study once located in this area have now been re-framed in the United Kingdom and North American parlance to be areas of study, which come under the classification of visual art and design.

My own engagement in Moscow was investigating the designed space and movement in that space but addressed from the choreography of scenography and in particular this choreographic quality in opera. This research was presented again as part of the Ferens Fine Art Lectures[4] at Hull University and, later, when the presentations of the series were curated by Robert Cheesmond and formed an edition of the online journal *Scenography International*. This journal was set up with the express purpose of publishing work about scenography, which developed from the International Federation and international scenographers. With many publishers refusing in the early nineties to fund publications, which relied on colour photographs as part of their discourse, the use of the Internet and web publication was the perfect answer. The journal continues and has been recognized internationally as a valued journal of academic debate related to Scenography.

As with many areas of inquiry in academic life, scenography has been investigated from the point of view of the artist and the impact of technological change on the art of designers. Whilst many of the advances of technology and technological change have been advantageous to theatre production, there have over the last twenty years been advances in technology, which have not always been seen as conducive to the success of theatre performances as a whole. It was important, therefore, for scholars and practitioners to debate whether these advances had contributed to the sales of gadgets of spectacle, which in turn could be blamed for the reduction of the quality of writing and theatre presentation. This particular belief was borne out by the popular press, reviews by more distinguished theatre reviewers and modern playwrights themselves, who felt swamped by the technology rather than inspired by the possibilities created by it. The debate has often been badly focused on the 'chicken and egg' principle of production versus intelligent writing. As practitioners and spectators have become more accepting of technological change this has proved to be unhelpful, as it reduces the argument to the pejorative use of technology and the positive use of the 'muse'. What I believe has become clear is the need to discuss these changes and developments, especially in the light of the social and economic pressures of the late twentieth century and the burgeoning embrace of change in the twenty-first century. This view charts a continuing aesthetic of performance, which can be valid for both technological and literary works and what scenography has enabled as expression in visual terms, contributing to the development of holistic theatrical experiences and new terms such as Total Theatre.[5] I was once fortunate to be working with a PhD student, who was interested in the connectivity of scenography and performance, which led to us playing in a pseudo-scientific manner with a formulaic idea of what constituted Total Theatre.

> Scenography and Physical Theatre = Total Theatre
> S + P = TT (this is for the scientists)
> TT = S divided by P (only joking!)

However, what was exemplified by our discussion was the binary vision of semiotics and phenomenology, which seemed to demonstrate the conflict between scenography and physical theatre theories of deconstruction. Although we determined that phenomenology was certainly a more appropriate theory from which to explore a physical theatre language, with the detail of Edmund Husserl's work, it is difficult to make a precise and all encompassing definition of phenomenology.[6] However, in the basic sense, we were endeavouring to describe basic human experience, and phenomena, derived from the Greek for appearance, so it is clearly an appropriate theoretical application for Scenography. Phenomenology is most helpful as an explication of design activities, as it attempts to describe the world stripped of all presuppositions and culturally imposed expectations and naturally requires a 'suspension of disbelief'.

So what is the discussion?

- Scenography developed into a recognized theatre art in the latter part of the twentieth century?
- Physical theatre developed out of a reaction to spectacle theatre of the late twentieth century?
- Is physical theatre 'alternative' to spectacle theatre?
- Do both scenography and physical theatre collide in Total Theatre?
- What is Total Theatre?

These questions are still under investigation and the rich seams of scenographic research provide us with activity for many years to come. Christopher Baugh's book *Theatre Performance and Technology*[7] gives a romp through developments related to scenography and some of the particular inheritance of practice, however, there is much more detail to be uncovered and debated.

Painting and the Theatre

The history of a painterly style and the rise of the role of the designer are inextricably linked. For centuries the backgrounds and scenographic presentations, if we may use such a modern term to describe them, were ascribed to one person, quite often the producer, who may also have been the actor-manager. However, these visionaries were not totally alone in the presentation of the theatrical piece. The scenic artists, who were inevitably part of that team, whose own style and ideas became part of the production, made a major contribution to the production. These people are very rarely credited and so we recognize instead, the work of Inigo Jones and Henry Irving as revolutionary in scenographic terms. This mimics the hierarchical structure not that indistinct from the patriarchy of the monarchy for which the Stuart Masques were created. We see the artistic and aesthetic vision of one artist brought to performance at the Stuart Masques, written by Ben Jonson, and designed (and in many senses directed), by Inigo Jones, as their relationship charted the debate in the 1640s of poetry versus spectacle at its most virulent and vitriolic. Jonson frequently commented on how his work was swamped by spectacle. The effects created were technologically fantastic; however, the masques were of their time and were superseded by a written theatre in England of the late seventeenth century. From then on the kinds of scenographic presentations presented were in the form of backdrops to the action. During this period the influence of the Fine Arts was paramount and thus an array of artists was commissioned to provide backdrops to scenes. Indeed, a number of artists were used for a particular play, as unity of space was not a consideration. The artistry of the artist was celebrated; the fine detail and depiction of nature and light were acclaimed.

Martin Meisel in his book *Realizations*[8] examines the changing relationship between art and theatre in the nineteenth century. He suggests that Irving's Lyceum production in the 1890s was the culmination of this relationship. The work of the Grieves family right through the nineteenth century also illustrated the link between the classical rules of art, which prevailed, rather than rules of theatricality. The subjects to be painted and how they should be organized, on a vertical or horizontal axis, and the way in which the paint was applied with no visible brush strokes and a highly varnished finish,[9] illustrated the symbiotic relationship between the two-dimensional art and the three-dimensional performance. The symbiosis was destroyed when technology and philosophy crashed in on the gentle art and this took the form of revolutions in many different areas. The industrial revolution during the eighteenth century had changed the nature of the landscape in which people lived. It was no longer a tranquil and beautiful environment and people were herded into cities to work in an environment of chimneys and engines; England moved from a rural to an urban society. By the end of the eighteenth century the playhouses had increased in size to accommodate the popular performance genre of spectacle theatre, which was a combination of music, opera and ballet with acting that was not very subtle because the playhouses were enormous: 'Without subtlety in acting, fine characterization, upon which modern tragedy and comedy of manners both depend, is impossible.'[10]

The profit motive and commercialism of the theatre as a leisure industry became more prevalent. Audiences of the eighteenth century enjoyed all manner of special effects created by instantaneous changes of elaborate scenery in plain view: 'One cannot argue that the emphasis on scenes and machines came solely as a response to commercial drive. Rather the impulse was, at least in the beginning, theatrical.'[11] If this heritage of the mechanistic is linked to commercialization, then it may go some way to explaining the early questioning of technologies of spectacle used in the late twentieth century and their gradual acceptance in the twenty-first century. These early flirtations with technology suggest that the antithesis of literary performance to spectacle theatre may well be rooted in the prejudices from both Jones and Jonson, and the nineteenth century. As the quote above suggests there are excesses to everything, and the flooding of the Lyceum for battles of ships in the nineteenth century, is perhaps one of the larger excesses.

However, there was a direct relationship to practice in the Fine Arts, and with the addition of mechanisms during the nineteenth century. As products from the industrial revolution penetrated the theatre walls to be used as a greater means of creating theatrical effect, the work of painterly artists still filled the large expanses of space for scenic decoration and it was the verisimilitude of the effect which was celebrated: 'The splendour of the scenes the ingenuity of the machinist, and the rich display of dresses aided by the captivating charms of music, now in a great degree supersede the labours of the poet.'[12] So, we return to the concern, which first reared its ugly head with Jonson and Jones, of conflict between text and image. The image, the effect, becomes synonymous with the technology and, as such, is to be damned because in our time, a time of the electronic and digital image, it is seemingly so easy to produce a visual experience, the image does not have the weight of the word, and yet, as we shall see from further research, the image is often even more powerful.

The Economics of the Image for Theatrical Production

Inherent in the power of the image and the visual presence of scenography was also the investment in the image over the word. Over the latter part of twentieth century theatre production, companies have invested in technology, hardware, software and mechanisms, to provide instant emblems of production. What has occurred is the visual image as the unique selling point of productions rather than an investment in the written word. This sort of investment is not unusual in the economic climate of global capitalism, which has enabled the development of spectacular productions for a world market, either on tour or in a production of the famed original, in the capital cities of the world. This is not to say that the image makers, in this instance the scenographic team, have seen the investment in their art but the larger producers (as with their eighteenth century counterparts), have seen fit to fund theatrical tricks that will bring an audience to the theatre.

It is here where the discussion of contemporary performance reaches a new polarity. Are we talking of a conflict between writing and design? Or, is it that the notion of the written performance is now a form which looks less and less like a screenplay with fewer scenes of dialogue and more scenes of action or illusion, metonymy and emotional hook?

The modern scenographic team made up of set designer, costume designer, director, lighting designer and sound designer has, in fact, evolved due to the rise of particular technologies, which in their initial phase were thought to enable a particular 'auteur' to produce a signed piece of work. The developing technologies and the changing of the theatre spaces has meant that we now more legitimately speak of a scenographic team rather than the single director-auteur.

Whilst practitioners in the profession have for some years been discussing their work from the point of view of a scenographic team, the popular media and even more erudite theatre critics and academics still refer to the auteur of a particular piece as the director. Whilst the image versus word conflict has been well documented as a problem for theatrical effect in previous centuries, it is worth noting that this conflict becomes most apparent when artists (and I use this term for the collective of people of different skills and backgrounds who work in the field of performance) from other backgrounds wish their own skills to take supremacy and be of popular appeal. This is apparent in the conflict between Ben Jonson and Inigo Jones. There are no complaints documented of Jones' concern that the poetry of Jonson would detract from his design, but rather the reverse. It is clear that the scenographic team combine their skills and understanding of their specialisms to produce a piece of performance, the value of which is not more or less enhanced by one or other artist's signature on the production, but is enhanced by the cohesive use of all theatre arts to create another three-dimensional live one; this being the difference and the strength of the word and the image; the light and the sound and substance of performance.

In this volume there is the opportunity to review the work and working practices which have operated over the twentieth century, but there is also an opportunity to understand new attitudes to the process of production; a consideration of the relationships of creativity, which are made from the politics of the time but also of the people designers are with, in the room. This was an area which we discussed in our original meeting in Moscow in 1994, and which comes up again and again in this volume: the relationships of directors and designers and how the working partnerships progress. In many ways, this volume documents the struggles of those relationships. Struggles in production processes, which are usually fore-grounded by later changes of practice, have destabilized some creative practices but few established and funded, building-based companies can countenance moving away from the capitalist structure by which theatre and performance is made, in specified production periods, and it is this structure which rarely allows for experimentation. So after more than 100 years of research and practice begun by Appia[13] and Craig,[14] we still have structures for making theatre and performance which preclude the experimental and limit the confluence of practices that permeate the creative process of a rehearsal space, where not only directors and actors are working on the floor, but so also are designers and technical specialists and an array of other talented creative practitioners. In a recent Platform Event interview at the Royal National Theatre with the director Declan Donnellan,[15] his interviewer Alison Oddey[16] asked him about his new company and relationship with actors in Russia. He was passionate about, '...my Russian company...Cheek By Jowlski...', but what he was most emphatic about was the freedom created by those funded companies with full-time actors and a company of permanent practitioners who, as within any factory, are specialists who are passionate about their product.[17] Performance practices are directly influenced by the means of production, as is demonstrated by different modes of operating for devising, or directing. However, space must be given to the ideas of individuals, as they attempt to express our culture through performance, if a performance is to act as a voice of the human spirit. For what is the job of the director and the designer, the scenographic team?

In the St Petersburg of 2004, capitalism has changed the nature of the Russia that I saw presented in Moscow in 1994. In ten years, the enthusiasm for the arts has become a middle-class pursuit and there is poverty on the streets, the like of which was not present a decade earlier. What does the theatre of Russia project to the rest of the world? A marvellous production of Chekhov's *Uncle Vanya* directed by Lev Dodin,[18] which is now a global product touring Europe and America? Whereas, in Moscow in 1994, I saw a moving production of Eugene Ionesco's *The Chairs*, the auditorium filled with workers who had just left the factory when the show started at 7pm. They seemed to arrive from out of nowhere and it was completely sold out. The content was raw as the old man and old woman of the story died, unable to hear the message or understand the communication intended at the end of the play. The audience stood on its feet for 10 minutes, clapping, and then left in an instant as one unit of emotionally charged individuals. They disappeared into the streets as magically as they had arrived for the start. In St Petersburg of 2004, we celebrated the production values, the sound of the language and excellent performances, but the middle-classes had toned down this message; it had been absorbed in their outer apparel and did not reach into their hearts.

In this introduction I have talked of scenography, as a dynamic for performance; if it is to touch the spectator, then it must sing as well as move. It must touch the core of the spectator so that the scenography is spoken of again as the whole experience rather than its parts. That is the job of the scenographic team.

My thanks to my original companions for their inspiration and communications:

Eric Alexander, Martin Drier, Francis Reid, Roswitha Flatz, Robert Cheesmond, Erik Ostuud, Jerry Bangham, Elena Strutinskaya, Heather McCallum, Octavio Rivera, Jan Erik Leijon.

Notes

1. IFTR/FIRT, the world organization for theatre research, which has annual conferences and meetings to discuss and present research in theatre and performance.
2. Christopher Baugh's theory is that this word directly relates to Josef Svoboda and his work as a visionary of the kinetic possibilities of scenography. See *Theatre, Performance and Technology*, Palgrave 2005. However, for alternative views, see also Howard, *What is Scenography?*, Routledge, London, New York, 2002.
3. Known as the PQ, this competition is put together and incorporates design elements from all the theatre crafts alongside architectural design for theatre spaces. The Golden Triga is awarded to the winning country to celebrate their country's entry of top work from the previous 4 years.
4. Ferens Fine Art Lectures are themed events celebrating aspects of fine arts practice. This was an interesting series as it included scenography within the fine arts context. The lectures in this series are published in *Scenography International*, www.scenography-international.com.
5. Originally a concept from the Bauhaus, Walter Gropius designed such a theatre space for the director Erwin Piscator. It was an attempt to combine different architectural stage forms in one space. However, the funds were never available to make Gropius' plans reality. See Gropius, W., and Wensinger, A.S., *Theatre of the Bauhaus*, Baltimore, John Hopkins University Press, 1961.
6. Husserl, E., *The Crisis of European Sciences and Transcendental Phenomenology*, Evanston, IL: Northwestern University Press, 1954, 1938.
7. Baugh, C., *Theatre Performance and Technology:the development of scenography in the twentieth century*, London: Palgrave Macmillan, 2005.
8. Meisel, M., *Realizations:Narrative, Pictorial and Theatrical Arts in Nineteenth Century England*, Princeton NJ: Princeton University Press, 1983.
9. Hamblin. J., *The artistic approach of the Grieve family to selected Problems of Nineteenth Century Scene Painting*, The Oliver State University Ph.d. 1966 Speech – Theater, Ann Arbor Published University Microfilms International.
10. Hamblin, p. 14.
11. Kenny, Shirley S., *British Theatre and The Other Arts*, 1660–1800, Washington: Folger Press, 1984, p. 18.
12. Ibid.
13. See Beacham, R., *Adolphe Appia:Artist and Visionary of the Theatre*, London: Routledge, 1993.
14. Craig, E.G., *On the Art of the Theatre*, London: Heinnemann, 1911; reprint Mercury Books, 1962.
15. Director and founder of the touring theatre company Cheek by Jowl; Associate Director Royal National Theatre.
16. Oddey, A., *Devising Theatre*, London: Routledge, 1994, 1996; *Performing Women*, Palgrave, 1999, Palgrave Macmillan 2005; *Re-Framing the Theatrical: Interdisciplinary Landscapes for Performance*, Palgrave Macmillan, 2007.
17. Platform Event, Royal National Theatre London, Cottesloe Theatre Interview by Alison Oddey, 9 November, 2005.
18. Director of the Maly Theatre, St Petersburg; See also, Shevtsova, M., *Dodin and the Maly Theatre*, London: Routledge, 2004.

Part II

Performing Partners

Chapter 2

Hand In Glove: The Designer as Director as Designer

Charles Erven

If the goal of a production is to achieve a proper form for a dramatic work of art, it must be organized into a cohesive unity. This fundamental idea transformed twentieth century theatre. Theatre artists experimented with various collaborating teams in search of this elusive goal of perfect form. The Director and The Designer emerged as dominant players in the creation of this form. Although actors remained the focus of the drama, such visionaries as Gordon Craig and Adolphe Appia helped us understand that they were, in fact, another of the elements to be orchestrated and composed into the final truthful shape of the drama. How this organic form is to be realized underlies the evolution of the wide variety of director/designer relationships and approaches at work in the theatre today.

As a serious design student in the early 1970s, I, like many other stage designers, adopted the artistic goals set forth by Appia and Craig at the turn of the twentieth century and brought to the United States by Robert Edmund Jones. The concepts of three-dimensional scenery and lighting composition rhythmically connected to the dramatic conflict and movement of the script were ingrained in me by my teachers who traced their line of teaching directly back to Donald Oenslager, Jones's assistant in New York in the 1920s. My course work also included a serious exposure to directing, in theory and in practice. Since that time I have worn both hats from time to time, although I am primarily a professional stage designer. Understanding the nature of the designer-director relationship has been an ongoing process for me. Most of my knowledge about this relationship comes from practice and explorations of twentieth century artistic theory through production. I have worked with a variety of American and international theatre artists, sometimes as the director, mostly as the designer, over the last thirty years. In preparation for writing this chapter, I asked several of these artists to reflect on the nature of the director/designer relationship. Their responses confirmed a wide range of approaches to understanding this dynamic interchange. While they all acknowledged that the primary responsibility for the final choices of a production lies with the director, how a production's final form emerges is as varied as the individuals involved. Some of the productions we have worked on will be used to demonstrate the dynamic of the director/designer relationship being discussed in this study.

Since Gordon Craig first presented his vision of a new theatre over one hundred years ago the question of the fundamental nature of the relationship between the director and designer of theatrical productions has lead to a variety of answers. Craig, echoing Appia, called for a greater integration of scene with voice in crafting this new theatre. In 'The First Dialogue' of his book, *On the Art of the Theatre*, the Stage Director informs the Playgoer that the father of the dramatist is the dancer and not the dramatic poet because dramas are created to be seen by audiences, rather than to be read by listeners. It is the movement, the gesture and the sweep of colour which captivates audiences, '…more eager to *see* what he [the dramatist/ actor] would *do* than to *hear* what he would say'.[1] In other words the interaction between the actor's body, the design of space and the visual imagery is paramount for a theatre audience, the literary less so. As evidence, he notes that even audiences far in the rear of playing spaces, sometimes out of ear shot, can be captivated by action, be it poetic (dance) or prose (gesture). Even for these distant viewers, the empathetic recognition of human shapes moving through a space can draw the human imagination into the consciousness of the performance. Craig clearly championed a new vision for the role of design in theatre. If visual images of actions received by the audience are perfect, the highest levels of dramatic art can be attained and a form actualized. For Craig, this perfection involved the correct rhythm of movement and scene, along with colour line and action, and the artist who ultimately crafts it is the director, who in essence orchestrates the design of the production.[2]

This idea was succinctly communicated to me by Christopher Catt, (Chair of the Theatre Programme at Wagner College and former artistic director of the Lambs Theatre in New York City), when we first collaborated on a production of *Cabaret* for a summer company in Southern California in the mid-1970s. He noted that the more he worked with actors who could act (versus having to teach craft in rehearsals), the more he realized the process of directing was actually one of design, in which the director organizes all of the component elements of a production (of which acting is one) into a cohesive whole: the final form. He was, of course, referring to the creation of the total *mise-en-scène*, which includes but transcends the more pragmatic issues of creating ground plans, models, costume sketches and light-plots. Moreover, his comments go directly to the question of where lies the boundary between the respective domains of director and designer.

This chapter uses the metaphor of a hand in a glove to describe the designer/director relationship. Which is the hand and which the glove depends on one's perspective. If the designer is the glove, or the form encasing the production, it must fit the hand, have a good shape and be flexible. If the designer does not understand the needs of the director and actors the glove may be too tight, rigid and restrictive, or it may be too large, ill-fitting, loose and sloppy. It might actually fall off. If the director is the glove, having a clear image of the final form of the play, the hand of the designer must be managed so the resultant content fits (or fills) the shape or concept of the glove. In this case, the director must guide the hand (the design) using its own tools and terms – space, proportion, movement, colour, texture, light – in toning the design to fit the preconceived glove. Therefore, the designer who directs and the director who designs best understand this fit.

Inevitably the stage designer directs options for movement by providing levels, entrances, physical obstacles and motivational objectives for actors. Directors exploit these options to design and create compositions which reveal the conflicts and action of the play. Designers provide textures, colours and volumes, line, highlight, shadow and contrast to stimulate the senses of actors and audiences in kinaesthetic and visual ways. Directors integrate actors into and out of the environments created by designers. Designers plan for and accommodate the needs of actors, directors and audiences to precisely encapsulate and express emotions, attitudes, conflicts and ideas. Collectively, a sensual form emerges, capable of containing the content of the play. Ultimately, it is the inclusion of the actor into the composition which enlivens the scene and, around which, all of the production should be designed by both director and designer.

If the ultimate purpose of directing is one of design, putting all the pieces of a production (actors included) together, then a designer who understands directing can also fashion and guide the production into its final form. To fully participate in the creation of this final form, the designer directs by anticipating and offering directorial choices, providing spatial and compositional options and laying a foundation for the final shape and image of the production. In this way, the stage designer actually meets the director half-way and may, at times, so significantly solve problems of form that the director needs only integrate the actors and acting into the spatial arrangement provided. I have experienced this situation many times, both as a director and as a designer. Two examples will demonstrate the power of the design to direct a production.

At our first meeting to discuss the previously mentioned production of *Cabaret* in 1978, the director, Christopher Catt, presented me, the designer, with a photo of a contemporary design of Wilfred Minks. He offered this as a style he liked for the show. Such was the power of his suggestion that I was able to design the production quickly and present Catt with a storyboard layout of the entire show, its shifts and timing, the next day. Using flown practical doors and oversize painted panels and portraits, projections and easily shifted scenic units, the design so completely resolved issues of blocking, transitions, timing and placement of obstacles that Catt remarked at the opening of the show that this was the first time he'd ever had a show directed or 'blocked' by a designer. He seemed surprised that such a thing could occur. The scenic solution provided such a solid foundation for the form that the show blocked itself and the director was able to concentrate almost entirely on developing the acting and integrating the conflict and movement into the scenic structure. The resultant style was risky and everyone was challenged to push beyond preconceived boundaries to assemble a show so integrated that audiences sat through the entire production during an air-conditioning breakdown in 100 degrees heat. The makeup melted on the actors' faces, but the audience remained in their seats until the end.

In 1996 the tables were turned when I was the director of *Dr. Faustus*, for which the sets and costumes were designed by Lucie Loosova, a scenographer from Prague. Loosova wrote that: 'When the hand is [the] director and [the] glove [the] designer I do not think that the designer is just [an] executor – he or she has creative ideas for the costumes and stage, which have to go together with the story.'[3] Her understanding of the designer as a powerful creative force in determining the final form of a production was clearly demonstrated in the costumes and set she created for this play. She further notes the, '...designers effect on the piece is BIG...because I am creating the art world, which is meaningless without the director.'[4] The art world created for this production consisted of two inches of sand filling the entire stage floor in a thrust configuration assembled in a wonderful black-box theatre. Large panels at the rear opened and closed to reveal Hell, and scenic units were reduced to the barest minimum, usually easily-shifted furniture. The rough power of this primitive playing space was immediately evident and transformed my entire approach to the production. Her design released my imagination into a vastly more mystical and theatrical realm. Suddenly, actors could wrestle, fall and perform all sorts of physical action safely, as if at the beach. Scene shifts became virtually instantaneous and choreographed. Locales flew around the space. Focused and dynamic movement of mood-enhancing light rapidly followed the progression of the action around the enormous playing space. The possibilities became endless. Although I, as director, actually determined the blocking and composition, the design powerfully directed the pace and timing of the show. Her scenographic solutions for *Dr. Faustus* fully displayed the directorial and conceptual ability of a truly theatrical designer to solve the issue of form for a play.

Within this great openness, Loosova's costumes provided the anchor and structure necessary to keep focus on the content and style of the play. The mystical transformative and transcendental effects of costume, makeup and mask are well known in the theatre and Loosova used them to great advantage in costuming this production. Most of the characters of Marlowe's play are symbolic, rather than individualized, and Loosova's costumes helped transform actors into archetypes. Some of the costumes were so rigid and iconographic as to make all the necessary statements about character simply by putting the actor inside and asking him or her to move or just stand appropriately in the sand. This was especially true for the many small characters (such as the Duke and Duchess of Vanholt, Helen of Troy, and the Emperor) who populate the play but who are provided with very little textual support to develop into fully-rounded characters. They became expressive images, revealing more of the costume designer's insight than the playwright's description. Other costumes (especially the revellers in the tavern, the jester and Wagner) were very loose and conducive to a full expression of clown-like body movement, which was further facilitated by the sand floor. Again, the costumes revealed a directorial concept and method in the design. The main characters wore very simple, historically-contemporary costumes, which made them relevant to a contemporary audience, and which, allowed them to enter in and out of the variety of physical, mental and spiritual states of the play. Finally, the small vignettes of the seven deadly sins were transformed into a pageant of moving tableaux built around the costumes. Of particular note was the costume for gluttony, which included a fully laden table suspended from the actress's hips and which could travel with her wherever she walked on stage, and the dominatrix-driven cart pulled by a large muscular man representing lechery.

The designs were so powerful and visual that actors were immediately inspired to become specific characters and my role as director could be focused primarily on the orchestration of movement into dramatic confrontations, which were visible and well lit. This was a case where a powerful scenographic vision guided the play. It reflected in the designer a thorough understanding of the theatrical and dramatic, of how magnificently-costumed characters organized in a space could be capable of telling a powerful story.

A conscious awareness of the ultimate integration of the other's efforts provided the most beneficial foundation for the work of both director and designer. As the director guides actors toward character actualization, an awareness of the contribution of the design can fruitfully underscore and enhance that development. In addition, a director who understands the potential of the designer's domain to provide actors with additional stimuli to abandon self and assume character encourages the use of scenographic technique as a dynamic interactive tool.

Among Adolphe Appia's great contributions to the *mise-en-scène* was his insistence that scenic space and objects become three dimensional, fully lit and active on stage. His work with Jacques Dalcroze at Hellerau in the 1920s explored the interactive nature of scenery, levels and space with actors and action. Directors and designers who know how to exploit this kinaesthetic potential collaborate to bring the most powerful form to a piece. Several of the directors and designers who provided commentary for this chapter specifically identified as central to their work, the dynamic ability of scenery to become an additional actor.

Both Lucie Loosova and Danila Korogodsky, a St. Petersburg stage designer living in Los Angeles, speak about the designer creating a unique world or theatrical space, in which stories may unfold for audiences. As Loosova states: 'The designer is creating a new world for the director to live in…I, as the designer, have to bring the audience out from [the] real world…to another reality…to live the story through.'[5] Korogodsky sees his function as, '…a helper, a servant of a story (not a director, but a story).'[6] He further states: 'I create spaces in which stories happen, so when I talk with my directors, I like to talk behaviour and how the worlds we create will influence character's behaviour…So you talk actions and situations, and motives and psychology…That leads me to the invention of the world.'[7]

For Korogodsky, however, the most important part of the designer/director relationship occurs during the initial meetings to discuss the play. He wrote: 'I like directors who do not tell me what to do, or what their needs are, but the ones who are scholars of life and who trust me to do my job, but provide me with exciting humane challenges connected to the stories we deal with.'[8] For him the reason to do any play today requires determining the conceptual core of the show beforehand. This discussion should not be about theatre, but about life and it should use the, 'language of poetry and visual associations' rather than mere logic.[9] As a designer, Korogodsky, is very forceful in his use of poetry and visual associations to create spaces, in which stories can be told. They are always connected to a deeply-felt conceptual impulse. Once this is established he provides fully committed and complete visualizations, which demand recognition by director, actors and audience. For Korogodsky, designs should be metaphoric instead of merely illustrative. When a director encounters one of his designs, the scenographer has already made a profound statement about the content and purpose of the production. Much of the final form is already there, waiting only for the contextual conflicts of actors integrated into the space.

I directed three productions in the mid-1990s designed by Korogodsky. Each of the sets and all of the costumes were firmly rooted in a clearly thought-out artistic metaphor. Each demanded a fully experimental commitment on my part in order to direct on them. Our second collaboration, a production of *The Adding Machine* by Elmer Rice, most dramatically demonstrates how a design powerfully affects the direction. The metaphor for this 1920s American play was a merciless capitalist meat-grinder throwing Mr. Zero and all ciphers of the world into a pit after devouring their energies and replacing them with the newest labour-saving technologies: the adding machine. Along the way the scenes include the office, the home, a court, a prison, a graveyard and a rendezvous in heaven. The scenic solution was a large ramp about sixteen feet wide (4900mm) at a very steep angle of about 35 degrees rising to fourteen feet (4300mm) off the stage floor at the back. At the front of the ramp all of the traps in the stage floor were removed to form a huge hole around, which smaller six-foot deep (1830mm) ramped platforms of a similar angle formed a continuous walkway around the pit. The ramps were steep enough to require focused concentration by actors as they moved and always presented the imminent danger of falling into the eight-foot deep hole (2450mm), which contained huge gym mats at the bottom to protect actors who actually fell into it.

The tension produced in actors, trying not to be discarded while navigating an unnaturally angled floor, was deliberate and mirrored the underlying fears of the characters in the play. In addition, the central section of the highest upstage ramp rotated like a grinder and could be used for entrances in a very expressionistic manner. Swings suspended from the catwalk over the hole created heaven and the pit itself became the prison. Finally, small trap doors in the smaller ramps allowed actors to enter anywhere on the walkway by crawling through the tunnels created under the ramps themselves. With a set like this, any conventional blocking and stage presentation was not possible. This design, based on a clear conceptual metaphor, determined from the start the final form of the play. It required a style of directing and acting suitable only to it. By providing unconventional solutions to space, movement and composition, the designer significantly 'directed' the production.

A director too strongly wedded to the overarching control of a production may have difficulty in adapting to such a powerful design. When an answer is provided in one fell swoop, the director's prerogative may appear to be threatened. In order to be successful, this type of collaboration requires a strong conceptual and artistic commitment by both designer and director from the start. It also requires acknowledgment of and trust in the other's theatrical sensibility, craftsmanship and commitment to the presentation of the story in a genuinely artistic form. This is not a design approach which allows for significant tinkering of concept or physical form as the rehearsal process evolves. The conceptual connections uniting the final design form cannot be individually dismantled or reorganized without serious damage to the entire metaphor. The acting and performance must be made to work within the design. In this type of situation the commitments forged in the initial meetings must be well thought-out, fully visualized and firm. The process of bringing the play to the stage focuses on making the conceptual, actual. The glove is designed from the start and the hand works to fit neatly into it over the rehearsal period.

In contrast to this approach, Ron Sossi, founder and Artistic Director of the Odyssey Theatre in Los Angeles, identifies flexibility as the most important quality in the designer/director relationship. He wrote:

As the play takes shape during the rehearsal process, I strive to keep the final form as open as possible for the longest time possible, so that it can really grow into what it should be…I very much appreciate designers who don't so much 'own' their sets that they are unwilling to let something go or radically change it even if at the very end of the process.[10]

For Ron, the design can be altered even up to the last minute to accommodate the evolution of form. Although he confers with designers on the issue, the final decision about the form remains firmly in his hand. In this case, the director clearly is the glove, even if initially the shape of the glove is unclear. He continues: 'I find that the best way to talk with designers early on in terms of sharing my vision of a piece is to speak in metaphors and the "feeling" of the piece.'[11] This fundamentally intuitive beginning, not unlike Korogodsky's preference for 'the language of poetry and visual associations,'[12] allows the production to develop in any number of ways, requires a relatively long gestation period and precludes quick scenographic answers and commitment. Rather than arriving at a clear conceptual commitment before rehearsals and set-construction have begun, the form is not finalized nor even fully visualized until just prior to opening.

Nevertheless, the task of making the poetic concrete falls to the designer. Sossi freely admits that he usually doesn't have '…the visual sense to initiate a specific design in my head. I need the designer for that, but once I see it, I know if it's right or wrong…or close or not close.'[13] In other words, he understands his relationship with the designer to be one of initial inspiration, continuous critical evaluation and final approval. Sossi continues: 'Once presented with basic sketches, which I prefer, the set can really become more of an active collaboration on a day to day basis.'[14] The scenery is viewed as participatory with actors in the evolution of the final shape but only so far as the process works to gradually concretize a less precise image originally in the director's mind.

For a production of Caryl Churchill's *Far Away*, which Sossi directed and I designed, an initial scenographic treatment was agreed upon and then systematically pared down over the next several months of rehearsal. Whole scenic units were discarded as the production evolved. Pieces were rearranged and rebuilt even as the show was about to open. The final form beautifully fit the production and received rave reviews in the *Los Angeles Times*, but it was able to do so only because of the willingness of the actors, technicians and designers to accommodate the constant re-evaluation of the director. Throughout the process the director remained the gardener, pruning the bush as it grew. Although he will readily acknowledge the contributions of the entire creative team, Sossi's stamp was clearly on the final outcome.

In this type of working relationship, the director determines the glove or form of the production throughout the process. The designers (and the actors) are asked to flesh out the hand until it fits the glove, even as the silhouette of the glove is evolving. This organic process puts intense practical pressure on designers and technicians, who must be willing to adapt, discard and re-visit up to the opening of the show, and to defer to the director's aesthetic taste and the needs of the production as he/she sees it evolving. It is imperative when working in this method for the director to be able to clearly communicate, using the vocabulary of the designer. The elements and principles of design (line, proportion, position, shape, colour, angle, silhouette, time) provide a clearer language than, 'that doesn't work' or, 'try something else'. Using this visual language under the increasing pressure of an imminent opening makes the process of re-working precise and efficient. The designer, in turn, must be willing to defer to the vision and authority of the genius-director envisioned by Wagner and Craig.

Katharine Noon, Artistic Director of the Ghost Road Theater Ensemble, also in Los Angeles, is an ensemble theatre artist who sees herself as a conceiver, whose job as director is to, 'mediate and contribute to the fundamental conversation' between designer and actor as they provide and react to each other's 'creative gifts' on a daily basis.[15] The initial concept originates and stays with her. It does not vary. The process of implementing the concept is fluid until a form emerges or must be established for some reason. In her work, ensemble and improvisation are critical as both designers and actors mutually influence each other's contributions on a daily basis. She sees the designer as, 'key to this collaboration' and a full contributor to the ensemble from the very first days of the project. For her: 'The director and the designer challenge each other to look at the material with fresh eyes.' This challenge is conveyed to the actors who 'look at their work and the piece in new ways.' In her work, the designer becomes one of the actors in the ensemble, which is collectively searching for a form to express their work. The, '...constant dialogue between action, image and text yields work that is alive and immediate,' work that speaks directly to the time in which it is being created. The final result is collective without an overt directorial stamp. It is one in which the designer works with the group to conceive and give form to the piece rather than working to concretize an evolving vision of the director alone. The process she uses requires a profound collaborative trust in which the interaction is fluid as the form of the play evolves both in conceptualization and physical reality. There is a lot of room for experiment, chance and discovery in this manner. To those used to directing already-fully-scripted plays such as *A Streetcar Named Desire* the process appears inefficient. Its effectiveness, however, serves the ensemble's goal of collectively creating a totally new work of art, which is fresh and alive. The difficulty lies in the, 'quantity and quality of constant communication that has to occur.' For her, 'the design is integrated into the piece as something essential to the telling of the story and the movement of the action as opposed to a backdrop or something that is layered on to the play, once it is conceptualized and rehearsed.' Although she as director retains the ultimate final say, the designer and the director (along with the actors) are both the glove and the hand throughout the process.

According to Mark Weil, the Artistic Director of the Ilkhom Drama Theatre in Tashkent, Uzbekistan, there are no standards or principles to which the director/designer relationship must adhere. Sometimes in his mind a strong visual idea originates, which he precisely communicates to a designer; sometimes the designer responds with such an 'unexpectable interpretation' that he abandons his original idea. Sometimes he waits for the designer to respond to the briefest suggestions from him before engaging in a scenographic dialogue.[16]

Nevertheless, for Weil to direct any piece there is the, 'necessity of form of design to connect to concept of production.'

When he came to Wisconsin in 1997 to direct a production of *Rhinoceros*, he was presented with a given playing space in an experimental black-box already built as a scenic replica of an Italian Renaissance Theatre and previously used to mount both *Tartuffe* and *Guys and Dolls*. In this case, a basic, already-built stage design was given to the director who then had to find a way to integrate it into a third, stylistically-different production. The set, as given, was unsuitable for *Rhinoceros* because it had no organic connection to the script. Yet budgetary and other concerns required that it somehow be incorporated. Alteration of the structure allowed the resolution of this dilemma but, first, a conceptual basis for the choices had to be determined. The elegant arch, which had framed the seventeenth century opulence of *Tartuffe* and worked as a traditional Broadway theatre for *Guys and Dolls,* was stripped bare to suggest a bombed-out contemporary theatrical space. All of the masking was removed and the arch with second-story balconies and ground-level proscenium doors stood nakedly abandoned centre stage; a situation not unlike the world in which Berenger finds himself. A fountain/planter lined with clay slip was built centre stage to simulate the town square, but also, and more importantly, so actors could transform themselves into Rhinoceri by rolling in and covering themselves with the mud in the fountain. Once turned into rhinos, the entire cast pranced and played throughout the wide-open space in their underwear covered with mud. The concept allowing this to occur focused on 'skeletonizing' the space to make it more generic and providing a method to transform the cast 'rhinocerotically'.

In this case, the designer had presented to him a pre-existent glove, which did not fit. The director, responding to what was already provided, visualized alterations, which were then carried out, so that the final shape became an excellent fit with the content and style. The solution for transforming the characters into rhinoceri (the muddy fountain) was retained when the production toured to Tashkent three months later. Here was a case of an ill-fitting glove altered to fit through a director/designer collaboration based on trust and common vision for the production. The design ultimately influenced the direction and the director purposefully corrected the design based on an organically-envisioned concept. As Weil wrote:

> But if it occurs, that having received a draft discussed in works, I feel that we are going in the wrong direction then I begin, as in this case, a quite complicated and long dialogue with a designer, in the result of which we come up with an absolutely new, third interpretation, that is not similar with our first suggestions to each other.[17]

Rather than entrenchment and battle, a new solution is found which meets the needs of all involved. Such was the case with *Rhinoceros*.

The traditional domains of director and designer often divide along the manner in which each deals with actors. Directors are primarily concerned with the evocation of character in all its psychological, emotional, kinaesthetic and expressive aspects, both vocally and physically. It is a process of incarnation of the spiritual and cosmic into an already existent, but different, human physical form. Designers are primarily concerned with the creation of visual and spatial images, and environments in which actors move to establish relationships, with characters and audiences. The best designs compositionally formalize and momentarily hold profound experience in a series of 'snapshots' capable of being understood, stored and later recalled by audiences. Ultimately, the unfolding dramatic action occurs in a designed space. In an ideal world, this designed space is unencumbered by mundane considerations such as budget, personnel, available talent and deadlines. A grand vision without adequate resources is doomed. Therefore, an essential ingredient in the majority of production endeavours is the ability of the artists involved, especially the director, to conceptualise the form without damage or serious compromise to fit within given restrictions.

Believing that 'Directorial vision is primary.'[18] David Molthen, Chair of the Theatre Arts Department of Carroll College in Wisconsin and a recognized international expert on Central American Theatre, was exceptionally capable of re-imagining complex scenographic problems into concise and manageable solutions suitable to smaller venues with limited resources. For the director to initiate a pragmatic down-sizing of scale is especially helpful to the designer, who can then focus on creating a workable theatrical space unencumbered by unrealistic expectations. Molthen refers to himself as, '…a most traditional director of theatre…in which the director forces the concept/metaphoric nature of a design onto the scenographer.'[19] His vision of the glove always precedes discussions with the designer, but once that is communicated, he is content to allow the designer to find the solution, to flesh out his concept of the design. Having determined the final form in his mind, he is able to direct the rest of the production in a systematic and efficient manner. Underlying his approach is a clear visual sense and a practical understanding of what it takes to get productions mounted.

Sometimes the constrictions on production are so severe that the resultant form is seriously compromised. At other times this approach forces transcendence, which is remarkable. Such was the case with a production of Stud Turkel's musical, *Working*, which presents a series of musical vignettes, extolling the virtues of working people in America. Produced in a college setting in the mid-1980s, Molthen's image was one of industrial materials, a variety of levels and a presentational dance space. He wanted it to be simple and direct, capable of rapid shifts from one occupational motif to another, in a unit set with shifts accomplished by lighting and simple hand held props. Everything was to be open and visible to the audience. With these needs clearly in mind, the set emerged as a raked wooden floor in front of a pipe scaffold of several levels capable of supporting actors. Access above was via a circular staircase and traditional escape stairs. Fireman's poles to slide down and a proscenium arch made of industrial materials completed the space. A great variety of visual images could be created in which a rapid-fire sequence of small scenes, were juxtaposed to large choral numbers staged on the open floor. *The Milwaukee Journal* critic called it one of the ten best productions in the area that year. Done on a minuscule budget, its scenographic success began with a clear, pragmatic directorial vision of the design.

Designers and directors, who understand and respect each other's domain, can arrive at a mutually conceived form for the production (the glove), which best suits the action and content of the play (the hand).

Jan Dusek, one of the originators of Action Design in the Czech Theatre and Head of the Scenography Programme at the Czech Academy of Art, spoke to a group of designers in Long Beach California in March, 2004. In his prepared remarks he stated: 'My attempt… was to prepare a theatre design, which would not be defined and created by the actors' movement only, but would also become a real part of the dynamics of the performance, basically the stage design would become an additional actor.'[20] For him the primary focus of the design is to be found in the main dramatic moments, the real dramatic action, of the script from which the entire scenography evolves. In Action Design, this search for a real dramatic action replaced psychology as the main motivation for actors, directors and stage designers. In Jan's method of designing, serious and respectful dialogue must precede all the work and provides a constant avenue of exchange whereby the final form may be achieved. As such the form becomes a truly shared vision of collaborators. He concluded the discussion of his work by clearly expressing his preference for a working relationship in which the scenographer had control over the spatial and visual aspects of the production, distinct and separate from the director who is focused primarily on the needs of actors. Once the idea is agreed upon, each person focuses on the area of their expertise, with full trust that the other is equally committed and capable of bringing the form to fruition. Such a relationship, he observed, requires a high level of artistic integrity, complete trust and a demonstrated competence for both director and designer to defer and delegate with confidence to the other. Dusek noted that such collaborations can be difficult to establish but afford fantastic results as all involved are personally and more highly motivated to struggle together to arrive at the best revelation of dramatic action. In his mind, it is the only way for designers and directors who are artists, to work. Due to the fact that his designs so directly engage the human actors, the final form becomes more plastic and unpredictable than the initial drawings or models might suggest. How the director and the actors manipulate the space and costumes determines the ultimate shape of the play. For him the hand in the glove should do something surprising and unexpected, which enhances the dramatic moments and expressive meaning of the play.

Designers plan and organize space, colour, light and options for dramatic action. They encase actors in costumes, which liberate or confine character. Directors and actors exploit and enliven the potentiality of the design elements, which in turn are capable of further inspiring the actors. All work to incarnate an honest 'gestalt' for the production. Ultimately, directors evaluate and guide these elements into a unit. Collectively the efforts of all those involved merge into the resultant form, which reveals the levels of aspiration, artistry and ability of the contributors. Audiences receive the designed results of each of these collaborations, and hopefully, a theatrical exchange of energy occurs and a sensual memory is recorded. The exchange is stored as a visual and visceral image/experience capable of being retrieved as memory in the consciousness of the audience, collectively and as individuals. In this collaboration, the process of production design becomes paramount and assumes high levels of competency, technique and artistry from all the participants. In this situation, the designer becomes a partner with the director who, nonetheless, by definition, retains the final authority for the outcome. In the best of situations, the glove exquisitely fits the hand and allows a fully plastic and dynamic manifestation of the content, conflict and intent of the play.

Notes

1. Craig, E.G., *Craig On Theatre*, (Ed.), Walton , M.J., London: Methuen, 1983, p. 53.
2. Ibid, p. 55.
3. Lucie Loosova, interview by Charles Erven, e-mail, 26 February, 2004.
4. Ibid.
5. Ibid.
6. Danila Korogodsky, interview by Charles Erven, e-mail, 17 March, 2004.
7. Ibid.
8. Ibid.
9. Ibid.
10. Ron Sossi, interview by Charles Erven, e-mail, 17 February, 2004.
11. Ibid.
12. Korogodsky, e-mail
13. Sossi, e-mail.
14. Ibid.
15. Katharine Noon, interview by Charles Erven, e-mail, 14 February, 2004. All quotations here are from this interview.
16. Mark Weil, interview by Charles Erven, e-mail, 31 March, 2004.
17. Ibid.
18. David Molthen, interview by Charles Erven, e-mail, 22 March, 2004.
19. Ibid.
20. Jan Dusek, 'Action Design', unpublished paper read at United States Institute for Theatre Technology Conference, 17–20 March, 2004, Long Beach, CA, pp. 3–4.

Chapter 3

Political Performing Partners: Director Lee Strasberg, Scene Designer Mordecai Gorelik, Playwright John Howard Lawson and the Group Theatre

Anne Fletcher

In his work with the Group Theatre, Mordecai Gorelik's use of the active metaphor is a design process coalesced. He worked several times with his friend and playwright, John Howard Lawson, across the 1920s, but it was with 'the Group' that his methods met with those of Lee Strasberg. The three artists collaborated specifically on two productions, *Success Story*, (1932) and *Gentlewoman* (1934), and it is in these production processes that their political and aesthetic similarities and differences can be observed. It seems that on these projects, Strasberg's directorial intent and Gorelik's use of the active metaphor collided with Lawson's political stance. Perhaps Mordecai (Max) Gorelik bridged the gap between Strasberg's method and Lawson's political meandering, and/or Strasberg and Gorelik's strong and persistent personalities were able to overcome the inchoate forms of Lawson's middle plays and wrench from them more commanding productions than they would otherwise have attained.

No designer collaborated more energetically than Max Gorelik and his instincts were generally correct about John Howard Lawson's pieces, with regard to their playability and the inherent messages. Together in the earlier work on *Processional*, and with the New Playwrights they tried to 'break the fourth wall,' and to introduce contemporary European styles in America. They shared an aesthetic that embraced theatricalism. As Gorelik's design theory matured and Lawson's politics became paramount, the fabric of Lawson's plays, on the surface at least, evolved into more of a socialist realism than the presentational theatre he had previously practised, but a social realism in which the protagonists waffled politically as much as their creator. As a result, it became incumbent upon the designer and director to interpret the pieces and it would propel them forward into fully realized productions.

Lee Strasberg characterizes his years with the Group as an opportunity for him to test his active training techniques, drawn from Stanislavski but heavily augmented by Vaghtangov's work, to a company over time.[1] In these years, prior to his seminal work at the Actors Studio, he was to hone his personal adaptation of Stanislavski's 'Magic If', to develop his idea of 'adjustments,' and to utilize what many others today call 'parallel improvisations' through which actors tap into the emotions explored in hypothetical experiences.

Surprisingly little correspondence among the collaborative triad of Lawson/Gorelik/Strasberg seems to survive, but while their professional interaction cannot be exactly reconstructed, enough material is available on each, individually, to draw some significant conclusions about their collaborations. Most importantly, it appears that at this point in their careers these three theatre practitioners, while more philosophically divergent than one might suspect, all passionately sought a dramatic expression that would reflect the tenor of their time, and one that would have an impact on its audiences.

The Group Theatre's power struggles, poverty, inter-personal relations, artistic triumphs and failures are well documented elsewhere, but studies of the company seldom addressed the collaborative processes. Morsels of information lie scattered amidst the countless pages on and by Group participants; but most written depictions of the group's controversies focus on casting issues and on the famous battle between Stella Adler and Lee Strasberg over the Groups' deployment of Stanislavski's system. Max Gorelik is lauded retrospectively as the designer most compatible with the company's ideals and processes,[2] but when he worked with the Group, its directors considered him 'scrappy'. Strasberg is frequently betrayed as brilliant but a bully, the temperamental genius who pushed Group actors beyond what they considered to be their breaking points in his efforts to achieve artistry worthy of comparison to the Moscow Art Theatre. John Howard Lawson's playwriting career, which he abandoned in 1937, is only significant when read against his politics. So, it is from intermittent comments by the key players and through an exploration of their theories, Gorelik's considerations of the efficacy of scene design, Lawson's political manifestos, Strasberg's emergent acting theory, that this study is drawn.

It is of special note that on the heels of *Success Story*, the Group earned critical acclaim with their production of *Men in White* by Sidney Kingsley, directed by Lee Strasberg and designed by Mordecai Gorelik. In Gorelik's papers, or in third person accounts of the production processes for both *Success Story* and for *Men in White*, there is no indication of anything but cordial collaboration between director and designer. In fact, the two men are remarkably consistent in their reflections on developing the operating scene in the latter, in particular, utilizing similar vocabulary in their descriptions. For example, each explored and theorized about ritualistic aspects of theatre long in advance of Richard Schechner and

Success Story – painters elevation and renderings.

Success Story – rendering and production photgraph.

Performance Studies. So, breakdowns in communication on and concepts for the other two plays cannot be attributed to long standing animosity between director and designer. Perhaps, with his propensity for polemics and his insistence upon the efficacy of a script sometimes at the expense of its stage-worthiness, Lawson became, 'odd man out' in such a synchronistic production process.

Despite some recognition with *Men in White*, though, the Group was experiencing growing pains and malcontent, sources of which may be sought in managerial disagreements and in the increasingly leftist ideology adopted by many Group members. Concerns festered until after *Success Story* and then they erupted. While the company often viewed the directors collaboratively collectively, (although it defined the company, the Group's organizational structure sometimes made it much more troublesome than the traditional model of the single director at the hub), their major irritant appears to have been Harold Clurman, not Lee Strasberg (or Cheryl Crawford). With both Lawson pieces, (although he received no additional programme credit), Clurman also acted as dramaturg, poking and prodding Lawson with regard to text revisions, so Clurman remains lurking in the background of

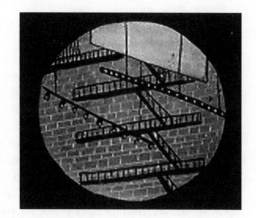

The Pure in Heart.

the production team as discussed here. Clurman even claimed that he had, 'practically collaborated on'[3] the writing of Lawson's *The Pure in Heart*!

Group legend has it that Harold Clurman literally 'talked' the organization in to being, and it was he who set the philosophy, the 'Group Idea' as it was called, of a repertory company bent on producing new American drama with the social message. It was not long, 1931 to be precise, before Max Gorelik questioned the efficacy of the Group motto and even asked the founders to consider an alternative to Broadway. In retrospect, Clurman credits Gorelik's insights.[4] In any case, the 'Group Idea' was the glue that held the company together, what got them over the bumps and hurdles they faced, and what constituted 'membership'. Participation, in such a collective, demanded brutal honesty, implicit trust, and a tireless collective vision. All retrospective analyses of the Group point to its tempestuous times as moments when honesty, trust and collectivity foundered, or when an 'outsider' was hired for a role, the design, the creation of a dramatic piece. Playwright Robert Ardrey wrote this humorous account of his work with the Group on *Thunder Rock*:

> They give you what amounts to temporary membership…If somebody in the company gets a divorce, you discover yourself on the witness stand. If the switchboard girl has a baby, you find yourself in labour pains. The light man has a brainstorm. He floods the stage with evil red light. You run shrieking to the director. Go talk to the light man, says he…An actor discovers a bad line in his part. Do you find out about it, in nicely tempered terms, from the director? No, in the midst of rehearsal the actor speaks his line, comes to a halt, looks about. 'Where's the author?' Ardrey, this line stinks. You find yourself with the business manager, worrying about the budget. You find yourself with the publicity man, worrying about the press release. You share [Max] Gorelik's headaches, while he works over the model of the set, trying to find room in the base of a lighthouse for a half a dozen vital group actors to express their vitality…A regular Broadway production finds the author on the outside, looking in. The Group Theatre production finds the author on the inside, looking cross-eyed.
>
> This process, no doubt, was not right for everyone![5]

Max Gorelik was well suited to the Group for a number of reasons, not the least of which was his intellect. As Wendy Smith explains: 'Like the Group he rejected the idea that an artist created in an unconcious frenzy of inspiration; he believed in analysing a script carefully and totally in order to create scenery that conveyed its essential message.'[6] He felt he contributed significantly to the Group and after four, then five of his designs for the company were realized, he was insulted that Clurman would not acknowledge him as a full member. Clurman, it seems, would talk in terms of principles, but in practice was often petty and personal. Personality clashes and a volatile discussion of Group principles ensued during the production processes of these Lawson plays.

On its surface, *Success Story* is not imbued with the particular brand of socio-political immediacy most commonly associated with the Group Theatre's fare. In its interpretation of the script, the Group seized the historical moment and transported the play far beyond its printed page, further in the direction its playwright had anticipated. In fact, the Group intended to 'out Marx' John Howard Lawson with the play's ending, and he fought them.

A traditionally realistic piece, especially for Lawson, *Success Story* tells the tale of the economic rise of Sol Ginsberg from his impoverished beginnings on New York's Lower East Side to the presidency of a prominent advertising firm. As radical as a youth, regularly attending cell meetings, Ginsberg adopts the cruelly capitalist philosophy that 'nuthin' matters but get your hands on the cash'[7] and proceeds to 'step on' everyone in his path, ultimately blackmailing his way to usurp the presidency from the boss who showed him kindness when he was young and brash and bright but not yet jaded. The characters in *Success Story*, although the piece is given to melodrama, are drawn with dimension, depth, and warmth. Even the seemingly demonic Ginsberg has moments of truth and vulnerability. The other principal characters include: Raymond Merritt, the boss, who has amassed a fortune, largely through his personality but who adheres to some sort of code of ethics and would never 'hit a man when he was down'; Sarah Glassman, Ginsberg's long-suffering girlfriend from his kinder days, who stands by him for close to three acts (six years), hoping the old Sol will return, but, in the end, shoots him; and Agnes Carter, Raymond Merritt's hard-boiled, realistic mistress who becomes Sol Ginsberg's wife. The cast is completed by the sorts of corporate characters one would expect to find in an advertising agency; the gum-chewing secretary with limited vocabulary; her attorney, a Yale graduate who possesses the appearance, but lacks the skill and determinations to 'cut it' in the advertising world (he appears later in the play as the epitome of the 'down and out man' of the Depression); and Rufus Sonnenberg, a millionaire Wall Street banker who warns Ginsberg that he should find some sort of outlet and enjoy life. Surprising as this sounds, the play is not peopled by stereotypes. Even in print these characters have charm and, if not dignity, humanity. They were played with passion by the Group Theatre actors: Luther Adler as Sol, Franchot Tone as Merritt, Stella Adler as Sarah. As we will see, their passion was not necessarily commensurate with the playwright's intent.

The Group's intensely emotional interpretation of *Success Story*, specifically its final scene, is where the company led by Lee Strasberg in their portrayals, most differed with Lawson: '...the utter pessimism of the last scene troubled the Group; they wanted to see some redeeming note of hope in Sol's debacle...Clurman argued that, while Sol has lost his integrity, Sarah has been true to her moral obligations and that the difference between them must be made explicit in the scene preceding the shooting.'[8]

Lawson's political sentiments were, to be sure, not antithetical to those of the Group. 1932 was a particularly poignant year of the Depression, with the Dow Jones average swooping to all-time lows, and the United States government's use of violence against its veterans' peaceful protest. As would be the case with the Vietnam War several decades later, and the war in Iraq, it became impossible for well-read artists and intellectuals to turn a deaf ear to perceived injustices. In the climate of the Depression, however, and in the theatrical world in particular, artistic and socio-political answers seemed to stem from the same sources, Germany and Russia. Perhaps it was the conflation of politics and art, combined with the overall naiveté of the Group that led so many of them to Marxism and, in turn, to Communism. Mordecai Gorelik tells an amusing tale, corroborated elsewhere, of an early meeting with Harold Clurman in which Clurman claimed that the Group would not be 'restricted by Marxism'[9] to which dramatist Sidney Howard responded, 'Marxism is a pretty roomy philosophy, Harold.'[10]

In 1932, as he re-wrote *Success Story*, John Howard Lawson, although an avowed political activist and long-standing writer of the leftist press, had not yet joined the Communist Party. Many of the Group actors had been, or were, on the cusp of joining. Clurman, although he wrote for *The Daily Worker*, would never join and came to eschew political writing as Lawson fully embraced it. Gorelik forced his first wife to destroy her membership card and, having read Marx in the original, tried to persuade his friends, (often in vain), that Communism was not the panacea they sought. In total, though, Group members and friends' leanings were to the left, and their political bent affected Lawson's re-writing of the text and their reception of his work that summer. In addition, March 1932 marked the first National Workers Theatre Conference. Many Group members, including Strasberg and Gorelik volunteered with workers' theatre agencies, and Gorelik wrote for *Workers Theatre*, aligning himself with the Theatre Collective as well. Group members would devote increasingly more time to these projects, but in the summer of 1932 the artistry of the Group and its purpose preoccupied their minds.

The Group's radicalism, affected their improvisation and summer 'skits' while they awaited Lawson's re-writes. Lawson, much like Clifford Odets although with less fame, would always be assessed in terms of his potential. Clurman believed Lawson to be 'the hope of our theatre,'[11] and a good match for the Group, 'not only by his contribution of the playwright, but by his love of discussion, even of dispute.'[12] Lawson and Gorelik hoped the Group Theatre would become their artistic home. In the summer of 1932, John Howard Lawson ruminated over his political commitment; the double-failures of *Gentlewoman* and *The Pure in Heart* would push him away from playwrighting and into the political arena altogether. At the time of *Success Story*, however, his decision had not been made.

Led by Harold Clurman, the Group pushed Lawson toward a less ambiguous ending, one in which the character of Sarah would spell out her rationale to Sol before he died: a well-made-play *scene à faire* of sorts, testimony to actor Bobby Lewis's assessment that the Group was caught in the world of nineteenth century realism.[13] 'Lawson was appalled. He didn't want the finale to be exultant; he considered Sarah as confused and neurotic as Sol.'[14] Lawson's prevalent theme in his major plays was confusion, personal and political. Unfortunately, the playwright persisted in insinuating his personal point of view in the plays' action, long before tampering with point of view was in vogue and, thus, his plays were perceived as confused rather than as depicting confused characters. Lawson viewed Sarah's radicalism as an escape. He did not create her to be a serious Communist. The Group, however, sought a resolution to the action of the play. They had no problem dealing with the play that sported an anti-hero, but their newly-discovered Marxist (read Communist) tendencies made them crave a solution to the problems expressed in the play, as did their moral and theatrical instincts. (Gwen Ballantine, the protagonist in Lawson's *Gentlewoman*, presented the same sort of problem for the company.)

Lawson responded with a printed manifesto of sorts entitled, 'Communism in Relation to *Success Story*',[15] in which he stated that the character of Sarah was pushed to her emotional breaking point; that her action was not politically motivated. In an odd twist, Lawson's characterization sided with the emotionalism inherent in the Group, while the Group desired a clear-cut political perspective. Ironically, Lawson would take abuse from the leftist press for his lack of commitment. He failed to incorporate the requisite 'conversion ending' of Marxist drama, or to clearly convert the character of Sol into a martyr figure.

'Method' acting, as codified by Lee Strasberg during his time at the Group, was in its infancy in America but the director and his actors knew intuitively that it was impossible to play a negative objective and that vacillating or, worse yet, mixed emotions are seldom if ever clearly and accurately portrayed onstage. Lawson's personal political ambivalence would take its toll on the production, and Strasberg's interpretations of plays, as well as their casting, would further complicate matters. In fact, in both plays, we find the American theatre's emotional appeal winning out over its possible polemics, and we find, curiously, that in America emotionalism often equals economics in real life, and at the box office.

While Strasberg's exercises often enabled the Group actors to stretch beyond the boundaries of typecasting, sometimes they flexed the script beyond the bounds of the playwright's intent. Such was the case with Strasberg's direction of Stella (and possibly Luther) Adler in *Success Story*, in which he returned to his focus on 'affective memory'.

John Howard Lawson was disappointed in the Group's casting of Stella Adler as Sarah Glassman. He saw her more for the role of the sex-pot girlfriend, Agnes,[16] as were some of the other Group actresses, who felt they were often passed over for Harold Clurman's 'girl'.[17] With her fiery temperament and long-standing affair with Clurman, Stella Adler seemed to get her way. The resulting double standard of company rules, applied to others yet not Adler, had caused an understandable bitterness in some of the other actresses. Known for her propensity toward strong, even over emotion, Lawson found Adler unsuited to the more demure, long-suffering Sarah Glassman. Nonetheless, Strasberg (and Clurman) were 'hell bent' on her playing the role and Lawson's opinion was overlooked, as was often the case in Group dynamics. It remained Strasberg's task to tone Stella Adler down and to mould her into the character needed. In retrospect, Strasberg was quite pleased with his results. In his own words:

Stella Adler...had an unusual emotional intensity, expressiveness, and physical vitality that the playwright felt was wrong for the character of the meek Jewish secretary, who was secretly in love with the stock boy. Lawson wanted Stella to play the role of sensuous and glamorous wife of the corporate head. We perceived in Stella, however, the presence of the emotional colours needed to create a controlled but dynamic character. I wanted a deep emotion – which Stella had – but contained in the pure, lovely, ethereal quality. It was very difficult to get that from her because of her natural tendency was to 'burn up the stage'. In one sequence, Stella's character was supposed to show concealed longing for the stock boy, but for Stella, the notion of a repressed, hidden-cam romance was alien to her own behaviour. All of her attempts were overdone, or without personal truth.

She was finally able to achieve the character by means of an unusual adjustment, which I called the 'shipboard adjustment'. I gave Stella the following instructions: 'You are on a boat, alone, it's night-time, moonlight. There's a man there, and you talk. But you know it's not going to last. And therefore, you tell each other things that you would never tell anyone you know. You don't spill your guts to somebody you don't know, but you share it. You romance the other person, and on the fifth day, you say it's been very nice, let's meet again sometime, and you leave. It's very real. But it is pure, it doesn't seek anything else.

The adjustment worked for her. She was to think that everything on the stage was actually happening on the ship; she had to create and retain the sensation of being on board the ship: the moonlight, the water, the romantic mood. Thus, she brought nothing of the way she would behave in an office onto the stage. Not only did the adjustment work but people came backstage and didn't recognise her. Friends told her that she was so different, so changed, so calm. It was probably her most distinguished performance.[18]

Strasberg worked similarly with Luther Adler as Sol, recognizing that the actor needed an in-road toward the rage this character feels, toward his humble beginnings and toward all above him in social class. However, Adler had never experienced such a reaction, so as Strasberg asked him, 'What makes you angry?' Luther Adler found outrage in witnessing wrongs to other human beings, and Strasberg began to play off that reaction. He asked the actor to substitute an injustice toward someone close to him for the onstage circumstances that were to propel him to anger. This private motivation allowed him to portray the character's anger onstage.[19]

Little is written about Max Gorelik's setting for *Success Story*, but much can be deduced from his other work and from his theoretical writings. All of the action takes place in the advertising agency office, and Gorelik's setting was in keeping with Lawson's basic stage directions. Critic Bernard Hewitt noted Gorelik's particular use of texture.[20] The designer himself later described the set as, 'one of the first modernistic interiors on the Broadway stage',[21] and Wendy Smith asserts that the set was inspired by a painting by Braque.[22] In any case, the set was sleek, shiny, modern, and high-tech for 1932, appropriate, functional, and aesthetically pleasing. It well represented the opulence associated with the upper class and by extension with corporate capitalism. Gorelik had proven himself to the Group with his remarkable set for *Men in White*, which was a unit setting that exemplified his dexterity in the area of scene changes and put into practice his idea of scenery as a machine. *Success Story's* office setting epitomized the corporate executive's wealth and taste, illustrated by the modern art on the walls and remains surprisingly contemporary some eighty-plus years later in the post-Enron world. To emphasize the rapaciousness inherent in the plot, Gorelik added corporate signage. Gorelik selected a monochromatic brown colour scheme for the play as well, emphasizing the masculinity of the office. His rendering indicates the extreme height of the office ceiling, evidenced in the production photograph.

The audience's response to the play, despite the mixed notices it received, was enthusiastic. Encouraged by the audience reception, the Group was determined to keep the production alive, despite financial exigencies. They began a publicity campaign they could little afford; further lowered ticket prices; implemented a group sales policy; and even 'papered the house'. Group members took on speaking engagements and actively pursued an audience. One of their most successful enterprises was a symposium for subscribers in which not only Gorelik and Lawson participated, but the stage electrician as well! A lively debate ensued over the despicability of the character of Sol.[23]

Committed to continuing the project, the Group actors voluntarily accepted cuts in pay, ultimately working for almost no pay at all when the corporate producer Lee Shubert, their backer, insisted on 'getting his take' directly from the box office. Harold Clurman railed against the reviewers, but as Wendy Smith so aptly puts it: 'The idea of theatre as a public arena for the social commentary and intellectual debate wasn't just foreign to Broadway reviews, it was anathema.'[24] Individual actors were praised with Luther Adler critiqued as displaying, 'precision, definition,'[25] and his sister as 'warm, simple, and vibrant.'[26] Both comments further supporting evidence for Lee Strasberg's directorial process.

The socio-political fervour of the left, its pertinence to their theatre and their audiences struck the Group hard. While the financial state was to swoop even lower with the ignominious *Big Night*, and still farther before they even began the runs of *The Pure in Heart* and *Gentlewoman*, their newfound political commitment, although often muddled and misguided, would not falter. The failure of *Big Night* forced the Group directors to free their actors for other engagements, undermining the guiding Group precept of continuous work.[27] An acrimonious and contentious atmosphere prevailed. There was even talk of moving the Group to the city of New York. These conditions set the backdrop for more turmoil to come.

Gentlewoman posed problems for all concerned. Once again reflective of Lawson's political indecision at the time, the play itself waffles in terms of attitude and genre. At face value, it appears to be written in the drawing-room mode. Its settings are three interiors, the first, a drawing-room, but beneath the play's polished veneer lies the teeming class struggle. 'Ostensibly [*Gentlewoman*] tells the tale of a love affair between a wealthy woman and a bohemian writer with radical tendencies, but it is really an examination of the nature of personal complete commitment.'[28] Unfortunately for Lawson, and for all the participants in the Group's production of the play, this examination of commitment was unclear, even with laborious re-writes.

Gwen Balantine, the upper class wife (soon widow) of a wealthy businessman and aspiring politician, is the title character in the play. She is a woman of taste and breeding, admired by all. She remains aloof and will admit true feelings to no one, until she is confronted with Rudy Flannigan, an autobiographical Lawson of sorts, spouting radical ideas. Gwen's husband, bankrupt and psychologically impaired (both unbeknownst to her), commits suicide. Gwen is left penniless and alone, despite her entourage. She has an affair with Rudy and they take an apartment together. Details of their life reveal that neither can really adapt to the other's class. Gwen thinks that she has curbed her desire for the finer things in life she has scrimped and budgeted to have. Actually, she has simply learned to take handouts from her wealthy aunt, guilt free. The little extravagances she flourishes on Rudy (fresh flowers, a steak), despite the Depression, are indicative of her still-cavalier attitude. Rudy is forced to 'sell-out' and write propaganda for money. He is constantly faced with the typical intellectual's 'writer's block.' He has a brief fling with Connie Blane, a meaningless young thing motivated by her intense jealousy of Gwen. At the end of the play, Rudy and Gwen part. She does not tell him that she is pregnant with his child.

Lawson felt that this message in *Gentlewoman* was apparent and that only through commitment to the Communist Party revolution, 'can one achieve honour in life.'[29] It was not. Neither the script, nor the Group's playing of it purported anything close to a party line. The character of Rudy is overcome by self-doubt to such a degree that he cannot be viewed as a revolutionary example. Actor Lloyd Nolan's emphasis of the character's debauchery at the expense of his politics undermined Lawson's intent. The casting of Nolan, a non-Group actor, while he was willing to learn the 'Group way', caused further unrest amongst the regular players. They also took umbrage at the posting of actors' biographies in the playbill, an unprecedented practice in the formerly egalitarian Group Theatre. Stella Adler was hopelessly miscast as Gwen, and the sincerity with which she infused the role worked against any negative view of the capitalist character. Gwen became, instead, ennobled. Once again, other actresses in the company, especially Eunice Stoddard, resented the casting of Adler in yet another lead, and one seemingly outside her range. Wendy Smith's assessment makes sense: '…Stella was unhappy and uncertain of her faith in the Group, Harold wanted Stella to be happy and remain with the Group; therefore, she would play Gwen.'[30]

Lawson failed to confront issues of form versus content and this troubled Lee Strasberg who openly acknowledged to the other two Group directors that the drawing-room style was not his strong suit as a director.[31] Strasberg was forced to indoctrinate the non-Group actors into his rehearsal practices. This time he struggled less successfully with Stella Adler than he had in *Success Story*. Even this directorial giant could not determine the adjustment that would rear up in Adler's overly emotional portrayal of Gwen. The difficulties exacerbated the actress's wholesale questioning of the efficacy of the 'method'. The playwright admired her skill in other vehicles but viewed the method, in this instance, as detrimental: 'In trying to immerse herself in the part through such devices as affective memory, she gave Gwen a 'soul' and made her love from Rudy pitiably sincere, and thus eliminated the basic reason of their separation, their inability to love.'[32] Yet again, the playwright's form and his message were muddled. References to collective farming,[33] Colonel Fowler's trip to Russia,[34] bread lines, Haven's (the butler) visit to a radical meeting,[35] stevedores,[36] the farmers' league,[37] and even Gwen's final speech about walking, 'towards a red horizon,'[38] with 'blood in the sky,'[39] fail to infuse the play with a firm ideology. They were inorganic and seemed grafted onto a realistic play. Sam Smiley fights unsuccessfully but nobly to defend the play on its rhetorical principles:

> Each of *Gentlewoman's* five scenes ends with a crisis that involves conflict, and in each a decision resolves the conflict...She (Gwen) decides not to go to bed with Rudy; to go away with him; to leave him; and to send him away. Each of her decisions illustrates a crisis in the class war... Since each decision points to the total argument of the play, the central thought dictates the organisation and supporting action the play illustrates... Money, breeding, culture, love, and even intelligence do not really matter; commitment to the Marxian cause is man's only salvation, according to *Gentlewoman*.[40]

Sadly, none of the key players involved with *Gentlewoman* dissected its structure in such a fashion. Harold Clurman recalled: 'Every aspect of the play betrayed an ambiguity that derived from Lawson's intense groping. The social problem that was at the centre of the play's meaning could not be identified with any particular situation, for what was clearly visible struck the audience as merely the depiction of a rather stupid love affair.'[41]

Clurman's retrospective analysis of the text, however, reveals him, too, some twelve years post-production, to have been, as unaware of Lawson's authorial intent as the audience he describes. Harold Clurman saw life and literature inevitably in emotional terms, and he argued with John Howard Lawson over revisions from that standpoint. While he understood Lawson's personal and socio-political empathy with both the characters Gwen and Rudy, Clurman still viewed the piece as the story of a neurotic woman who arrived at the given circumstances of the play, 'through emotional disuse and lack of connection with the world.'[42] He viewed the affair between the gentlewoman and the 'poet', as he calls him, as arising from their desires 'to resolve their lack of fulfilment'[43] and not as a physical/romantic metaphor for the political ideologies. In addition, Clurman served as the Group's chief representative to the playwright during the re-write process. Clurman was still stinging from hurt by the other members of the company's directorial triumvirate's (Strasberg and Cheryl Crawford) out of hand rejection of him when he suggested he might direct Lawson's other piece, *The Pure in Heart*.

Clurman describes his personal disappointment in John Howard Lawson's reaction to the play's poor press. At first, the playwright battled the press, openly duelling with his friend Michael Gold in the pages on the *New Masses*, but gradually he acquiesced. The Group took a few hits from Gold as well, regarding its pandering to the box office. Lawson accepted a speaking engagement at a radical literary club where he was subjected to 'a host of indictments, the burden of which was that though undeniably a writer of parts, he was confused.'[44] To Clurman's dismay, Lawson virtually apologized for his dramaturgical (read Marxist dramaturgy) qualities and vowed to do better! As for Clurman, his contributions to the radical press ended shortly after the run of *Gentlewoman*.

Mordecai Gorelik's renderings for the set for *Gentlewoman* are housed at Ohio State University and at Southern Illinois University Carbondale. William Brasmer's description and analysis of the set: 'Early Stage Designs of Mordecai Gorelik', finds Gorelik, like the rest of the Group's production team, grasping for a metaphor: '...in Gorelik's designs...we sense Gorelik trapped within the confines of two highly prescribed realistic sets but also unable to create a metaphor which would relate the action in the play to wider social conflicts.'[45] The design for Act I, a finely polished wood-panelled library, was an orange-wash drawing with the set and colonial furnishings outlined in pencil. The design for Act II, a highly feminine sitting-room, is a purple wash drawing with the outline of the set and furnishings in white tempera paint. Preliminary sketches for the scenes that take place in Gwen Ballantine's home illustrate Gorelik's ability to render realistic detail, a talent for which he is seldom credited. Gorelik attempted to suggest in his choice of colours two sides of the central female character in the play. First, the grasping entrepreneur and, second, the seductive woman, but the design subordinates line and mass (two of Gorelik's strong points) to the use of colour, and therefore, makes the designs inconclusive in what they attempt to impart.

Gorelik himself seems not to have commented on this design experience. What can be deduced from the extant renderings is that, despite the constraints of the script required settings, Gorelik attempted to comment on the play's characters and to support its action through his use of colour. His experimentation with Lawson's middle works and colour is proved by his designs for *The Pure in Heart*.

The closing of *Gentlewoman* marked a low point in the Group's existence. Tempers ran high. Gorelik forced the issue of his membership and the actors expressed that dissatisfactions and desire to participate more actively in setting Group policies were welcome. While the actors backed Gorelik, who had designed five shows by then, the directors later pulled rank and revoked the membership bestowed upon the designer at a particular Group meeting. Furious, Gorelik disassociated himself from the Group for a full three years.

So, what conclusion(s) can be drawn from an examination of these productions beyond the rudimentary idea that personalities infect production processes? They can be viewed productively as a microcosm of Group praxis and even more beneficially as a portrait of politics and production of the early 1930s. We can discover in *Success Story* and *Gentlewoman* hints of the Group at its best, when Strasberg's adjustments and affective memory practices gelled with his actors, when Gorelik's metaphors were retained, and when Harold Clurman let well enough alone. We can recall the twists and turns of John Howard Lawson's career, remembering his non-realistic forms, which appropriately satirized American life of the 1920s and forecasting his complete abandonment of playwriting as he struggled with the mastery of a prescribed Marxist structure. Above all, we can witness the development of the American theatre's distinctive voice, playing to its distinctive audience a voice that would soon awake, and sing, allowing for the emotionalism and the positive endings the Group sought, and yet ringing true with a social conscience, in the future work of Clifford Odets, Arthur Miller and beyond.

The Pure in Heart was, in the words of Malcolm Goldstein a, 'two-time loser.'[46] Written in the 1920s (and still more reflective of the Jazz age than of the Depression era), revised in the 1930s, the play was attempted by the Theatre Guild, the same week as *Gentlewoman*.

Critics reviled it, with more just cause than *Gentlewoman*. Marxist critics considered the play 'retrogressive', with *New Masses* inquiring as to why Lawson was 'willing to finish and produce such a pretentious and muddled play in 1934.'[47] While Lee Strasberg did not direct the play, Theresa Helburn did,[48] it is included here because Gorelik first designed it, and it illustrates the difficulties Lawson experienced in settling on a style at this point in his career.

Sam Smiley defends the piece on rhetorical grounds, claiming that '...when it is understood that the incidents and their sequence establish an environment and build to a climactic scene in which the socio-economic system can be blamed for the errors of individuals, then the structure of the whole becomes apparent.'[49] He asserts that the cast in the form of the melodrama, the various scenes purport the central thought given to didactic drama, in this case that 'there is more to life than the rapacious clawing toward financial success.'[50] Smiley does admit the characters' actions are unmotivated. Characterization in this piece, perhaps, is its biggest flaw. Maybe if the characters were more believable, more sympathetic, the rest could be forgiven, but as Jonathan Chambers argues, Lawson's intention was not necessarily the creation of believable characters.[51]

The play's implausible plot centres on the almost rags-to-riches rise of Annabel Sparks, a post-adolescent would-be actress who runs away from home in favour of the bright lights of New York. The theatre is Lawson's metaphor for life, or microcosm of it, with all its falsity. All in the space of a week, Annabel charms her way into the chorus of a musical; has an affair with its director; climbs into bed with its philandering but realistic producer; is fired because he is involved with the play's star; persuades a new-found funder of the play-within-a-play to finance the future acting lessons; and use it all up because she falls 'in love at first sight' with the philanderer's down and out gangster/murderer brother. In the end, police officers shoot down her and her beloved gangster. Annabel's view of the glitz and glamour of New York, as represented by the city's skyline, is contrasted with the philanderer Goshen's only honest scene in the play. Gerald Rabkin's evaluation of the text is an accurate one, even charitable: 'The obvious difficulty with the play...is that its melodramatic structure is unable to sustain the weight of Lawson's social criticism. Lawson not only uses the theatrical metaphor; he succumbs to it, and the very theatricality of the play dissipates the seriousness of his criticism.'[52]

Ironically, Mordecai Gorelik appears to have been the only participant in the production process to recognize that the play's theatricality was a matter with which to be reckoned and he was fired. Gorelik, Lawson's friend and collaborator on the non-realistic vehicles *Processional*, *Loud Speaker*, and even *Nirvana*, was the logical choice to design. Gorelik's extensive correspondence and diaries do not reveal his response to his firing, but his continued friendship with Lawson is well documented by his correspondence and anecdotally by his widow and by mutual friends. Earlier, Gorelik's designs for the New Playwrights' production of *Fiesta* were pulled as well, even with Lawson as a founding member of the organization, which makes one wonder whether Lawson's personal associations might have been as uncommitted as his ideologies.

William Brasmer rightfully suggests that the producers, 'misjudged Gorelik's sets' and the drawings indicate, 'that Gorelik had partially caught the fake romanticism of theatre life in his garish green wing flats which formed a background for the "play within the play" scene...'[53] Surely Gorelik did not miss the irony and the humour of Lawson's character Homer, the play-within-a play's set designer, a recent graduate of Yale, full of big design ideas he was eager to implement? To contrast the inner world of the theatre and the play-within-a-play with the external circumstances that affect the characters' lives, Gorelik designed and had hand-painted slides to be utilized as projections of that external world. The subjects of these slides included: (1) the tops of the telephone poles set in perspective against the sky, as one sees from a moving train for Act I, when Annabel leaves home for the big city; (2) scaffolding for Act I, Scene 2, the theatre; (3) the top of the city skyline for Act II Scenes 1 and 2.

Gorelik's settings were utilized through at least one dress rehearsal of *The Pure in Heart* when, although his sketches and models had been pre-approved, Gorelik was fired. The designer later commented that 'the producer, director, and author...were so taken aback when they saw the settings on stage that they had Jo Mielziner design the show.'[54] Probably Gorelik's design concept could not have saved *The Pure in Heart* from being the critical debacle it was but the renderings clearly indicate that he had a design concept that was in keeping with the theme of the play. It was a bold scenic metaphor, reflective of a bold theoretical mind at work. Gorelik the dramatic critic even more than Gorelik the designer is evidenced in the slide projections. In them, he sought a device for foregrounding that social commentary that is implicit in Lawson's clunky and melodramatic script.

Notes

1. Strasberg, L., 'The Voyage Continues: I, Discoveries at the Group', in *A Dream of Passion: The Development of the Method*, E. Morphos, (Ed.), New York: Penguin Books, reprint 1988.
2. Harold Clurman in Smith, W., *RealLife Drama:The Group Theatre and America* 1931–1940, New York: Alfred A. Knopf, 1990, p. 73.
3. Harold Clurman to Paul Strand 30 December 1934, in W. Smith, *RealLife Drama:The Group Theatre and America* 1931–1940, p. 166.
4. Clurman, in Smith, p. 73.
5. *New York Times*, 9 November 1939, in Smith, p. 391.
6. Smith, p. 71.
7. Lawson, J.H., *Success Story*, (photocopy personal property of Paul Mann), courtesy of David Krasner.
8. Smith, p. 97.
9. Gorelik, M., *Toward a Larger Theatre*, Landrum, MD: University Press of America, 1988, p. 7.
10. Ibid., p. 7.
11. Clurman, in Smith, p. 93.
12. Ibid, p. 93.
13. Smith, p. 91.
14. Ibid., p. 98.

15. Ibid, p. 98.
16. Ibid, p. 102.
17. Ibid, p. 114 and p. 165.
18. Strasberg, p. 88.
19. Ibid, p. 87.
20. Hewitt, B.,'Mordecai Gorelik', the *High School Thespian,* November 1941 in J. Palmer, *Mordecai Gorelik's Theory of Theatre* Dissertation, Carbondale: Southern Illinois University, 1967, p. 101.
21. Gorelik, M., 'Design for Stage and Screen: An Illustrated Slide Lecture', produced at Southern Illinois University of Carbondale.
22. Smith, p. 110.
23. Ibid., p. 111.
24. Ibid., p. 109.
25. *The New Yorker,* 8 October 1932, in Smith, p. 110.
26. *New York Post,* 27 September 1932, in Smith, p. 110.
27. Smith, p. 117.
28. Ibid, p. 163.
29. Smiley, S., *The Drama of Attack:Didactic Plays of the American Depression,* Columbia, MO: University of Missouri Press, 1972, p. 176.
30. Smith, p. 164.
31. Ibid, p. 166.
32. Lawson autobiography, p.308, in Smith, p. 166.
33. Lawson, J.H., *Gentlewoman* in *With a Reckless Preface:Two Plays by John Howard Lawson,* New York: Farrar & Rhinehart, 1934, p. 125.
34. Ibid., p. 125.
35. Ibid., p. 179.
36. Ibid., p. 203.
37. Ibid., p. 218.
38. Ibid., p. 220.
39. Ibid., p. 220.
40. Smiley, S., *The Drama of Attack:Didactic Plays of the American Depression,* Columbia, MO: University of Missouri Press: 1972.
41. Clurman, in Smith, p. 133.
42. Ibid, p. 132.
43. Ibid.
44. Ibid, p. 133.
45. Brasmer, W., 'Early Scene Design of Mordecai Gorelik', Ohio State University Theatre Collection, Bulletin No. 12, 1965, p. 47.
46. Goldstein, M., *The Political Stage: American Drama and the Theatre of the Great Depression,* New York: Oxford University Press , 1974, p. 90.
47. Mather, M.W., Review of *With a Reckless Preface…*17 July 1934, in G. Rabkin, *Drama and Commitment,* Bloomington, IN: Indiana University Press, 1964, p. 148.
48. Ms Helburn does not actually name *The Pure in Heart.* I have concluded that she directed the piece based on her mention of a play by John Howard Lawson in Theresa Heburn, *A Wayward Quest: The Autobiography of Theresa Helburn,* 1st edition, Boston: Little, Brown and Company, 1960, p.194 and Smith's reference to Elia Kazan serving as the Assistant Stage Manager for *The Pure in Heart,* Smith, p. 104.

49. Smiley, p. 176.
50. Ibid.
51. Chambers, J.L., Messiah of the New Technique: John Howard Lawson, Communism and American Theatre 1923–1937. Carbondale: Southern Illinois University Press, 2006.
52. Rabkin, G., *Drama and Commitment: Politics in the American Theatre of the Thirties*, Bloomington: Indiana Press, 1964, p. 147.
53. Brasmer, p. 47.
54. Gorelik, in Brasmer, p. 49.

Chapter 4

The Director, the Designer and the Ghost/Creative Team in Site-Specific Performance Practice

Kathleen Irwin

I n this chapter I will discuss aspects of collaboration between the creative team and adjacent communities in site-oriented performance, addressing specifically how a community claims ownership of a site and insinuates these claims into the space between director and designer. I ask the question: in such cases, does the nature of the creative collaboration differ significantly from that of conventional conceptualizing teams?

While creative dialogue in traditional performance models does, in fact, involve a community of artists who bring pressure to bear, the nature of site-determined performance is such that the dialogue expands to include stakeholders, beyond the creative team, who have a defining impact on the process and resolution of the concept. While initial steps necessitate the free-wheeling search for an emblematic host space, typically by director and scenographer, what follows is an interaction with the site, now defined by material boundaries as well as by the memories, dreams and desires of a multitude of interest groups. These include all landlords, tenants and clients, both alive and dead.

Central to this investigation is the notion, not of conceptual or artistic authorship of an event by the creative team, but of community ownership of a given site designated for performance and how these, sometimes vying, claims impact and politicize the event at all stages of conceptualization, development and reception. This chapter will investigate briefly how claims of ownership, acts of transgression and hopes for transformation determine the interaction between the creative team, the community and the ghosts that inhabit the site.

The Weyburn Project, a project mounted in September 2002 on the site of the old Weyburn Mental Hospital, represented a mad labour of love by creative team, Andrew Houston and Kathleen Irwin.[1] Issues central to the project were place, representation and performativity. The process, which resulted in a large-scale, site-specific, multi-disciplinary performance, necessitated an outreach into the community that profoundly influenced the final event.

In the 12 months leading up to the performance, Houston and Irwin invited a diverse group of theatre professionals, academics, students, musicians and performers, video and visual artists and a community of volunteers to engage in the development of a site-specific installation/performance at the Souris Valley Extended Health Care Hospital (formerly the Weyburn Mental Hospital) This community-linking effort was entitled *The Weyburn Project*. It carried, as well, the subtitle, 'The Excavation of Silence and the Discourse of Madness', revealing some of the issues we wanted to circumscribe.

The project represented a genre of performance that uses a found space as the starting point for a devised work that is specific to and inseparable from the site for which the piece is developed. Here the mental hospital took focus and became the background for devised texts that braided together both local and global issues. The eroding building provided an ideal archaeological site of research and investigation and the performance was, for actors and audience alike, an act of walking, looking and digging. The research and the community involvement stripped away layers, exposed histories of institutionalization and brought to light issues of economy, gender, mental health and universalized healthcare. It dealt, primarily, with the 'ongoingness' of this site as a powerful metaphor in the municipality, the province and in the country.

Within the community of Weyburn, the project responded to the stigma that the mental asylum represents. There remains a strong constituency that wants to demolish the asylum, not realizing that, by doing so, the stigma would only be magnified. Those that wish to recuperate the building are developing an action to transform the site into a museum or cultural centre. Either way, the project witnessed and reconstituted the personal stories embedded in the walls of the site and problematized the accepted narratives.

Although the event is complete, it has become woven into the collective memory of the community. What remains from this performance intervention is the interactive website that functions as a growing repository of oral history and will remain so, indefinitely. As well, the project seeded future projects including a published photographic collection, a new media exhibit and an orchestral composition. As well, a full-length video of the project in development has been completed for broadcast through the Saskatchewan Community Network.

The next example project is *The Dionysian Lear* site-specific performance in an old brewery.[2] The object of this community-based performance was to explore the links between space, text and self-exploration, focusing on the Dionysian aspects of ritual and performance. Initial research investigated the continuum of self-discovery that positions the use of stimulants (psychotropic drugs, alcohol) to induce, at one end, stupor or trance and at the other end, ritual, performance, catharsis, revelation, and enlightenment.

The anticipated result was a site-specific performance event that braided together this investigation with a devised text, using multiple revisions of the Lear story including Shakespeare's *King Lear*, Howard Barker's *Seven Lears,* Joan Ure's *Something for Cordelia* and Edward Bond's *Lear*. The aim of this work was to exploit the notion of spiritual blindness and self revelation to investigate patriarchy and power through one of Canada's foremost industrial families. The performance site was the abandoned Molson's Brewery in Regina, Saskatchewan, a heritage building dating from 1908. The use of the brewery expanded the concept of Lear's blindness to include issues relevant to a community where substance abuse is a significant problem. The genre of performance was large scale, site-specific and interdisciplinary in nature, incorporating the work of artists from across many disciplines including music, video, installation, sculpture, painting, ceramic and performance.

This project offered an opportunity for practical performance-based research into the relationship between site-specific strategies and issue-based interventions. In addition to the themes of substance abuse and blindness found in the Lear/Molson narratives, the site itself took a central role. Due for demolition, the performance attempted to focus the attention of the community on the passing of a building, replete with memory and history. The project hoped to educate public and municipal authorities to the notion that transitional buildings and neighbourhoods may experience sustained economic re-development when re-zoned for cultural and artistic use. Here, the initial impulse and momentum developed by the creative team was re-directed by more pressing community concerns. The sudden placing of the Brewery on the retail market and its subsequent demolition halted the project but raised public awareness and outcry.

The final project was *The Claybank Project: Crossfiring.*[3] This was a large-scale, site specific, community-based performance planned for August 2006 at the Claybank Brick Factory, National Historic Site near Avonlea, SK. What was proposed was a multi-phased project that started with a creative concept focused on performance but eliciting and utilizing community involvement and support at every step of the way. The site was again a contested one on a number of levels and it was anticipated that the communities would shape the result significantly. From the outset the project intended to develop links following a proscribed strategy.

In Phase One, an interactive web site mapped out the proposed conceptual and aesthetic approach and attempted to develop consensus in the community by communicating with stakeholders through the interactive component of email address. It elicited and archived the oral history to be woven into the performance event at strategic places. On a practical level the site served as a source of information for potential funders.

In Phase Two, the process reaches into the wider community, bringing on board artists from across a range of disciplines. This multi-disciplinarity complements the complex nature of the place itself, which functioned as a site of aboriginal spirituality and creativity as well as a site of intense industrialization that spanned the twentieth century, ending with the Free Trade Agreement in 1989. At this point, the website chat room was the discussion forum, which connected both professional artists and the interlocking communities of aboriginal and European descendents.

In Phase Three, the performance, the artists and volunteers moved onto the site, and through a workshop/rehearsal process, the performance began to take shape. The website now functions as an information centre for the media and general public and serves as a box office providing ticket information, site maps and start times.

In Phase Four, the event was mounted (running over two weekends). Afterwards, the website remained as an archive of the event and a repository for local narratives to be linked to other similar websites. Typically, as with the other works cited, all phases of the project are documented on still, video and movie camera. The film footage is used to produce documentary for commercial and festival distribution.

Community Links

The development of a community-based, large-scale, site-specific performance at Claybank was significant on a number of levels. This event focused attention and attracted artists, historians, academics and eco-heritage-tourists regionally, nationally and internationally because of its diverse approach to a complex past that included aboriginal and colonial histories as well as more current issues of industrialization and globalization. *The Claybank Project* supported issues of economic as well as cultural sustainability and addressed the acute current situation surrounding rapidly-diminishing rural populations. It bridged communities in south-western Saskatchewan, linked diverse communities of interest, artists, academics, historians, tourists and sought commonalities among indigenous and colonizing cultures who had invested this place with meaning.

How the Creative Team Works With the Community in Site-Specific Performance Practice

Scenography inscribes space in performance and has, for the better part of the twentieth century, implied the spatial organization of a play-text in a stage space to support the philosophical and ideological content of the play and the specific vision of the director. However, what can be said of scenographic strategies in site-specific performance, a hybrid form of presentation that takes its initial impulse from the material world? How is meaning deployed in a context that, while 'theatrical', is not confined to a staged experience and may embrace a variety of critical strategies for interpreting place materially and phenomenologically? What is the nature of the complex exchange between such performance and the place in which its meanings are defined? What are the contingencies that impinge on the traditionally-defined creative team when local community and individual interests intervene vociferously?

Within the traditional creative team of director and designer(s), what a scenographer does defines an approach and a practice that is wholly integral to the process. A scenographer deals with the production and reception of the visual text of a performance, including such physical considerations as the site of the performance and, together with the director, determines how the spectator functions within the framework of the performance. As such, the creative team functions collectively as a dramaturg whose jurisdiction is both aesthetic and practical. While this activity describes a recognizable function in text-centred performance in conventional venues, it plays out differently in devised, site-oriented performance. Here literary text does not take centre stage. Rather, place is privileged and the desires of the surrounding community become the chief organizing agent. While the creative team is instrumental in determining and negotiating the use of a particular site, the public's relationship to that site is a determinant. The creative dialogue opens to include an ever-expanding group of individuals as well as the multitude of clamorous ghosts that emanate from the site.

This complex unit, lead by the director and scenographer, begins to negotiate the multiple dimensions of the specified place through a process of uncovering meaning; in the terminology of site-specific practitioners, Michael Shanks and Mike Pearson, this way of working is called theatre archaeology.[4] Through this process, a place reveals, what I call, a 'spatial performativity'. I use this phrase to discuss the accretion and emanation of meaning in a particular place through time and across adjacent communities, and the subjective, reading of place in performance. There may be a better word but 'performativity', like site itself, has accretions that are useful.

The devising of site-determined performance is one constituted, more or less, on the notion of collaboration, interactivity and community/audience participation. The relationship between the creative team and the communities among which the collaboration occurs is shifting and continually re-negotiated as a variety of roles are assumed in the process that develops the performance. Employing a variety of interactive skills, the initial role of the creative team is that of the 'experiencing being', initiating a phenomenological exploration of the site through physical encounter and innumerable conversations with individuals. In the words of Suzanne Lacy:

> [in works] that take place largely within the territory of experience, the artist, like a subjective anthropologist enters the territory of the Other and presents observations on people and places through a report of her own interiority. In this way, the artist becomes a conduit for the experience of others and the work a metaphor for relationship.[5]

In this process, the individual anecdotes that are uncovered are given political value and these subjective stories provide an authenticity that has profound social implications.

Throughout the summer of 2001, using an interactive website, taped interviews and innumerable conversations, the creative team collected anecdotal data for *The Weyburn Project*. These stories recounted memories, hearsay, second-hand tales, rumours and the like. All were given equal weight, used in a variety of unmediated ways in performance and archived verbatim in the still-functioning website. In this instance, the creative team played the role of empathic witness to the community's private experiences, their needs and desires.

The creative team functions, as well, in mediating, selecting or framing certain specific information used in performance by drawing attention to details but not analysing or commenting on them. This activity provides a common ground for artists and community to come to consensus, collaborate and corroborate information. For example, in *The Weyburn Project*, daily nursing journals, patient rosters and rules of conduct were recited verbatim in performance. The strength of this recitation lay in the sharing of this with participants and audience who understood this information on a profound and direct level. The affirmation of certain lived experience frequently lays the groundwork for a critical analysis. As Suzanne Lacy suggests, '[a]s artists begin to analyze social situations through their art, they assume for themselves skills more commonly associated with social scientists, investigative journalists and philosophers'.[6]

In the uncompleted performance project, *The Dionysian Lear*, the creative team encountered a problematic situation in the early stages of research into circumstances surrounding a local brewery. This forced the early conclusion to the project but launched a political action to stay the demolition of the building. Rather than allow the local artistic community to acquire the historical space for its own use, the brewery unilaterally chose to level it for re-sale. In this instance, although the creative project was thwarted, artist activity was directly translated into community activism in an attempt to save the heritage site. Given adequate time, this transition might have been accomplished through performance strategies. Circumstances being what they were, the artists instead approached the situation through municipal government, proving, predictably, that one cannot fight city hall.

To take a position with respect to the public agenda, the artistic team must act with an understanding of social systems and institutions and in collaboration with people. The entire process is a collaboration that undertakes the consensual production of meaning with the public at all stages. This last example represents the ultimate in consensus-building between artist and community and exemplifies how ownership claims made by a community surrounding a particular site and given approbation through the process of performance development, can provide an opportunity for transgressive strategies that lead to transformation. Through this active engagement, the aesthetic practice is locked to the political practice.

In the early stages of development for *Crossfiring*, the creative team moved from the initial stage of locating a site that resonated, an abandoned brick factory, to the next stage of initiating interaction with the community to assess interest, ascertain community agendas and areas of contestation. This interface was achieved through a variety of means: an interactive website, addressing community groups and local press and, most importantly, meeting people one-on-one. All had a vested interest in the project and many wanted to represent the interests of those no longer able to voice theirs, including colleagues and relatives long deceased but still requiring attention. Typically this community of voices are far from passive, and rarely form a passive audience. They are participants who consider their investment part of the art; many believe, in fact that it is in this space of interaction between the artist and the audience that the performance happens.

Certainly audience participation forms and informs the work; how it functions is integral to the work's structure. Complexly structured, non-hierarchical, flexible and changing, the audience comprises the active collaborators without whom the work would not be realized, the volunteers and performers, about, for and with whom the work is created and, finally, the spectators who, unlike most audience members, have a direct experience with the event. Due to the collaborative process of the community-based performance, this group is well informed and actively engaged.

For example, it was frequently the case that audience members attending *The Weyburn Project* had contributed their own work journals and personal memoirs to the process and later heard them repeated in performance. As a result of the performance, individuals expanded the reach of the event by becoming politically active surrounding certain key issues pertaining to the future of the mental hospital. By connecting with a past through the very active present, the performance entered into the collective memory by retrieving and examining, partially re-assembling and problematizing fragments of the past, using both real and fictitious fragments. At least a part of the audience carried the artwork forward over time as myth and memory. In this way, such events become woven into the fabric of the community and, as Lacy writes, become 'in the life of the community, a commonly held possibility'.[7]

Places, especially places that resonate, signify and emanate complex meanings in reality and even more potently when framed by performance. Individuals and communities, whose lives are closely linked with specific sites, understand this and may become willingly co-opted, even complicit in unlocking meanings. The act of creative collaboration does not flatten meaning, rather it allows for a multiplicity and ambiguity that tends toward the social, political, universal and is sometimes transformative. When such a relationship achieves demonstrable effects, community-based, site-oriented performance is at its most powerful.

Reality Claims – From Realism to Reality

How space is mediated and embodied through time is central to the production of meaning both in archaeology and in site-specific performance. The mediation with the past, also central to the negotiation and practices of everyday life, is something we routinely do using an 'archaeological imagination' to bridge knowledge gaps and to interpret the past in the only way possible, by engaging quotidian objects and observing them through a prism of present interests and values. The results of this imagining are subjective, provisional, interpretative and phenomenological. According to site-specific practitioner theorists, Mike Pearson and Michael Shanks, this practice is also central to the production and reception of meaning in performance where site is experienced and laid claim to and contingent on the local circumstances, memories and expectations.[8]

What this section attempts is a brief theoretical investigation of the changing spaces of dramatic performance across the twentieth century. It situates the notions of site-specificity and performance against a phenomenological and psychoanalytical reading of 'home' in the literature of dramatic realism and in relationship to a postmodern, heterotopic reading of the liminal space used as performance site. In such latter-day engagements with specific places, resistant practices contest and invert the utopian notion of home within the binary of local practice and global rupture. Employing, finally, the trope of home/not home, I propose a performative reading of site to discuss spatial engagements, eruptions and excesses that characterize the fundamental dynamic of found space in performance.

Pearson and Shanks' process, 'theatre/archaeology', is to de-familiarize what is taken as given and reveal the equivocal nature of this experience in performance. This process involves an attitude suspicious of orthodoxy that acknowledges the impossibility of any final account in making sense of what we perceive cognitively, of that which was never certain in the first place. This phenomenological dilemma ponders how much the perception of reality can tell us about what is real and this ambiguity is, in fact, central to their practice. In performance terms, the spotlight of observation that brackets a situated event catches these elements temporarily in a reality based on a spatial relationship that is also temporal (containing a remembered past, present and an imagined future) between the observer and the observed. This relationship implies a performative way of being in the world, a complex way of interacting with the material word that allows for contingencies and encourages reading, as it were, against the grain, in the gaps and between the lines.

In *The Practice of Everyday Life*, Michel de Certeau reaffirms the contingency and restlessness inherent in spatial relationships specifically in such daily practices as urban pedestrian travel. These practices, he claims, reveal a non-linear narrative in the loose sieve-order of material/rhetorical detail that these actions provide. He writes:

> These heterogeneous and even contradictory elements fill the homogeneous form of the story. Things extra (details and excesses coming from elsewhere) insert themselves into the accepted framework, the imposed order. One thus has the very relationship between spatial practices and the constructed order. The surface of this order is everywhere punched and torn open by ellipses, drifts and leaks of meaning: it is a sieve-order.
>
> The verbal relics of which the story is composed, being tied to lost stories and opaque acts, are juxtaposed in a collage where their relations are not thought, and for this reason form a symbolic whole. They are articulated by lacunae.[9]

Citing the city's surface as an example, he writes that there is a charged topology of street names and places that may or may not still actually exist but remain, detached from actual places, 'a geography of meanings held in suspension'. Emblematic and emptied of their original significance they are filled up by a, 'second, poetic geography on top of the literal… meaning'. These place names imply certain promises concerning aspects that are not wholly present. The perception of such named places is complex and ambiguous in that they claim a reality but the reality is not totally given. Rather, it reveals itself in, 'successive aspects, never simultaneously'.[10] Like a child's game of peekaboo, as one aspect seems to be revealed, it simultaneously turns away.

This playfulness is effectively employed in site-determined performance, which is most comfortably, hence most frequently, situated within the context of the late nineteenth- and early twentieth century urban/industrial environments. Here, performance occupies these spaces of indeterminacy, engaging with material specificities to nudge memory, tell stories, and draw out legends, myths and dreams. What is essentially a phenomenological approach to these material specificities is, at the same time, performative, characterized by a myriad of possible hidden, contested readings and mis-readings. Herbert Spiegelberg states, 'the actual reality of non-subjectival phenomena of reality never excludes the possibility of illusion and error'[11] or, in locutionary terms, of 'misfirings'.[12] Austin writes, 'the (materialities) promise something beyond their actual content and this transphenomenal promise may, in theory, always turn out to be deceptive…'.[13] Already, within their reality, is the promise of 'irreality'. To extend the field of signification beyond Austinian linguistics, this suggests a resemblance to 'citational performativity' in that certain materialities signify or re-enact a way of being in the world but in every iteration or re-examination clear the way for other possible readings that sometimes misfire and sometimes hit their mark.

In *The Poetics of Space*, Gaston Bachelard argues that there is a sort of 'attraction for images' surrounding a valued space that transcends both the subjective or objective descriptive analysis of that space and works on a poetic level of memory, imagination and dream.[14] He claims that the phenomenologist seeks the essential nature of that space at the same time valourizing the role of the imagination in augmenting its reality. The subject experiences the space, 'in its reality and in its virtuality, by means of thought and dreams. It is no longer (only) in its positive aspects that (it) is really 'lived', nor is it only in the passing hour that we recognize its benefits. An entire past comes to dwell in (it)'.[15] Bachelard illustrates this with a thorough-going investigation of home, claiming that the constituent signification of 'the house' as the primal 'shell' colours and is the de facto paradigm for all future spatial experience. This claim is central to the strategy of site-specific performance, specifically how it engages site to explore and exploit the complexities and engagements of 'home', 'belonging' and 'disenfranchisement' for performance ends.

Bachelard's notion of the embodied house as a metaphor of conscious and subconscious human experience dove-tails handily with Una Chaudhuri's thesis on the power of place in twentieth century dramatic developments. In *Staging Space, The Geography of Modern Drama*, she links the inherent centrality of space, specifically domestic space, to the notion of modern dramatic realism and the subsequent involvement with found space that characterizes a range of postmodern performance models including site-specific work.

The shift, according to Chaudhuri, marks a movement in dramatic literature (and in signifying practices including scenography), away from realism and toward the real, defining a re-alignment in theatre and cultural studies, in which space increasingly replaces time as the significant focus of analysis. Chaudhuri foregrounds the figure of home within the broad schematic of place in drama and traces the movement in theatrical practice away from the ideationally defining notions of home and belonging within the boundaries of the proscenium stage and into dislocated sites of indeterminate signification where these ideas are inverted and contested. She writes: 'From the experience of place as one dimensional and fully determining, to the experience of place as multi-dimensional and creative, the stages of drama recount an ongoing experiment with place (reflected in – though not mechanically parallel to – the ongoing experimentation with stage space)…'.[16]

Chaudhuri examines the motifs that mark dramatic realism, the myths and symbols of the house and family, in a psychoanalytical analysis that is fully grounded in the physical setting of the realistic stage and echoes Bachelard's treatment of home as both nurturing and as a well-spring of all spatial embodiments without which 'man would be a dispersed thing… cast into the world'.[17] In both analyses the theme of home is fundamentally significant. In dramatic realism, in the discourse of psychoanalysis and phenomenology, it represents the starting point, cradle, site of our intimate lives, the localization of our memories and the place to which we all would return, if only in reverie. Bachelard's notion that all inhabited space bears the essence of home suggests that the relationship between people and place is profound, fundamental and conveys meanings that include the tropes that Chaudhuri employs of belonging/exile and ownership/transgression. She makes the claim, in fact, that the complex relationship between people and place, contained in the imagining of home space, has been the defining trope of dramatic realism and continues to be examined through the lens of post-realist dramatic experiments. The investigation of this she labels 'geopathology', employing the term to link the themes and the problematics of plays and place with the numerous spatial experiments that tested 'the possibilities of plays and place' over the span of the twentieth century. The experimental impulse that, 'began with Dadaism, continued with Artaud's Theatre of Cruelty and Brecht's epic theatre, and eventually exploded in myriad forms variously known as happenings, environmental theatre, performance art, and finally site-specific theater',[18] reflects the increasing engagement of theatre with resistant practices, marginal populations and transgressive spaces including 'liminal space, third space, not-space, impossible space, the city'.[19] Her statement that, 'this new dogma is rooted in a phenomenology of space according to which the position and orientation of bodies in a specially designated…environment add to or mould the meaning of what those bodies say and do',[20] is an elaboration of the terms of site-specificity, which began to emerge in performance and exhibition strategies in the 1960s and 1970s when, as Nick Kaye claims, site-specific work began to engage space to explore and articulate the exchanges between the work of art and the places in which its meanings are defined.[21]

Reflecting, as well, on the problematics surrounding the relationship of people to site, Bachelard employs the term 'topoanalysis' to analyse space through, 'a systematic psychological study of the sites of our intimate lives',[22] and to fully investigate the memories and desires surrounding the notion of home. These images must, he claims, have to be understood phenomenologically in order to give them psychoanalytical efficiency. By this he means that the houses of our earliest and most intimate memory are oneiric; they exist in the unity of imagination and memory and, in order to recreate the enhanced geography of early childhood, 'we are constantly reimagining its reality'.[23] The profound desire to fulfil the longing surrounding this early 'shell' enters into all spatial relationships, determining our engagement with and ways of perceiving all environments. All space, however temporarily inhabited, is claimed and measured against the initial experience of home.

Chaudhuri's dialectic surrounding the locus of home is, like Bachelard's, both phenomenologic and psychoanalytic. She states that the domestic focus of realism maps out a symbolic system that characterizes its 'interiority' as feminine and problematic within a dominant and normalizing, patriarchal, order that retains melodrama's oedipal family focus. Like topoanalysis, geopathology engages the notion of 'home' in all its psychoanalytical complexities, 'replete with all those powerful and empowering associations to space as are organized by the notion of belonging'.[24] Geopathology defines the terms and problematics of spatial representation; the reference of home involves notions of victimization, departure, exile/ruin or escape and is complicated by an unquenchable longing for (an impossible) return.

The movement away from 'home' in the development of twentieth century narrative drama exists parallel to a physical movement from the enclosed and totally visible stage of early naturalism and realism, to the open and indeterminate environment of experimental and devised performance. Chaudhuri frames the departure of theatre away from 'naturalism's famous four walls', as a shift so radical that it seems to symbolize a universal condition[25] that embraces the (double) drama of immigration and multiculturalism emblematic of our time. This kind of theatrical imagining, Chaudhuri writes, marks a moment in which mapping the site vies with or displaces conventional narrative as a technology of identification, 'who one is and who one can be…are a function of where one is and how one experiences that place.'[26]

Displacement, dislocation, homelessness, and disenfranchisement have characterized much post-realist, postmodern performance and the scenographic impulse to situate performance in transgressive locations is a concrete engagement with these tropes. The strategy involves the use of transitional sites that are read as liminal spaces (disused factories and abandoned warehouses), which signify in complex ways at the intersection of politics and poetics. The resulting fragmenting of perspectives reflects a polyvocalization and an absence of stable signification that characterizes, as far as this is feasible, postmodern forms of expression. Site-specific performance participates in this polymorphism by extending, physically and ideologically, the figure of home well beyond the local situation into city/district/country/world. In doing so, it largely abandons the traditionally-staged discourse of home, which began to unravel, according to Chaudhuri, as far back as mid-twentieth century, under pressure from the utopian efforts to reconfigure society and in response to the reality of diaspora and immigration.

The radical migration of art and performance, at this juncture, away from conventional galleries and theatres contained the notion that newly emergent marginal groups had the right to reflect and respond in their own voice, with reference to a specific space or locale. That these voices be accepted as authentic became essential to the ideology of politically-focused performance genre as did the notion that new and diverse audiences might be engaged through experiences reflecting their complex, fused and shifting identities. These audiences comprised individuals revised as autonomous and flexible, not confined to a seat in a darkened auditorium but negotiating new sites of performance as readily as international borders and the virtual landscape of cyber space. Chaudhuri's vying and defining mythologies of 'home' and 'journey' here coalesce into a transcendence with globalization and multiculturalism now defining its very nature in terms of multi-media and multi-dimensions. She describes this state of being in this world as, 'thorough going and ubiquitous is this dispersal of subjective experience, wandering over vast global distance daily as they change channels, fax letters, leave messages on answering machines…'.[27]

The tropes of belonging and exile that Chaudhuri considers the significant characteristic of the shift in the spatiality of modern drama addresses themes central to Bachelard's analysis of space as always marked by profound yearning for home; that which is always sought but never regained nor left behind. The symbolism is particularly potent at this juncture, characterized, as it is, by global Diaspora. Recognizing this, Chaudhuri positions the shift from realism's encompassing, normative, euro-centrism to post-realism's subjectively-reflexive, hybrid inter-culturalism alongside seismic shifts in global politics and migration practices.

The concurrent movement away from traditional sites of representation towards liminal sites is a move clearly marking new spatial alignments, from the circumscribed, bi-directional experience of the proscenium theatre to the ambivalent, multi-valenced experience of the site-specific event that reflects a new way of experiencing the world. This re-direction from realism's stage to an engagement with 'real space' acknowledges change and instability as normative and recognizes the impossibility of constituting identities based on totalizing signifying systems and utopian ideals. It employs the strategy of choosing surroundings that are both familiar and not familiar, home and not home, hence proposing a kind of place/ness, not as the absence or erasure of place but as the combination and layering of many different places: 'a heterotopia as a place in which all the other real sites that can be found within a culture, are simultaneously represented, contested and inverted'.[28] These sites, that Foucault calls third spaces, are dense, contested spaces of resistant practices, where cultures and ideologies collide. Describing performance's purchase on the terms and conditions of 'real space', Chaudhuri writes that 'the theater posits a new kind of placement, not in any one circumscribed and clearly defined place but in the crossroads, pathways and junctions between places'.[29]

Both materially and ideologically, 'between places' represent the material terrain of site-specific practice. Practitioners Shanks and Pearson propose a way of engaging these sites using an archaeological methodology that uncovers specific local identities, histories and ideologies, at the same time attempting to situate this within a global context.[30] Archaeology, they claim, has long performed the role of providing material correlates for stories and myths of identity and belonging, relying on these to unify people around a common story of their national identity. These narratives or 'cultural geographies of the imagination' unify and flatten history, and fail to cope with the diversity of genuine local narratives. To deal with this, a fundamental point of departure in their approach is

> an encounter with materiality and regional focus, the ruins of a local past, setting the homogenization of processes like nationalism, colonization and imperialism against the peculiarities of history and geography. This is about the relation between local past and those global methods, frameworks and master narratives, which may suppress, under a disciplinary and cultural uniformity, the rich pluralism and multicultural tapestry of peoples and histories.[31]

What emerges through this approach is a patchwork of narrative fragments resistant to the insistence of universally-read meta-narratives and stereotypes that gather around national identities and specific localities. In their practice, material site is used to signify a representational fixity that denies itself at the same time as it affirms its presence, opening itself to the twin strategies of dispersal/containment, absence/presence operative in any given sign. Whereas a mimetic perspective, characteristic of the modernist stage, tended to reify absent referents in performance, for example, detailed naturalist stage design, thus sustaining an illusion of full presence, a phenomenologic encounter with site offers a perspective tending to favour the generative and ludic capacities of visual negotiations in the material world, reliant on local specificities and the interplay of audience and site in the joint production of meaning. Here, site is read in relationship to a myriad of embodied practices (colliding, converging, convening) focusing on the singularity of events outside of any monotonous finality. As a strategy for generating meaning, it takes its pulse from a specifically Foucauldian sense of history as a discontinuous recurrence of disciplines and practices, of interpretations incorporated in history as events centred in the human body in sentiments embodied both in their presence (love, conscience) and in their absence or unrealised state (longing, desire). Centred in the body, this history erupts, in breaks and ruptures, as the story of living bodies claiming and contesting space at both macro- and micro-political levels.

Chaudhuri's notion that to theorize a geography of theatre centred around such terms as borders, limits, rootlessness, territoriality, nomadism, habitus, home, homelessness, and exile is to, 'bring…[it] into alignment with a considerable body of contemporary cultural theory, in which space is increasingly replacing time.'[32] This implies a more subjective and ideologically-engaged relationship with the spaces of performance, these characteristics being most visible when the traditional, passive, fixed alignment of actors and spectators is inverted. Over the twentieth century, such re-alignments have been rehearsed by Artaud, Grotowski, Brook, Schechner and a host of site-specific practitioners and theorists, who have found ways to insinuate their own resistant meaning into performance and to position their practice subversively within networks and structures of power.

Cultural geographer Steve Pile engages the notion of resistant space focusing on acts of subversion across a range of power relationships, everyday embodied practices and orders of magnitude; acts of resistance made visible in the smallest ironic gesture in acts that temporarily re-inscribe the dominant narrative. These acts are frequently constituted through the idea of movement where mobility is seen as radical and transformative.[33] Although he does not directly engage performance practice in his discussion, his characterization of liminal space or third space, is pertinent to the performance strategies discussed. Pile writes:

…if de Certeau is right, resistance cannot be understood…as a fight that takes place only on grounds constituted by structural relations – because other spaces are always involved: spaces that are dimly lit, opaque, deliberately hidden, saturated with memories, that echo with lost words and the cracked sound of pleasure and enjoyment. The spatial practices of resistance are not just the mobilization of a class across space, not the mobilization of an interest group in a particular place, but about insinuation…[34]

Like de Certeau, he argues that contradictions lie within the ideological organization of spatial structures: while exaggerating differentiations, spatial strategies also, consciously or unconsciously, leave room for the transgressions and subversions that valorize the individual. While maintaining and enforcing rigid structures of control within its strictures, individuals seek and practice alternative strategies. Following de Certeau, Pile claims that the central strategy of authority is to force people to play its game by its rules, thus forcing people to find innumerable ways round this; he writes that individuals, 'rat run through the labyrinths of power'. From this perspective, resistance is less about particular acts, than about the ludic desire to act out in a power geography where space is denied, circumscribed and/or totally administered.[35]

Site-specific work makes choices that mark out spaces of indeterminacy, contingency and strive for meaning that is shifting, dense, referential, and provocative. It situates transgressive behaviour within systems of power, temporarily privileging or bracketing certain spaces and marking them indefinitely. Such performances do not reinforce the status quo but are, to employ Elin Diamond's use of the term, 'performative' in that they circumscribe:

> …cultural practices that reinvent the ideas, symbols, and gestures that shape social life. Such reinscriptions or reinventions are, inevitably, negotiations with regimes of power. Viewing performance within a complex matrix of power, serving diverse cultural desires, encourages a permeable understanding of history and change [and]…can expose the fissures and ruptures, and revisions that have settled into continuous reenactment.[36]

If spaces, like acts, can be experienced as politicized/historicized/embodied, to what extent is the coherence and articulation of identity based on historically and socially-instituted norms embedded in spatial practice and in discrete places? To what degree is identity expressed through practices insinuated between, 'the cracks and fissures' of structured and marked space? Through a range of performance gestures, marginalized groups, immigrant populations and individuals all seek, and frequently succeed in finding ways, to inscribe their presence within physical structures, to over-write normative practices and, however temporarily, voice counter-narratives in a myriad of creative ways in order to displace meaning represented in and by specific sites. Space records a set of norms that both challenge and open themselves up to acts of resistance that are embodied and performed. Performance, as a gesture bounded by signifying space, reiterates the set of norms across, against and through a spectrum of possibilities. Considering one of these possibilities, Pile states, '…resistance may take place as a reaction against…but it also involves a sense of dreaming and remembering something better…find[ing] new ways, elaborat[ing] new spatialities, new futures.'[37]

Judith Butler's notion of 'performativity', as distinguished from performance, is important here. She writes that performativity, 'consists in a reiteration of norms which precede, constrain and exceed the performer and in that sense cannot be taken as the fabrication of the performer's "will" or choice; further what is "performed" works to conceal, if not disavow, what remains opaque, unconscious, unperformable'.[38] What Butler's notion of performative addresses in site is the ineffable excess that oozes out and triggers memory, nostalgia, desire to belong, desire to leave, guilt and fear and all the overwhelming associations attributable to home. To enter into these spatial engagements in performance is to embody these associations in all spaces we inhabit, however temporary. Hence, place can be exploited in performance, can be read performatively, making meaning parallel to, in opposition to and in excess of, performance. Furthermore, all temporal referents (past, present and future) triggered by the phenomenological experience of place extends signification well beyond the constraints of performance.

Notes

1. *The Weyburn Project: The Archaeology of Madness*, A Knowhere Production Inc. Production, Creative Team: Director – Andrew Houston, Scenographer – Kathleen Irwin, the Community of Weyburn SK.
2. *The Dionysian Lear,* A Knowhere Productions Inc. Project Aborted Creative Team: Director – Andrew Houston, Scenographer – Kathleen Irwin, the Community of Regina, SK.
3. *The Claybank Project: Crossfiring,* A Knowhere Productions Inc. Project in Development, Creative Team: Director – Andrew Houston, Scenographer – Kathleen Irwin, the Community of Avonlea, SK.
4. Pearson, M., and Shanks, M., *Theatre/Archaeology,* London: Routledge, 2001.
5. Lacy, S., (Ed.), *Mapping the Terrain: New Genre Public Art*, Seattle: Bay Press, 1995, p. 174.
6. Ibid., p. 176.
7. Ibid., p. 180.
8. Pearson, Mike and Shanks, M., *Theatre/Archaeology*, London: Routledge, 2001, p. 11.
9. de Certeau, M., *The Practice of Everyday Life*, Berkekey: University of California Press, 1984, p. 107.
10. Spiegelburg, H., *Doing Phenomenology: Essays on and in Phenomenology*, The Hague: Martinus Nijhoff, 1975, p. 137.
11. *Spiegelberg, H., The Phenomenological Movement: A Historical Introduction. The Hague: Nijhoff*, 1960.
12. Austin, J.L., *How to do Things With Words.* Cambridge: Harvard University Press, 1962, p. 16.
13. Ibid, p. 137.
14. Bachelard, Gaston, *The Poetics of Space: The Classic look at How we Experience Intimate Places,* New York: Orion Press, 1964, p. 3.
15. Ibid., p. 5.
16. Chaudhuri, U., *Staging Place: the Geography of Modern Drama*, Ann Arbor: University of Michigan Press, 1997, p. xii.
17. Bachelard, p. 7.
18. Chaudhuri, p. 22.
19. Ibid., p. xi.
20. Ibid., p. 22–23.
21. Kaye, Nick, *Site-specific Art: Performance, Place and Documentation*, London: Routledge, 2000, p. 1.

22. Bachelard, p. 8.
23. Ibid., p. 19.
24. Chaudhuri, p. xii.
25. Ibid., p. xiii.
26. Ibid., p. xi.
27. Ibid., p. 4.
28. Pearson, M., 'The Dream in the Desert', *Performance Research*, Number One, Spring 1996: 6.
29. Chaudhuri, p. 138.
30. Pearson and Shanks, p. 35–37.
31. Ibid., p. 37.
32. Chaudhuri, p. xi.
33. Pile, S., in Keith, M., & Pile, S., *Geographies of Resistence*, London : Routledge, 1997, p. 29.
34. Pile, S., p. 16.
35. Pile, S., p. 15.
36. Diamond, E., (Ed.), *Performance and Cultural Politics*, London: Routledge, 1996, p. 2.
37. Pile, S., p. 30.
38. Butler, J., 'The Lesbian Phallus and the Morphological Imaginary', in *Bodies that Matter; On the Discursive Limits of Sex*, New York: Routledge, p. 57–92.

Chapter 5

Director Petr Lébl and Designer William Nowák: To a Man

Věra Velemanová

Motto: 'nevertheless, sometimes we have to admit that MORE can even be MORE. Why not raise your voice when you really need to and why not maintain that high note a little longer "than normal"?' Petr Lébl

It is no exaggeration to say that Petr Lébl (1965–1999), 'maintained that high note' throughout his very intensive, but unfortunately short, artistic career; although somewhat fragile, to all appearances quiet and non-aggressive, he provoked and amazed by his hard-to-capture style of perception, method of thinking, impossibility of classification, and obsession. The instinct for 'game' or 'play' through which he completely eliminated the boundary between his own artistic and personal life, in its end-result self-destructive, expressed itself on another level as a game with identity: on the outside innocent, charming, amusing; in its inner-self possibly more serious and more cruel than it seemed. It applied even to the method by which Lébl definitively chose to 'leave the stage', as though submitting to the rules of a game, directed with merciless, appalling efficiency.

As a designer he sometimes signed off as Arnold Lébl or Letitia von Brandenstein, but for most of his professional productions his set designer is named as William Nowák. The pseudonym seems bizarre thanks to just one detail, which turns the name into an anachronism, the diacritic above the 'a', in a surname which has otherwise been Germanized.[1]

Lébl once announced that he was not a designer. Why? For him, the staging of a play was an indivisible form where all the elements are closely tied together, conditioning and influencing one another; on the one hand they are the consequences of a thought-through concept, on the other, of possible accidents. At first sight Lébl's work in the theatre seems fundamentally visual, with everything that concept implies. It provoked, it was admired and cursed, simply for the supremacy of its visual quality. There is no other figure in the Czech theatre that combined so absolutely stage design and direction. By exaggerating a little, one could say that to some measure František Tröster, and Josef Svoboda in particular, 'directed' the whole production through their set design, but that comparison is rather inadequate. However, the striking visual quality of Lébl's productions could not be separated from, for example, the aural element, where the special intonation of the actors' speech fused with the music and with shades of light and colour, forcing us to perceive the production with all our senses. Ivan Vyskočil characterized Lébl's creative type as, 'director as composer, orchestrator and author'.[2]

He attended a secondary school for graphic design. It is characteristic (because, on the one hand, of the impossibility of his classification and on the other, the prejudice of the educated classes) that he applied several times to the Film Faculty of the Academy of Performing Arts and was turned down for lack of talent. He did not complete his studies in the Drama Faculty. School did not bind him, it did not upset his living roots by its academic staleness and tameness, divorced from love of the performing arts; it did not undermine his eternal, seemingly naïve, drive derived from the conviction that the boundary or horizon is not yet in sight. It did not intervene negatively into the heart of his work, whose beating could only with difficulty be confined by those prejudices, which often confine someone who understands education just as the instrument of some sort of perfidious advancement and power.

His first production on the professional stage was Egon Tobiáš's *Vojcev* in Prague's Labyrinth Theatre (Divadlo Labyrint), 1992, for which, however, he was credited only as director, although he had had a decisive influence on the final appearance of the design. Soon after the death of the director Jan Grossman, he was made head of drama at the Theatre on the Balustrades (Divadlo Na zábradlí), 1993. That was where he chose to end his life in December 1999.

He also worked for other theatres, the Mecklenburgisches Staatstheater in Schwerin (Brecht's *Irresistible Rise of Arturo Ui*, directed by David Levin, 1996), the Habima National Theatre in Tel Aviv (where he directed Rostand's *Cyrano de Bergerac*, 1996), the National Theatre in Prague (where he directed Bedřich Smetana's opera *The Brandenbergers in Bohemia*, 1997).

Lébl's era as an amateur (1980–1991), possibly regarded with greater indulgence by the critical public because it did not venture to include itself amongst the 'elite' of the professionals, was characterized by a strong visual charge. In the productions Lébl created with his companies DOPRAPO, Jak se vám jelo and JELO, for obvious reasons the principles of 'poor theatre', applied, that is, a special form of 'action scenography'. However, from the very beginning, he shifted this aesthetic to other dimensions and in a Baroque manner even developed it to further depths of the possibility of the polysemantic quality of the scenic object. Under the conditions of the ruling Communist regime, even the dramaturgy of his amateur era was pioneering and courageous: Vonnegut's *Slapstick* (1985), Eliade's *Snake* (1987), Kafka's *Metamorphosis* (1988) and Wyspiański's *Wesele* (The Wedding, 1989).

His professional productions with their alleged over-use of props, costume details, and so on, provoked some critics. Lébl's pictorial vision of the world to a considerable extent divided and irritated the critical community whose polemics Lébl humorously absorbed into the context of his work as an indivisible part, the process of its origin (and its end): 'Lébl's productions provoke over-reaction in that it is not easy (and perhaps not even advisable) to distinguish where the construction ends and the decoration begins, what is 'for real' and what is only the free association of the director, so that attempts at logical interpretation land on the uncertain ground of speculation...';[3] 'The film-clip poetics of permanent shocks and mechanical heaping up of ideas...the original charge is lost by rapid repetition and easily slips into stereotype.'[4] 'Lébl however cannot be understood...You won't want to understand, you will want to perceive, to breathe in, for *The Maids* or against it, or both together, that's best, just as long as you breathe in…Whoever finds it reckless, is right. Whoever finds it fabricated, let him look in the mirror.'[5] 'Shall I take part in a noble-minded contest, who in the shortest time finds…more poetic images and more impropriety – when impropriety often illuminates the meaning of things more than what is correct?'[6] One could continue – the flood of polemics which in the 1990s flowed onto the pages of Czech periodicals, and forms a substantial chapter of the book edited by Vlasta Smoláková (*Fenomén Lébl*, Praha 1995).

Lébl's visual invention went hand in hand with a tremendous musicality, possibly inherited from his musicologist father, and a sense of rhythm. The important, albeit apparently hidden, meaning here has music, sound, a particular 'a-rhythmical' articulation of the word (when necessary), which helps the visual element gain a special strength, dramatic quality, shifts of meaning and sometimes even shifts of function of the scenic elements.

William Nowák began to co-exist with Petr Lébl in connection with the staging of Tankred Dorst's play *Fernando Krapp Wrote Me a Letter* (Labyrinth Theatre, Prague, 1992). This drama of the mystery of the origin and ending of personal relationships, life-giving and destructive, does not, as Milan Lukeš noted in his review,[7] require an elaborate set. However, Lébl planted the surface with decorative, decadently handsome objects as though created from a sweetly-eerie dream at the turn of the nineteenth and twentieth centuries, in places evoking the atmosphere of Luchino Visconti's films, in places the canvases of Gustav Klimt. This at first sight is a delightful picture whose attractive, externally fragile and apparently passive nucleus is focused above all on the figure of the leading heroine, and is gradually tested, and broken, by sharp ironical incisions. The charming asymmetrical sofa placed at the centre of the acting area is just long enough to squeeze in all three main characters, but short enough for one of those characters to be mercilessly squashed over and over again. The splendid coach, enveloped in flowers, its enormous proportions causing irritation, has several functions, but is in essence a pretentious instrument of torture for the affected Julie: her 'lover' the Count is yoked to the coach; the coach serves as a table in the inn, during which Julie subjects her men for a change to mental cruelty. The frame of the portal mirror is made up of classical-style columns (one of Lébl's favourite elements) with decorative Corinthian capitals, shamelessly confessed mocked-up scenery. A light, ethereal curtain, fluttering between columns, becomes a wave of the sea. Lébl here shows for the first time how he is able to extend the invention of his 'poor' amateur theatre into imaginative transformations of the function of individual scenic elements – not in any way misappropriating it – and at the same time to enrich it with an apparently antithetical, Baroquely-generous, gesture.

Just as in his amateur projects (on the one hand the supremely imaginative, express-ionistically harmonized *Tauridus* from the author's own pen in 1985 and on the other Milan Uhde's extremely abstemious *Výběrčí* (*Collectors*) in 1990), so later in the professional theatre, Lébl, whilst still maintaining a personal style, alternated between a profusely Baroque linking of elements and association in his sets, and the implementation of a pure, precise, unified form.

Pokojíček (*The Little Room*, by J.A. Pitínský, Theatre on the Balustrades, 1993) contained in itself both forms: the decorative and the austere. Just like an equation, the poverty of cardboard high-rise flats on the one hand and, on the other, everything that influenced youth at that time. The miserable outer world meant that at times the inner life was that much richer, and was also endowed with a sense of the absurd. Such a life is like a sponge, sucking up everything including rubbish and symptoms of the wretched 'culture' and rituals of the time, reshaping them into a new value. So, on an otherwise austerely-functioning stage, at a closer look we find alongside objects designed in the poverty-stricken taste of the Socialist 1970s: the refrigerator in which Father hides; the furniture which could be found in most Czech homes simply because there was nothing else; posters of idols at the time, which belong more to the sphere of aspirations and dreams than to reality. The decorative wallpaper represents an attempt somehow to differentiate, to show that, 'we are a bit better', petty bourgeois and in vain, because the behaviour and environment of the characters ends in stereotype; only the conclusion with its sudden take-off resembles the 'dream of a Western' from the much later *Uncle Vanya*: the parents, having literally disposed of their descendants, triumphantly drive off on a motor-bike, a little like *Bonnie and Clyde*, a little like *Easy Rider*; Mother in a dress from the dances of her youth, the fateful weapon in her hands, Father in the pose of a lady-killer. It is more of a dream, the pious hope of the two protagonists, a striking, tawdry reminder of their ever-more distant and ever-more idealized youth, which actually was so carefree and full of freedom.

It was precisely that purity of form, based on simple symbiosis, on the interconnectedness of visual and directorial elements (here indivisible), which was characteristic of Lébl's production of Genet's *The Maids* at the Theatre on the Balustrades (1993). If we compare *The Maids* with his later *The Seagull* on the same stage (1994), it is possible, although always inadequately so, to identify what is essential in Lébl's work. I have, therefore, devoted extra attention to these two works.

Here as elsewhere, Lébl was reproached for the wilfulness with which he loaded the text. In point of fact, it was more of a disguised reproach that the production was not sufficiently comprehensible, sufficiently descriptive for the audience. Meanwhile, Lébl worked with the text as with an artist's model, whose inimitable expression can be captured only if he imbues it with something still more, from his own resources, from his own inspiration. According to Lébl's teacher Ivan Vyskočil, founder and one-time leading figure of the Theatre on the Balustrades, close to Lébl with his own inventive, associative playfulness, Lébl's playful *method* (if we can use this term about work so difficult to grasp), upheld the comparison of the principle of play and the principle of imitation:

There are said to be two anti-poles creating a dynamic oscillating dynamic pole, that mutually act on each other, supplement each other…before one predominates. Normally the principle of imitation predominates. It is also the principle of normality and sanity in general. It predominates because it is economical. Imitation is on every side more economical than play which needs and uses a lot of life's energy – and personal involvement

– and is thus (from the point of view of imitation) 'profligate', 'wasteful', 'unprofitable', 'expensive'. Although the principle of imitation predominates and determines our life style, the need for play continues.[8]

It was *The Maids* which led Lébl to implement a principle which was also typical for Genet's later dramas (*The Blacks*, *The Balcony*). It involves a sort of play-within-a-play (with frequent alienating detours), a 'psychodrama'[9] of two prisoners, who project their story and destiny into their performances, into a play about the fate of two maids, a fate which is similarly subordinate, similarly miserable, issuing (inevitably?) into an idea about a crime and its execution. It seems that the closeness of the date of Genet's pardon from a life sentence (1948) to the date of origin of *The Maids* (1949) was important for this solution – apart from this, Lébl one way or another projected into each of his productions facts from the biography of the relevant author. I do not know whether Lébl knew of Pierre Vicary's conversation with Jean Genet in 1982, and whether it could somehow have influenced the director's point of view a little. In any case, Genet answers the question of when and why he first felt the need to write:

> Because while I was in jail, I was bored. When one's in jail, stuck between four walls – six if you like, the four walls, ceiling and floor – what else is there to do but dream? So my first books, my only books in fact were dreams, just slightly better organised than the average dream. I dreamt five books on paper, if you like, while I was in jail. But now that I've been released, and released you will tell me *because* of my books (and you're right), I no longer have the inspiration to write a book, so I don't.[10]

Alas, the prologue in Lébl's production does not take place, as Genet's stage directions indicate, in Madame's room with its Louis XV furniture, but in the twilight of an underground prison cell with a steel door, blue-green like a feverish vision. As design it is immeasurably effective, the impressive ritual of a play about two beings, two naked human bodies, to the sound of disturbing music. It is a process of creation, fighting against the chill of a prison cell through its roster of bodily smells, passion, pain and delight, free associations. The two actors experience it in rhythm and in harmony with a strangely beautiful dance of words. The magic play with the hands, ('And those gloves! Those eternal gloves!'),[11] slowly and in detail follows the accelerating beat of the ritual. A tension is induced between word and action; the word gains in meaning and at the same time its weight is relativized. This duet creates a disturbing, almost 'sculpturally' conceived clenched monolith, gradually developing other associations, which materialize through the accumulating figures. The whole performance then continues in the spirit of a seductive ritual, more noticeably than other productions by Lébl.

Essentially the ascetic set of bare walls, pallets, wooden steps, a lift, has, in comparison with the histrionically splendid set design for the Dorst or the dreamlike, fragile design for the later *Seagull*, harsher and firmer contours, even a harsher conclusion, in which the set crashes down. Lébl alias Nowák, 'embellished' it with several decoratively conceived costume elements, props and masks. If the fantasy of the two prisoners leads us after all to 'Madame's apartment', the seemingly ever-present flowers are always only talked of. Madame travels pompously by lift from below via the stage trap, with the faded charm of an operetta soubrette, moving on the boundary of mocked-up loftiness and irrevocable decay, in a hat of Hassidic cut. In place of antique furniture, she eventually buries herself under a growing pile of superfluities, obviously presents from admirers, with which Madame, queen of trash, rewards her subjects, including an absurd muddle of radiators and medical lamps. The chilly space is gradually populated with the costume of an Egyptian pharaoh, a mangy fox's mask, as well as the guardians of the lift in red liveries. The poetry of Genet's alternating of the male and female element, the continuous changes from sex to sex, thus interpenetrate the 'Ubuesque' poetry of the drain, climaxing in superfluity as a principle of the life on which our world is built. At the same time, everything is purposefully used for the play, which is both tawdry and elevated: tawdry in the context of the reality in which it is played, elevated in the sense of overcoming this reality.

The production of Chekhov's *The Seagull* (1994) – like *The Maids*, one of the summits of Lébl's work – is a kind of secondary, handwritten antithesis to *The Maids*, whilst maintaining continuity and style. Both of them can be regarded as a materialized dream; naturally, in comparison with the 'sculpturally'-hewn, bogus, fiercely elemental staging of Genet's play, Lébl's *Seagull* is a dream about the fragility, flight and feverishness of life; a dream about the painfully acquiescent decline of life, its dissolution in a boundless universe. With this is connected another general theme, love and its transience, and the issue of the meaning of art, especially theatre. It is as though Lébl wanted to capture these difficult-to-grasp phenomena of human life pictorially by more volatile, although physically more permanent means than theatre has at its disposal. Film and its two-dimensional quality became an inspirational source and also the two-dimensional quality and subtlety of a print. 'Lébl's stage looks like an old film studio...Those theatrical qualities: Theatre here parodies itself, by comparing itself to film, which parodies it.'[12] Vlasta Smoláková, a specialist in Russian theatre, admirer of the director and his long-time colleague, in an article recalled a significant moment which was clearly key for Lébl: the fact that in December 1895, when Chekhov read *The Seagull* to his friends for the first time, the brothers Lumière premiered their cinema in Paris.[13] Lébl, who in his amateur work had drawn on film techniques of editing, lighting, was inspired by the early period of film: the American silent screen, the famous era of film stars and Expressionist film, not so much by its visual Cubist morphology, as by the masking and even at times the extreme 'horror film' expression of some characters. The character of Nina is thus exaggeratedly stylized as Mary Pickford, 'as a reminder of that legendary young lady, innocently romping around, whilst danger lurks behind the corner.'[14] Madame Arkadina (somehow analogous with Julie from Dorst's *Fernando Krapp*) is here, under a deposit of make-up, a platinum blonde wig à la Mae West, and ostentatious robes and hats, an affected, aging prima donna from a provincial theatre, spasmodically and in vain stylizing herself into the pose of a worldly-wise and simultaneously eternally-young film star; Trigorin is a languid, weary and somehow sexless screen 'lover' à la Rudolf Valentino; Sorin (in an excessively unkempt wig, beetling eyebrows and bristly beard) oscillates between the archetype of a comic old man and a treacherous villain. In the final act the characters (except for the hopelessly 'lost' Arkadina) gradually lose their wigs and masks, carried away by the rising wind which simultaneously rids the whole action of the protective dusting of parody and reveals the naked tragedy of unhappy, eternally-unfulfilled destinies, which here remain defenceless, rid of every sentimentality and theatricality. The colour of this act is white, evoking an environment similar to a hospital room where no one is cured but only dies; where beyond the thin tulle curtain they already move like some sort of shadows. The predominating colour combination here is black and white. Milan Lukeš notes: '...even the seagull, in the end, is white with black marks. Even the silver birches. Even the dreams are in black and white.'[15] However, black and white film, black and white photography at the same time present some kind of indisputable, constant quality. They preserve space for the imagination, they do not disperse attention, on the contrary, by their magical mysteriousness, they strip down to the concentrated essence of the story.

Through his staging, Lébl almost unwittingly identified another level of silent film – its melancholy, depth and oppressive dark tones, and the ability of this specific phenomenon to respond to the tragically-comic existence of man more truthfully than many 'serious', apparently profound genres of that time. The poetics of the first two decades of the twentieth century, which grow from the spirit of Chekhov's period, in an unexpectedly exact way, help to draw closer to the atmosphere of the nineteenth century; Lébl works with such paradoxical shifts in other productions as well. On the visual side he connects with the principle used in the staging of Dorst's play. He uses the same element, classical columns, which here are a gradually decaying mock-up; they disappear in the same way as everything else which up to then concealed the reality of stories about people. Its outcome is a deep, immeasurably imaginative and (in the best sense of the word) personally-engaged look at the roots from which the spirit and atmosphere at the turn of the nineteenth and twentieth centuries and that which followed is derived: with all the decadence, with all the tension between the high and the low, the cruel and the tender.

For Lébl, light is clearly an exceedingly important factor. The lighting score has a somewhat different rhythm and function in every production. The light in *The Maids* is a modelling factor, visually uniting the firm outlines of the production's appearance. It is also a discreet guide, as it differentiates the individual phases of the play-dream: the play begins to develop under sparse lighting, full illumination penetrating the space at the moment the ritual evokes, makes material, the idea of the two prisoners and their female alter-egos appear on the stage. Later the whole situation is again relativized, with the help of light and its numerous shadows and levels, which however, never lead the 'body' of the production into the twilight of uncertainty, but always emphasize contours and shapes. The light in *The Seagull* has, so to speak, two levels: one within the staging, having the features of film work with light (exaggerated mimicry, emphasizing of details, an Expressionist nature); the other, from outside, comprehends every actual stage space as it were from an overview, from the angle of a theatrical optic. At the same time, however, the direction of the lighting as a whole is founded on the principle of Impressionist volatility and fleetingness, of subtle, difficult-to-observe changes of registers, which deliberately blur the audience's eyes, make them uncertain, guiding them to the magic of the instantaneous originating and ending of images. Just like the coloured structure of the birches and the black and white columns, it is light deliberately softening, gentle, uneasy.

The subsequent production of Gogol's *Government Inspector* (1995), another work by the 'couple' Lébl-Nowák, appeared in the shadow of the much discussed *Seagull*. It was dedicated to V. E. Meyerhold, whose scandalous production of 1926 Lébl treated with honour and respect, albeit at first glance he was less inspired by the visual concept of the set (in Meyerhold's case full of doors) than by the spirit of the production. Apart from this, Czech theatre history, of which Lébl was certainly aware, can pride itself on, at the very least, two legendary re-workings of Gogol's play: Jiří Frejka's 1936 production with a set by František Tröster with Cubist, Expressionist decoration, expressing by its warped, 'drunken' architecture, the state of body and soul in which the eponymous hero finds himself and, thirty years later, the production by Jan Kačer with a set by Luboš Hrůza (guest artist Oleg Tabakov played the part of Khlestakov in this late-1960s production).

Lébl's production was, from the point of view of design, reproached for luxuriance, gaudiness, indulgence in practical jokes, exaggerated details. However, the director-and-designer-in-one completely followed the intentions of the author, more direct, more ironical, than Chekhov, who, although a 'critical realist', actually worked with exaggeration and a considerable dose of expressiveness. Lébl conceived the production with generosity and no less sharp irony; its morphology shifted it markedly in the direction of the Orient. The scenic environment had all the marks of getting into a 'marasmus': under a deposit of ornamentation and gloss, slumbered material and spiritual poverty. In place of a curtain and on the floor the audience could spy Persian carpets; there were dazzling oriental costumes with rich embroidery and a huge crystal chandelier as a symbol of luxury. At the same time they listened to an everlasting dripping tap. In the second half of the performance some of the characters changed their oriental costumes (by Kateřina Štefková) for 'European', to demonstrate thereby their 'sophistication'. However, each of these had some sort of ridiculous detail. Maybe Lébl's *Government Inspector* came too early; perhaps later its many-layered quality would have been uncovered more consistently and openly. As it was, for many it became more of an eccentric throwback to the 'Russian period' of Lébl's work. It is, however, an integral part of this, in fact in that very attentive, 'intertextual' method of reading the text.

Stroupežnický's *Naši naši furianti* ['Our' Our Proud Peasants], (1994) and the much later production of Wyspiański's *Wesele* (1998) create another 'interest group' of Lébl's studio, with their theme and the way it is treated. In a certain sense, although it may not be apparent at first glance, they are in their irony and principle of de-mythologization close to *The Government Inspector*.

Both of them are about attitudes towards national tradition and national myth, about the reflection of outworn clichés in which, during the years when, because of 'compulsory reading', 'national' texts are read only superficially or not at all, this 'classic' is packaged. The magic of *'Our' Our Proud Peasants* arises from the fact that in the course of Stroupežnický's play an enormous number of characters alternate on stage. Lébl added up these characters and put them all on stage at once. He filled the stage not only with those argumentative but kindly aunts and uncles, but also with typical characters from Czech legends such as the devil, and the water sprite with his seventy children. However, the production was not a parody. It was just that an effort was made, in the same way as one reveals a fresco, to get underneath the ritualization and deposits with which we have corrupted our national literature. Disposing of superfluous hindrances and over-done piety, an effort was made to show the timelessness, truth and charm of these texts. The set was made out of the mocked up perspective walls and thatched roofs of dwellings; downstage centre, a chopping block, which was also an execution block, a symbol of the village judgement seat. All the architectural elements of the set, the simple white benches, columns, walls and roofs of the houses – looked a little bit like an easily-taken-apart Lego construction. Against the pale background, the costumes played a leading role, richly decorated skirts, caps and hats from a variety of regions (the broad South Bohemian hats of the men, the decorative shawls and caps of the women); the beauty of the 'old' unsettled by inorganic accessories or situations: every woman, even in folk costume, wielded a handbag; the community policeman carried his handcuffs in a plastic carrier bag. The National Anthem, *Where is my home* was performed by a Jewish innkeeper on beer mugs. One of the villagers was played by a black actor. It seems crazy, but Lébl was working from reality, a Bohemian village was never a sterile environment full of 'pure-blooded' good-natured Czechs. It was only a concept of folklore and tradition imposed from above, long-lasting, well-nourished and deliberately life-denying, which tried to make it so.

The production of *Wesele* was essentially founded on a similar principle: the set was relatively sober with relief architecture of a building's interior, white chairs, a rocking horse and an enormous stove. The costumes were more modest than in the *Proud Peasants*. Lébl and his costume designer Kateřina Štefková mixed different elements and styles. An actor appeared in the armour of St. Wenceslas, the slightly-weary, gradually-tipsy patron of the Czech lands, the good-hearted Farmer in a typical folk jacket and white shirt with a white doublet, and the Farmer's Wife in folk costume; and on the other hand Čepec in a fool's cap, the intellectuals, for example the Poet, in bohemian men's wear, and with wings. The confusion and strangeness culminated with the presence of an English lady copying the style of Queen Elizabeth, or a lady similar to Lady Diana; human beings who gradually become symbols, signs, until the time when the influence of deposits, as well as mediatization ad absurdum, sentences them among objects of daily use. They here represent 'tradition' which, carried away by the surrounding mass stupidity, this time inoculated by another type of power, holds to its own integrity and content with all the more difficulty.

In the second half of the 1990s Lébl was invited to work as director or designer in prestigious theatres in Prague and abroad. More than before, he was forced to confront his ideas with the requirements and ideas of other creators and undoubtedly gained new impulses and experience. In any case, his productions at the Theatre on the Balustrade during this period made a more concise impression. Though their style unmistakeably indicates who their director is, their concept is founded on completely different principles from, for example, the 'boundless' *Seagull*. In these later productions, Lébl found a charm in the three-dimensional stage object, which is in itself a metaphor, or which could create an oppressive feeling in a closed space. One example is *Ivanov* (1997), again created for the Theatre on the Balustrades. Another 'actor', apart from make-up, masks and props, was the set itself, which was shaped like a boat, changing its form in subsequent acts and its angle, thanks to a revolve. Through separate shifts, it changed the acting area of the staging, whether inside or outside. So we find ourselves in the entrance hall, in Ivanov's room/cabin. This movement is confused, uncertain, and harmonizes with the helplessness of the characters, Lébl conceived it as aimless, incapable of riding the waves, which it would rather avoid. Therefore, the ship would never come to port, and if it did, only to gradual disintegration, just like its inhabitants.

The set for *Uncle Vanya* (1999), the last of Lébl's productions, premièred two months before the director's death. It did not appear under the name of William Nowák, but of Jan Marek. However, its style bears the clear imprints of Lébl-Nowák's firm ideas about the visual appearance of the production, its principle being similar to the preceding Chekhov production. In the small space of the Theatre on the Balustrades, *Uncle Vanya* at the same time returned, as it were, to the prison poem in *The Maids*. However, this time it was not a poem about longing for freedom, as *The Maids* was, but about a dream which could, through liberalism, destroy the scenery of inventions, traps and cells which people need, over and over again, to surround themselves with in order to tyrannize. The production of *Uncle Vanya* was about a dream, already long reduced to tatters, about playfulness long ago crippled and stifled. A dread of oppressive spaces, the intensified atmosphere of an unbearable summer sultriness, 'before the storm' materialized itself in several stage environments, presented by voluminous shapes which barely fit onto the small stage. They could be perceived as different forms of imprisonment from which, this time, there was no flight: an enormous bookcase in which no one could orient themselves, a giant gate, a roof (with chimney and roof light) on which Astrov and Yelena confess their love – 'however, Yelena, perfect for the salon in her richly frilled long dress, on the roof doesn't look at all like a bird, more like a clumsy dung beetle. Her awkward movement indicates a general maladaptation for flight, thus its illusory quality.'[16] Once again, it was possible to experience a feeling of freedom, lightness, for a while to enter the world of dreams and forget: what was originally the reception room with its inevitable decorative wallpaper turns into a Western saloon; the bunch of roses Yelena receives from Vanya, who becomes for a while the hero of some sort of dream-like dancing Western scene, associated with the legendary Czech version of the popular country song about the yellow rose of Texas. America, ever closer in the context of the time, is for the characters of Chekov's play and Lébl's production always a safely distant world; one can only dream beautiful dreams about it. If, however, the real possibility of flight occurred, they would be too frightened. This scene clarifies at the same time the masking of the female characters, as a reminder of the wider context in which the play originated: for example, Sonya and Yelena's hairstyles and hats are close to the style of *The Girl of the Golden West*. A feeling of virtual euphoria alternates with still greater disillusions. The complete awareness of the impossibility of freeing oneself climaxes in the last scene, played out amongst school benches. Vojnicki puts a dog's muzzle on himself.

Lébl was not a typical autocratic or despotic director who would bend the work of his colleagues to the mere achieving of his own aims and reduce them to puppets. However, the designer in him, Nowák, supplied an impressive wholeness and strength: his idea was sufficiently clear on the visual side and for Lébl's team clearly sufficiently suggestive for him in the end always to be able to assert himself as designer, discreetly and without force. Lébl's charisma certainly played an important role; it was no accident that he was able to entice onto the small stage of the Theatre on the Balustrades (as actors) Czech opera singers of the first rank, accustomed to the massive spaces of the National Theatre and chiefly to a radically different poetic.

Lébl worked constantly with the costume designer Kateřina Štefková throughout his professional career. Her sense for exaggeration and for the semanticizing ability of detail, and her sense of humour harmonized with Lébl's means of expression and interpretation. Štefková's costumes were indivisible from Lébl's set design; they served the production as a whole and helped to motivate individual actors to the expressive stylization of their performance, facial expression and dialogue. The costumes inspired them to achieve an overview of the character, to exaggerate a particular feature of the character. Head-coverings especially played an important role in creating hierarchy and characterization, always touching on irony in their shape, getting rid of established clichés, created around the reality the given character presents. For example, the ostentatious sable caps with a tail and typical women's Russian head-dresses in the salon society around Ivanov; the quaint wigs in *The Seagull*; the head coverings, 'of every nationality and period' in *Wesele*; the Egyptian mask and Hassidic hat in *The Maids*.[17]

Even when another set designer is named, Jan Marek, Lébl's hand shows itself; in addition, we read in the programmes of some of these productions named as, 'a Petr Lébl production'.[18]

Lébl's legendary predecessor Jan Grossman came to the Theatre on the Balustrade at the beginning of the 1960s with the concept 'Theatre of Appeal', which was primarily to 'pose questions for the audience, often provocative and over-stated, and count on an audience with the urge to respond to these questions. It is a theatre which believes in the meaning of theatre as a dialogue between the stage and the auditorium.'[19] After Grossman's death, Lébl quite impiously transformed the outer appearance of the theatre, but in content, without even declaring his aim, he actually connected with Grossman's idea. In whatever way, Lébl's rendering unfolded from an outwardly-differing kind of perception, it was similar in deriving from an internal, personal relationship to the text and from a compulsive need to ask questions constantly. Lébl's Baroquely-pictorial style was frequently described as postmodern, but this label seems to be only a construct, a crutch, a feeble attempt to squeeze this style into an incomprehensibly 'comprehensible' classification; just as the term 'Theatre of Pictures', which on the outside seems appropriate but in essence denies the inter-connectedness of all the components in Lébl's productions, where every detail has its story and is well-founded with regard to content.

The connection between Lébl's direction and Nowák's set designs was seamless. The form of the production could, in complete freedom, without compromise, originate as a stream, a composition which is the essence of associations, of apparently uncontrived connections, of a total decomposition of the stage means from which a completely new composition grows, rid of prejudices and barriers. 'The established hierarchy of values fluctuates; from time immemorial the history of art shifted on this oscillation.'[20] Morphologically, visually, Lébl's productions were noticeably inspired by the wealth which art and the social situation left behind it in the first half of the twentieth century: the nostalgia of silent film, the inter-war avant-garde and ethnic diversity. However, as a man of the second half of the century, he also imbibed and transformed on stage the reality which had influenced him from childhood, which he had experienced in the stagnant waters of the 1970s. The new dimension, which is then presented, is always grotesque, subordinate to paramount stylization. It also means a return to details which had apparently passed with time, but in reality, had remained deeply embedded for generations and only mixed with the new reality through an absurd method. This deliberation over the sources of our pop-cultured world, made all the more ridiculous by reckless aspirations to self-destruction, is a central theme of all of Lébl's work; it is clearly no accident that he devoted himself almost exclusively to texts from the end of the nineteenth century and the twentieth century.

It could be said that he took up the principles of 'action scenography'[21] changes of function, the inclusion of the actor into work with a stage object, from his amateur work but developed them somehow unperturbedly, in his own, 'overdosed', way, with a drop of irony. What was essential, which could be seen from the performances of his productions, was the attentive listening to a dream, to associations which were outwardly linked together very freely, but in fact in connection with that 'listening to a dream', with iron logic. These constantly-repeating dreams, but on each occasion different, harmonize with the presence of favourite elements on stage: the fragile, wintry birch trees (*Vojcev, The Seagull*); the motif of 'incomparable' Egypt (*The Maids, Fernando Krapp*); the three-dimensional angels derived from a hearse, *Vojcev*, the production dedicated to Kurt Vonnegut, 'angels of my time', *Fernando Krapp, Our Proud Peasants*, in Act 4 of *The Seagull* one supports the leg of a table; 'classical' columns made of paper, their model taken from the fly-leaf of an old book (*Fernando Krapp, Seagull*).

Elements and objects passing from one production to another sealed Lébl's style and also his sentimental relationship with these items, with the environment where the production was created, with people. They were not fruitless instruments of provocation, practical jokes, but essential talismans, living objects with which the designer-and-director-in-one needed to maintain contact, communication, relationship; and with them, to experience and to create the PLAY.

Notes

1. It may also have been inspired by the name of a painter born and working in Bohemia, Willi (Vilém) Nowak (1886–1977).
2. Vyskočil, I., 'Byl jsem ohřmen' (I was overwhelmed), *Svět a divadlo* (World and Theatre) 3, 1992, nos. 1–2, p. 26.
3. Mikulka, V., on the production, *The Maids*, *Denní Telegraf,* (Daily Telegraph), 17 November, 1993.
4. Just, V., on *The Seagull*: 'Chudák Anton Pavlovič' (Poor Anton Pavlovich), *Divadelní noviny* (Theatre News), 1994, no. 11.
5. Karban, P., *PRO*, 1993, no. 50.
6. Ptáčková, V.,'Svět podle Petra Lébla' (The World according to Petr Lebl), *Svět a divadlo* 5, 1994, no. 6, p. 41.
7. Lukeš, M,. 'Hra o pravdu' (Play about Truth), *Svět a divadlo* 3, no. 9-10, 1992, pp. 28–33.
8. Vyskočil I., *Racek* (*The Seagull*), *Svět a divadlo* 5, 1994, no. 6, p. 53.
9. Hořínek, Z., 'Služky jako vězeňské psychodrama' (*The Servants* as a Prison Psychodrama), *Svět a divadlo* 4, no. 6, 1993, p. 102.
10. For the Australian Broadcasting Commission, in *Prague Writers' Festival*, catalogue, 21–25 April 2002, p. 50.
11. Genet, J., *Služky* (*The Maids*), Act 1, translation by Petr Lébl.
12. Lukeš, M., *Racek* (*Seagull*), *Svět a divadlo* 5, no. 6, 1994, p. 48.
13. Smoláková, V., 'Dobrý večer, hrůzná společnosti!' (Good Evening, Horrible Society!), *Český deník* (Czech Daily), 10 June, 1994.
14. Ibid.
15. Lukeš, M., *Racek* (*Seagull*), op. cit., n. 13.
16. Hořínek, Z., 'Strýček Váňa v tropech' (*Uncle Vanya in Pieces*), *Svět a divadlo* 10, no. 6, 1999, p. 85.
17. Programme copy.
18. Programme copy.
19. Paraphrased version of Grossman's original text of the concept of 1962 in M. Lukeš: 'Zastaralý vynález?', (Old-fashioned Invention), interview with Jan Grossman, *Divadlo* (Theatre) 18, no. 1, 1967, p. 57.
20. Ptáčková, V.,. op. cit., p. 40.
21. This term is used to define scenography which has a performative quality in its relationship with the performers.

Chapter 6

The Organics of the Rehearsal Room: Contemporary Directing Practice and the Director-Designer Relationship

Alison Oddey

In Helen Manfull's *Taking Stage: Women Directors on Directing*, (1999), Manfull argues that, 'One of the most fascinating areas of the directorial process is the delicate balance and relationship achieved between director and designer.'[1] This delicacy of relationship is described by the director Phyllida Lloyd as 'that point at which several talents and several art forms must merge, cohere, and find harmony.'[2] It is with this definition in mind that I want to explore and examine the collaborative, cooperative working relationship of different contemporary theatre directors and designers and how that particular relationship of two people as director and designer translates into the process of creativity, the working ensemble and the organics of the rehearsal room, which are dependent on a successful prior-rehearsal understanding of the selected story, play or opera and the place of production.

This chapter interrogates how rehearsal processes differ, in the full awareness that, for every production, this will always be a unique process and experience, which is dependent on the director's collaborative team, the play, opera or project chosen, the actors and the production team. In order to explore the various perspectives of the rehearsal room, I focus on the director-designer's relationship; of the director Phyllida Lloyd's collaborative approach to directing theatre and opera, with particular reference to working with the designer Anthony Ward and their specific processes of working on Friedrich Schiller's *Mary Stuart*[3] and Benjamin Britten's *Peter Grimes*.[4] I consider the differences between directing-designing for theatre and opera, how the process adapts according to scale and time, and how the designer is a central figure to the director in revealing layers of meaning of the text. I then examine the director-designer relationship further in relation to technology with regard to the designer Tom Pye's experiences of working with two directors, Simon McBurney and Deborah Warner, as the set designer, video designer, with the realization on the Royal National Theatre, London (RNT)/Complicite's production of Shakespeare's *Measure for Measure*[5] and on Warner's production of *The PowerBook*,[6] which was based on Jeanette Winterson's novel *The PowerBook* and devised by Warner, Winterson and Fiona Shaw.

In the director Phyllida Lloyd's inaugural lecture as the Cameron Macintosh Professor at St. Catherine's College, Oxford University on 6 March, 2006, Lloyd spoke of her experiences of the differences of the rehearsal processes of theatre and opera in relation to the actors, singers, designer, musical conductor and production team. The overwhelming essence of Lloyd speaking as a director of both text and music is of collaboration, creativity, curiosity, learning and ensemble. Lloyd's rehearsal room is one that gives time, space and silence to the participants to listen, discover and develop an individual response and understanding of their role, as rehearsals progress, whether as singers in Benjamin Britten's *Peter Grimes* or as actors in Lloyd's highly acclaimed production of Schiller's *Mary Stuart* in London's West End.[7]

Lloyd's awareness of different ways of working in rehearsal include the use of objectives and breakdown of intentions relating to words and the text, as well as the more pragmatic approach of getting up and doing, of improvising without prior discussion. Previously, Lloyd has been interested in the notion of process as being:

> full of tangible and intangible phases, and each of them excites me differently. The time spent before rehearsals begin, exploring the architecture of the play, often with the designer, is like amassing supplies for the journey – planning the route if you like. Being part of a new group of people and forging out into unknown territory with them in rehearsal is a fantastic privilege.[8]

She describes it as 'this tension between allowing something to happen in the rehearsal room and, on the other hand, grabbing it, shaping it and fixing it – that's my preoccupation.'[9] Lloyd describes the rehearsal process for *Mary Stuart* with regard to the actors as being those of the 'court of the mind' and those of the 'court of the heart'.

In April 2006, Lloyd worked with designer Anthony Ward on Benjamin Britten's *Peter Grimes* for Opera North in Leeds and in the pre-rehearsal period was behind with their 'designer deadline'[10] for the production, which was due to rehearse at the end of August 2007. Lloyd argued that logistical issues are pertinent in the world of opera, as opposed to theatre, making the processes of working very different. Opera demands design issues to be 'resolved much further ahead than in theatre', especially in relation to touring the work to different locations. Lloyd cites Benjamin Britten's opera *Gloriana* and Frederick Schiller's play *Mary Stuart* as two of the most important productions of her career for different reasons, 'the common factors are Elizabeth I and Anthony Ward.' Lloyd has also made a film of *Gloriana*, designed by Tom Pye, which was an attempt:

> to give a screen audience an experience which they could never have had in the theatre and it was inspired by the performance of Josephine Barstow as Elizabeth. It was a kind of deconstruction of the opera, an attempt to enter the imagination of the person playing Elizabeth I on a night in the theatre when the gap between her and the role had so closed there was no off-stage and on-stage, and the backstage world became the territory of the performance as well. We were mirroring the piece, which was about the way in which the public and private worlds meshed and bled into each other with the private and public world of a theatre.

The parallels of *Gloriana* being made for a physical world onstage and for film are about Lloyd's decisions and desire 'to peel back the things that would prevent the audience from participating in the experience.' She is clear that these questions are not about what period the piece is to be presented in, or about the concept, but about a set of cultural references for the audience to decode: 'I never start from that premise, because it's adding yet another layer of obfuscation to something that is already fiendishly complex.'

Mary Stuart represents the 'happy renaissance of our relationship' with Ward, and it is the second time that they have collaborated on a piece about Elizabeth I. Lloyd cites *Gloriana*, written in the 1950s, set in the sixteenth and early seventeenth centuries and *Mary Stuart*, written in Germany in 1800 about England in the 1580s, as indicative of a central question about design choices: 'Why did we choose to perform *Gloriana* in absolutely scrupulous Elizabethan costume, and *Mary Stuart* with men in suits and the women in period costume?' Lloyd states that everything goes back to the text. In the current example of the opera, *Peter Grimes* is both the music and the words. Lloyd believes that it is spiritually important to receive the texture of work that goes on in parallel:

We're always listening to the music but keep going back to the text, not always because text will reveal meaning, but will give us another kind of shape to the evening and prevent us panicking. The terror of designing *Peter Grimes*, is that the music of a storm or a sunlit morning on the sea is so overwhelmingly evocative that we're paralysed by our sense that every choice we make is inadequate. The only possible choice is one of stasis, just not to make a choice. Every mark we make on the canvas, every little straw we put into the model box is in some way a desecration and that in fact we might be better to bring in the curtain and listen to this music in silence as many previous productions have done – these musical interludes.

Lloyd and Ward have steeped themselves 'in the nourishment of the journey', which requires an open mind and a gathering of supplies for this journey. Lloyd and Ward immerse themselves in the text of music and word alone and together, whilst also in relation to the history of the opera, creating 'scrapbooks of reference', which might include 'racing around houses of Elizabethan England or listening to jazz.' Lloyd's sense of paring down a piece is vital to understanding how director-designer choices are made, as in *Gloriana*, where the pared down version of an Elizabethan world is an attempt 'to peel away all the things that stop you from understanding, hearing or participating in it, in the knowledge that the music is deconstructing the piece in front of your eyes, because it's not Elizabethan music, it's actually a post-war version of this.'

Lloyd and Ward spent a great deal of time discussing the space and use of the space for *Mary Stuart*. She describes the Donmar Studio as 'a very tricky theatre to work in' and how they were trying to strip away anything that would prevent the audience from experiencing the play. What specifically excites Lloyd is in what way the two women, Mary Stuart and Elizabeth I, are sharing the experience: 'To surround them by a court of ornately costumed men in high heeled shoes, doublet and hose, codpieces, swords and all the trappings that one would have needed to bring into that space…would have been to muffle the clarity of the aloneness of the women in their own worlds and their shared experience.' This resulted in further questions about the men and, if the Elizabethan was stripped away, what they would be wearing. Lloyd and Ward's research included looking at photographs of Thatcher's cabinet, an image of Thatcher 'at a Tory Conference, cake of white make-up on her face, surrounded by men in expensive Saville Row suits…not to draw a parallel between Thatcher and Elizabeth I but about the isolation of her.' This design decision was a huge strength of the production, and as Michael Billington comments:

> Lloyd has taken a bold decision. She puts Schiller's rival queens, Mary and Elizabeth, into period costume and the surrounding male courtiers into modern dress. Immediately this makes the point, like Andrea Breth's Vienna Burgtheater production that came to Edinburgh, that the two women are similarly isolated and imprisoned. Mary is literally held captive in Fotheringay.[11]

Consequently, it is this paring away process, which has become the journey of Lloyd's relationship with Ward and her relationship with design. However, Lloyd argues that design decisions are often required 'long before you want to make them, especially with a play.' She references a specific example of this with the National Theatre's Olivier production of Shakespeare's *Pericles*,[12] designed by Mark Thompson. This is the curse of the system, in her view, demanding the creation of a space and costume designs for a large, very diverse company of people. Some of the design decisions were made before the rehearsal process of about six to eight weeks started. Lloyd comments:

> This journey we were on – the beast we were creating – grew in directions I had never imagined. By the time we came to put this thing, which had evolved into this shape which had been pre-cast, it was a violent, harrowing experience, horrible for the actors…if I had had more courage I would have scrapped the set and the costumes, but actually I think that would have been a creative choice, because the piece in that space needed a huge amount of definition visually and we wouldn't have had time to repair what we would have destroyed.

In another example of Wagner's *Ring Cycle*,[13] which she describes as sixteen hours of opera that had to be logistically managed to be performed in one week and in one theatre, Lloyd 'was determined, where designs had to be presented ages before rehearsals began, that the biggest creative decisions and choices would be the ones taken in the rehearsal room rather than those taken in the Design Studio. The design would be such that it would go on releasing the direction in whatever direction the activity took us in the room.' For Lloyd this has meant working in a much more sparse way with each production that follows:

> I don't want to do staging, I want to have that process of discovery, a baton change of where the model leaves the designer's studio and is handed to actors and handed over to somebody to be built. I want the journey to start then, not think that's done, but it's with the designer that you discover the architecture of the piece. That's the mutual joy of it.

Lloyd perceives the organics of the rehearsal room as constantly evolving and shifting. In her role as the director, she wants to be able to continue releasing the work so that the opera or play comes alive:

> much of it will remain quite out of focus; there might be explosions happening, sights, smells and sounds coming into focus. As they do, you want to acknowledge them, find something…very often it's something that the actors in the room will all recognize. If you are all open and listening to each other, there will be something mutual…actors make that part of the building bricks…

Lloyd gives an example from *Mary Stuart*, where she was passionate about the staging of the sitting of Elizabeth I with her back to the audience through the whole of the court scene:

> Harriet [Walters] felt very vulnerable, her subtlety of listening was completely lost. Whilst alert and respectful to her fear, I felt sure these three speeches about England needed to be presented in this most dynamic way. Gradually, you begin to make arrangements to accommodate them – Mary Stuart's room, where the bed or chair is going to be – those things are not fixed until very late.

Consequently, Lloyd was not keen to have a run-through of the play too soon, and delayed the moment of running the play, as there is 'a tendency to cling onto something but it becomes hard to stand right back and see a scene like you've never seen it before.'

The transfer of the *Mary Stuart* production from the Donmar to a West End proscenium arch theatre made the dynamics of space different. Here, all the audience saw was a diagonal dynamic, the simple wooden bench along the wall and a chair: 'the image we kept having was of a row of men on a bench, either watching a woman sitting on a chair, or it was ambiguous whether they were supervising her or watching her from a position of power, or whether they were waiting, hoping to be chosen.' Lloyd describes it as getting to the essence of the wood and the thing in the centre. In the design process, they started with a lot more things, 'a complex floor with leaded crucifix in it, all kinds of signs that in the end we questioned why we needed to tell people that there's a catholic martyr at the heart of this.' Lloyd comments that there is so much going on that they just needed to have the space to let the actors speak, 'A lot of the agony went into the simple things, like how far onstage the side walls should be. A model box of Janet [McTeer] in the middle of the room, there, no, there, no, in relation to height, in matters of indefinable proportion.'

The production is to go to Broadway, New York in a year or so, which will be a fantastic opportunity for Lloyd to revive and renew it. She will be starting with the actors Janet McTeer and Harriet Walters and the text. The remaining company will be American actors and Lloyd's preoccupation is whether they all assume English accents: 'My feeling is that we should try to avoid that and have all the men talking American and see how that further throws their separateness into relief.' She is aware of a different context, where the audience's sense of relationship to Europe and their understanding or collective memory of catholic past will not be the same. The reward of the production will be to let the actors speak in their own accents, 'the fusion of all those elements to speak in the now.'

Lloyd is aware that the work between her and Ward is becoming harder as they attempt to have less on stage. She argues that simplicity is hard to achieve and knows that other directors prefer more design, so that Ward 'has an easier time with them.' Lloyd acknowledges Ward as 'a brilliant costume designer', referencing examples of choices he made to stylize and abstract what Walters wore as Elizabeth I, 'which was not Elizabethan at all, it was just a kind of silhouette, a version. She wasn't wearing a farthingale, her hair was incorrect because we wanted to use her own hair and add something to it. It was all completely abstracted. Much more of the energy went into the space, trying to create the empty space.'

Lloyd describes Ward as having a natural instinct for costume design and working from the people, citing their work on *Peter Grimes*: 'he can't start creating the costumes until he has every one of the fifty-five faces of the chorus in front of him. It's built on people.' She states that Ward feels less at ease in the rehearsal room and that they have never started in the rehearsal room with nothing, 'which is a source of grief between us, a bone of contention.' Lloyd's description of Ward is of somebody who is not a particularly live presence in the rehearsal room, which may be attributed to not quite knowing what his role is: 'he will have a relationship with the actors one-to-one, but he wouldn't partake in giving notes.' However, she is clear that if they have made their preparations correctly, 'then the space he's made for me will yield.' Lloyd suggests that Ward would rather be 'off in a little other boat, sailing aside fishing for fabrics, which are his speciality, whilst I am at work with the actors. When we come together in the theatre, when the aesthetic is being realized in tangible form, in costume and light and design, then we come back together, sit side by side and begin to work together again.' A huge contributing factor to the director-designer relationship of Lloyd and Ward is the lighting designer, so that a palette is created for the lighting designer to create a sense of space and staging. These collaborations are critical for Lloyd, as in the examples of Hugh Vanstone, who lit *Mary Stuart*, and Paule Constable, 'who lit part of *The Ring* and *Peter Grimes*.' Lloyd uses the term 'genius' to describe both Vanstone and Constable in using the space and light to bring to life whatever happens in the rehearsal room.

Technology and the director-designer relationship

The collaborative relationship of Lloyd and Ward utilizes the world of the computer in every sense, so that the tool of technology enables them to communicate with each other in the design process, such as, in the examples of how they amass their images and scrapbooks. In their design process of *Peter Grimes*, everything was abundant and accessible, so that Lloyd's attempt to storyboard a certain part of *Peter Grimes* without Ward resulted in opening her computer to look at characters in terms of thinking about them as people: 'we pluck these things out of the ether, being able to collage them…Anthony would have scanned that and sent it to me.' In the same way, their visit to Aldeburgh to look at and experience the beach experimented with technology towards the creation of design: 'We knelt down on the beach with his digital camera that takes video, and videoed the sea coming over the shingle. We rushed back to his studio, went onto I-Photo, made a slide show out of the frozen video and photographs we'd taken, set them to Benjamin Britten music, and we took DVDs of them.' However, when Opera North visited them and asked why there was nothing in the model box, Lloyd and Ward offered the DVD of their experience, resulting in the question: 'Where's the work?'

The physical experience of their designer-director relationship is about this dialogue through cyber space, 'this kit for the journey', which they grab very quickly. However, neither of them is interested in using the media of video or film on stage as a substitute for scenery. The speed and tricks of technology, the reading of imagery and the absorption of information makes the stark, simplicity of the theatrical experience of *Mary Stuart* become even more remarkable, according to Lloyd:

> My stripping away to the empty space, to the actor in the space is unconsciously because I feel that I don't need to accommodate this other thing and because there's something so unique happening in the live experience. As other experiences stop being live, as relationships start being in a chat room or across the internet, therefore, being in a room with the human, you want to try and take away everything that stops it feeling human.

The director-designer relationship of Simon McBurney, Artistic Director of Complicite and designer Tom Pye, however, suggests a more radical use of technology in the rehearsal room, as illustrated in the creation of Shakespeare's *Measure for Measure* for the collaborative RNT/Complicite production of 2004 and 2006. McBurney thinks of objects on stage as sculptural elements, which include the technology of microphones, cameras or video projectors. The technology is available for everyone, such as the forty-pound surveillance cameras used in the production, and McBurney believes that these elements are part of our lives and need to be seized on by all artists. McBurney uses video to write, playing with improvisations on screen, projecting it onto surfaces of the set or body of the actor, for example, in Complicite's production of *Mnemonic*,[14] needing to change things instantaneously 'otherwise for me they are dead'.[15]

McBurney works quickly with video technology in rehearsals as he does with lights and sound, 'we're over the cusp in the digital revolution...I use them because they are becoming cheaper and cheaper and more available.' In *Measure for Measure*, McBurney rehearses with an enormous amount of technology in the room with designer, Pye, and sound designer, Christopher Shutt, present from the start, and Sven Ortel from the second week. McBurney, Pye and Ortel worked in a collaborative process, which involved video from early on in rehearsals, integrating and weaving it into the work. Collaborating with everyone in the rehearsal room makes for an atmosphere and safe environment, as Pye suggests, for 'throwing in random ideas, not really knowing why you are trying them, to see what they produce.'[16] Pye cites an example of this playing process with regard to video, where they had a camera on the ceiling and projectors on the floor and on the back, and from this playing, the story of Mariana evolved. Ideas were tried out in rehearsal, for example, in terms of what could be filmed from above and what was useful for telling the story, to create the sequence of shipwreck projecting water on floor and back, as the actress rolls across the floor.

McBurney is interested in what happens with multiple realities, perceiving them as extensions of our consciousness:

> reaching out to the internet, our consciousness moves into the computer and through the lines of the computer all over the world. It's a curious image the internet; it's exactly like an extension of the human mind. All aspects of our darkest sexuality or violence are to be found on the internet; also the most wonderful things are to be found, the possibility of undermining governments and protesting at wars in a way that was never possible before.

McBurney is interested in virtual reality, the reality of celluloid, fiction and the play. He states that there is a curious contradiction in an audience believing more in film than theatre, and yet, 'theatre can become more like theatre than it's ever been; it can emphasise its theatreness.' In this sense, he is keen to alert people to the actual playing, using an actor at the start of a production to come out and talk to the audience, prior to the imagined world, 'because we are so aware that it is entirely fictional, created and false; how does it relate to reality, how is it virtual and how is it real?'

McBurney's filmic process of working to make theatre more like theatre relates to his absolutely focused understanding of the space to play in, questioning what happens when the play is taken apart and re-assembled. He perceives the director as a kind of map reader, a weather forecaster, a referee and a painter: 'each of those things has to be balanced in the room'. The excitement for Pye as the designer of *Measure for Measure* in the rehearsal room is to not know exactly where he is going, to not have stipulated every idea but to see what happens with the tools made available. The organics of finding the tools can be played with by McBurney and other members of the team right up to and including previews. Pye states: 'None of us really know everything about a text before we start rehearsing', and argues that this is what rehearsals are for, leaving options open, creating tools rather than set environments, so that 'we can go a lot further to backing up the text.' Pye suggests that the history of scene design is that the director and designer are supposed to know everything about the text, in terms of how the set will be used, but 'we don't know the complexities of the texts.' It is McBurney and Pye's approach to the text and how it is realized, which shocked and excited the audience reaction at the previews of the play's production, which in turn, invited them to make delicate changes, to fine-tune and to do some more work on the video technology.

Pye's experience of working collaboratively and as designer with the director Deborah Warner on the production of *The PowerBook*[17] was also evident in the rehearsal room, where video ideas were collected, for example, the horse projection and related story. At this point in the production the story turns to a representation of Sir Lancelot arriving at Queen Guinevere's bed-chamber. The arrival of Sir Lancelot is heralded by the projection of a beautiful white horse appearing ethereally out of the darkness and Sir Lancelot enters the chamber from a metal vertical ladder high above her, which enters the bed-chamber at the same time as he climbs down. All the time, his movements and those of the projected horse are both 'real' and dream-like in speed and quality. This raises the temperature of the love scene and creates a non-verbal and memorable scenic experience. Ideas evolved slowly at the start of this rehearsal process, so that the playing with technology brought a desire for 'almost a computer aesthetic', so that it looked contemporary, slick, sharp and refined, which is how the collaborative group came to the idea of a screen and the floor being a reflection of that, 'like a PowerBook'. However, the difficulties of this rehearsal process were to do with the technology, as it was the early days of software, according to Pye, and they were all new to it. Pye cites the technology as 'one of our biggest hurdles', which only came together towards the end of the rehearsal process, having 'cooked it up on stage'. It is the advance and development of the software that Pye attributes to the beneficial effect of collaboration with McBurney and previously Ortel in *Measure for Measure*.

Pye worked with Ortel on *The Powerbook*: 'we understand each other's aesthetics about what we do like on video and what we don't, and the difficulties of representation and non-representation.' Pye believes that video is very similar to set design when it is descriptive, two-dimensional scenery: 'when working with abstract ideas it's a delicate balance of what works and what doesn't work.' He cites the example of the Convent scene in *Measure for Measure*: 'and for a while we were projecting some convent gates up on the back wall, because Simon [McBurney] had this idea that as Isabella is pulled away somehow the image of gates would recede into the background.' Pye argues that he would never fly in a wheel or a pair of gates, so in projecting them he felt uncomfortable, and finally chose a Velasquez painting of 'The Immaculate Conception', 'so suddenly you're in a far more interesting world.' He states that it is Ortel who deals with the real technology, 'the nuts and bolts of the software, and he also did the design for the actual rig, where the cameras go, what projectors we're using; the real detail is Sven.'

However, there is no doubt that Pye's design for the production is received well, illustrated in the revived and revised production at the Royal National Theatre in February 2006:

Designer Tom Pye, presents an austere, bare, sloping acting area, with shallow steps at either side from which video cameras capture the action and transmit it to a number of overhead screens. This video, together with lighting that has a severe, steely edge to it and echoing sound effects, lends the whole production a kind of techno, 'Big Brother' feel to it. Not only does it connect with the intrusive TV show 'Big Brother' which monitors housemates continually through video, but there are also similarities with the original idea of 'Big Brother' found in George Orwell's novel, '1984'. And with images of George Bush projected onto the background, secret-service types with sunglasses to guard a

Duke who wears military uniform, this is a vision of 'Measure for Measure' not only brought bang-up-to-date, but also with the trappings of military dictatorship, rather than benevolent governance.[18]

Design is challenging for Pye when going into a new rehearsal room. Pye's background as a designer is in film and, for this reason, he enjoys the challenge of designing for both film and theatre, working in a different aesthetic and thinking in a different way about design. Pye is keen to do more film, to go back to having learned how to use one medium and comparing it with another, applying it differently. He is interested in the crossover of film and theatre and how the two mediums can be used, and is fortunate in working with directors, such as Warner, McBurney and Lloyd, who have experimented and tried ideas out. He believes that working in these ways that are more abstract and less representational enables exploration and showing what theatre can really do 'and why it can be such a profound and exciting art form.' Consequently, Pye enjoys working with directors and little information at the start, describing himself as being aesthetic and instinctive in the rehearsal room, playing with the latest tools, software, technology or real materials in scenic design as they become available.

For Pye, there is a difference when designing opera. He argues that the world of opera operates in a different way, varying from house to house: 'you design the set in advance; you even light it in advance and then you start rehearsing', which is in contrast to designing *Measure for Measure*, where Pye had not designed the set when rehearsals started. In this production example, there was the practical difference from opera, of a blank canvas and ten weeks of rehearsal, 'and because opera companies do work in repertory, they do need to get them built earlier and that's a tension we have to deal with – to try and keep things open.' Pye conceives opera as a great art form, feeling free to do scenic movements, to be abstract and to be more expressive, 'because you can follow the music and not the narrative, and often they don't always do the same thing.' He cites his collaboration with Warner on Britten's *The Turn of the Screw* at the Royal Opera House in 2002, exampled in Act Two with the planks, where there are interesting tensions in the scene and what the scenery is doing. Pye finds joy in directors coming to him with opera projects and the less he knows about them, he feels, the better.

The organics of the rehearsal room, according to both Pye and Lloyd, offer the same approach to working, whether it is opera or theatre, although each one is different. For Lloyd, the time factor per performer makes the organics different for the products created, for example, the difference between working with the 70 to 80 people on stage and 20 children in *Gloriana* and the eleven actors in *Mary Stuart*. Inevitably, with roughly the same amount of rehearsal periods, there is more time to spend with the actors of *Mary Stuart* to give individual scope and choice. Lloyd states that the choreographic aspects of the work require huge amounts of time and has to be very disciplined: 'The process adapts according to scale and time, but the intention is to give as much of that *Mary Stuart* process to all of it. One knows that gets the best out of people. You'd work the same way with opera singers, if there were eleven of them. You work the same with the principals, as with Janet and Harriet, providing that they are there for six weeks.' Lloyd is speaking about practical strategies:

> to get that un-definable thing to emerge, real practical things, which is why you can't talk about design. You have to get in the model box with bits of cardboard, it's very *Blue Peter*. You have got to get in there, and put something in there and look at it, whilst you're listening to the music, reading the text and downloading images from Google.

Lloyd acknowledges the many layers of meaning in *Mary Stuart*, which bring the audience closer to the experience or push them away from it: 'The designer is an absolutely central figure in helping those layers of meaning to be revealed rather than accruing layers, but actually almost peeling away.' As Lloyd explored her production of *Peter Grimes*, she is clear that Britten's naturalistic demands of a pub or a court room might now 'feel to us not necessarily helpful in releasing the meaning, because of our changing culture that everything is contextual and every big world event or every time the weather changes, our perspective changes too, it's all on the move.' At the time of interviewing Lloyd, she was quite stuck with *Peter Grimes*, but knows that it is part of the process of discovery, so that what becomes important are the things that are in focus for Ward and her: 'we have to go back to those, all human things, not a blue backcloth and a low wall, it's actually a picture of a wreck of Medusa; the things that are essential are all about people rather than the look of it.'

In fact, when the production opened in October 2006, it was clear from the reviews that this particular director-designer relationship had been successful:

> Using a subtle mix of costumes to suggest any era from the 1940s to the present, Lloyd concocts a chilling series of stage pictures…Lloyd achieves these effects with incredible economy of means. There is almost nothing to Anthony Ward's set apart from a few duckboards and an enormous, suspended net that represents everything from the manhunt to the billowing seas, and visually echoes the theme of Ellen Orford's embroidery aria, sung here with heart-stopping pathos by Giselle Allen. The turbulent, fluid conducting of Richard Farnes reinforces the notion that the chief character of Peter Grimes is the sea, and the Opera North chorus is magnificent throughout.[19]

This is the essence of each director-designer relationship, how the director relates to the designer, to the chosen text within a particular space, to the collaborative team responsible for the lighting, sound, costumes, to the actors and other production staff. It is for this reason that certain directors continue to work in partnership with specific designers, and indeed, lighting, sound and costume designers, knowing that their developed sense of shorthand, of language, gesture and vocabulary pertinent to their process of working together, can be depended on within the organics of the rehearsal room and the developing rehearsal process for each new production.

Notes

1. Manfull, H., *Taking Stage, Women Directors on Directing* London: Methuen Drama, 1999, p. 25.
2. Ibid.
3. Schiller, F., *Mary Stuart*, directed by Phyllida Lloyd, designed by Anthony Ward, Donmar Warehouse, 2005, and then transferred to Apollo Theatre, October-January 2005–6.
4. Britten, B., *Peter Grimes*, directed by Phyllida Lloyd, designed by Anthony Ward, Grand Theatre, Leeds and touring other Northern theatres and Sadler's Wells, London in October–November, 2005.
5. Shakespeare, W., *Measure for Measure*, a Complicite/RNT production, directed by Simon McBurney, designed by Tom Pye, 2004 and 2006.
6. Devised by J. Winterson, D. Warner, F. Shaw, *The PowerBook*, based on the novel by J. Winterson, directed by Deborah Warner, designed by Tom Pye, Royal National Theatre, May 2002 and touring production to Paris and Rome, September-October 2003.
7. See endnote 3.
8. Giannachi, G., and Luckhurst, M., (Eds.), *On Directing*, London: Faber & Faber, 1999, p. 57.
9. Ibid., p. 56.
10. Oddey, A., unpublished interview with Phyllida Lloyd, April 2006. All subsequent references are from this interview unless otherwise stated.
11. Billington, M., review of *Mary Stuart*, Donmar Warehouse, London, *The Guardian*, 21 July, 2005.
12. Shakespeare, W., *Pericles*, directed by Phyllida Lloyd, designed by Mark Thompson, Royal National Theatre, 1994.
13. Wagner, *The Ring Cycle*, directed by Phyllida Lloyd, designed by Richard Hudson, English National Opera, April 2005.
14. Complicite's *Mnemonic*, directed by Simon McBurney, designed by Michael Levine, originally devised for the Saltzburg Festival, production at Royal National Theatre, 2001, Riverside Studios, 2003.
15. Oddey, unpublished interview with Simon McBurney, July 2004. All subsequent references are from this interview unless otherwise stated.
16. Oddey, unpublished interview with Tom Pye, May 2004. All subsequent references are from this interview unless otherwise stated.
17. See endnote 6.
18. Brown, P., *Measure for Measure*, London Theatre Guide, 18 February, 2006.
19. Hickling, A., 'Peter Grimes', Grand Theatre, Leeds, *The Guardian*, 28 October 2006.

Chapter 7

Collaborative Models: Mielziner, Williams and Kazan

Julia Listengarten

W hat discoveries about past theatrical practices could potentially influence the shape(s) of the theatre in the twenty-first century? More specifically, what discoveries about past collaborative models in theatrical practice are integral to the theatre of the future? There are three collaborative models I would like to explore in this chapter: the relationship between designer and playwright, designer and director, and, perhaps most problematic, designer, director, and playwright. Particularly, I will examine the artistic partnership between Jo Mielziner and Tennessee Williams; Mielziner and Elia Kazan; and finally Mielziner, Kazan and Williams. In all three models, the designer plays an essential role. Does this prevalent role of a designer support or contradict the commonly accepted definition of the twentieth century theatre as a director's theatre, in which the single, usually directorial, artistic vision dominates?

Elia Kazan, one of the important players in the collaborative models I am examining here, writes in his autobiographical book:

A director is constantly threatened by the possibility of erosion in the goal he's set for himself. Since art is the product of a single vision, the director must, at all costs, maintain his grip on what he wants. Compromise is a trap. Always ready to spring.[1]

Although Kazan, as the director, is unmistakably a key figure in the collaborations with the playwright Tennessee Williams and the designer Jo Mielziner, it is the role of Mielziner and the effect of his artistic vision on playwriting and directing I would like to draw attention to.

In his article 'Simultaneity in Modern Stage Design,' Thomas Postlewait refers to Kenneth Macgowan's book, *The Theatre of Tomorrow*, in which the latter talks about the 'new synthesis' of the modern theatre, 'a complex and rhythmic fusion of setting, lights, actors, and play'.[2] As this romantic idea of artistic unity was more or less preserved in the productions born out of the collaborations involving all three key players: Mielziner, Kazan and Williams, the dynamic of their artistic partnership, a partnership that ultimately resulted in this synthesis, was not always one of harmony and unity. There have been, for instance, articles and books written on Elia Kazan's directing strategy of him usurping control over the material as well as the production team he was working with, especially when the material was a play by Tennessee Williams. Brenda Murphy in her study *Tennessee Williams and Elia Kazan* states that: 'Kazan's own drive to control the aesthetic process and its final product was ultimately as destructive to this finely tuned creative collaboration as were Williams' contradictory dependence on and resistance to his director, both emotional and artistic.[3]

Rather than accentuate the destructive side of the Kazan-Williams artistic as well as personal relationship, I would like to explore the constructive role of Jo Mielziner's scenography in the collaborative process and the changing place of the designer within this so-called 'new synthesis' of the twentieth century theatre. From an aesthetic if not financial point of view, Mielziner's role within the designer-playwright and/or designer-director collaborative models is no longer seen as that of a client to a patron. Indeed, Mielziner was not merely hired by a producer to visually execute the playwright's and/or director's ideas; he was a driving force in creating a stage language that defined the American dramatic theatre of the 1940s and 1950s.

Mielziner and Williams

The first collaboration between Mielziner and Williams took place in 1945 on the Broadway production of Williams' *The Glass Menagerie*. The play had previously premiered in Chicago a few months before, receiving excellent reviews from drama critics and establishing Williams as a young talented playwright. Mielziner, in turn, had already been recognized as an inspiring Broadway designer developing the innovative principles of the New Stagecraft. Commenting upon the Mielziner-Williams artistic union, Mary Henderson writes in her book *Mielziner: Master of the Modern Stage* that, '[t]he working relationship between Jo and Williams became almost mystical',[4] continuing for almost three decades and resulting in nine collaborations, namely the productions of *The Glass Menagerie* (1945), *A Streetcar Named Desire* (1947), *Summer and Smoke* (1948), *Cat on a Hot Tin Roof* (1955), *Sweet Bird of Youth* (1959), *Period of Adjustment* (1960), *The Milk Train Does Not Stop Here Anymore* (1963), *The Seven Descents of Myrtle* (1968), and *Outcry* (1972).

Not all of the nine collaborations were mutually happy and constructive but I would like to consider the first three Mielziner-Williams most successful collaborative efforts. Both the excitement and satisfaction that Mielziner felt while working with Williams on *The Glass Menagerie* are evident in Mielziner's personal account of this experience. 'Even as an inexperienced young writer', Mielziner writes, 'Tennessee Williams revealed a strong instinct for the visual qualities of the theatre. If he had written plays in the days before the technical development of translucent and transparent scenery, I believe he would have invented it.'[5] What is significant is that in *The Glass Menagerie* Mielziner immediately sensed and welcomed the poetic quality of Williams' 'memory play' that resisted relentless realism in design, which was characteristic of the majority of Broadway productions during the 1930s and 1940s. Moreover, Mielziner saw in the play the possibility of introducing the principle of simultaneity of interior and exterior scenes on stage through the use of scrim, a principle that Williams would later integrate in his plays, especially *A Streetcar Named Desire* and *Summer and Smoke*.

The Glass Menagerie (1945).

It was Mielziner's suggestion, according to Henderson, that

the first lines of dialogue, spoken by Tom, could be delivered outside (above) rather than inside the drab flat (below). Jo designed a transparent 'fourth wall' on scrim depicting an alley and fire escape, which would then allow him to light the interior and exterior scenes either separately or simultaneously, yet give Tom physical and psychic detachment from his mother and sister in their cramped world.[6]

The use of a transparent 'fourth wall' on scrim not only accentuated the poignancy and lyricism of the play and allowed for the relatively easy transition from Tom's outside world to the inside scenes of the story, the juxtaposition between the exterior and the interior also intensified the contrast between the past and the present, between the worlds of memory and actual reality. In the words of Postlewait, Mielziner's simultaneous sets created a sense of 'disruption, disassociation, and displacement.'[7] This sense that Mielziner masterfully introduced in *The Glass Menagerie* would pervade Williams' later plays *A Streetcar Named Desire* and *Summer and Smoke*, in which the real and the illusory coexist simultaneously on the same plane, at times widening the gap between them, at times becoming almost inseparable.

Having worked on the production of *The Glass Menagerie* with Mielziner, Williams understood the power of design and lighting to illuminate the inner, emotional lives of characters on stage and to unveil the ugliness of reality in contrast to the ethereal beauty of illusion. His subsequent dramatic works, therefore, imply the kind of poetic quality and spatial configuration that characterize Mielziner's design style. It is significant that the writing of *A Streetcar Named Desire* and *Summer and Smoke* coincided with the rehearsals for *The Glass Menagerie*. Not surprisingly, therefore, the playwright's initial idea for the staging of *Streetcar* was based on Mielziner's scenic design of *The Glass Menagerie*. Williams' original plan included a scrim or a transparent drop. He envisioned that

[t]he face of the building would be painted on gauze, and when Blanche entered the apartment the interior would be lit with blue light while the exterior light would dim out, making the gauze transparent. The scrim would be lifted into the wings during the first scene as it was in the earlier play, and it would descend at certain times.[8]

Mielziner eventually came up with a more complex and subtle design and lighting plan than the one he used in *The Glass Menagerie*, which, according to Williams, stimulated him to re-write the play. The concept of simultaneity in scenery was taken much farther in *Streetcar*, ultimately increasing the sense of disassociation and disruption already embedded in the play. There were different layers of exterior and interior sets coexisting onstage and being lit at different times. The street behind Kowalski's apartment was painted on a transparent drop and became visible only for a few moments when it was lit from the back; another layer of the exterior was created by the sidewalk running the width of the stage. Kowalski's

A Streetcar Named Desire (1947).

apartment comprised the interior layer of the design, which seemed brighter or more oppressive depending on the focus of the lighting and colours of the gels.[9]

It is well known that the text of *A Streetcar Named Desire* underwent multiple revisions before its premiere on 3 December 1947 in New York City and even though most of the revisions, (including cuts and alterations in stage directions and dialogue), were prompted by Kazan, some of the changes were indeed inspired by Mielziner's design. The visual environment Williams' suggests in the final version of *Streetcar* is based on Mielziner's design vision of the play which he executed, through his scenery and lighting. As Mielziner himself describes:

> throughout the play the brooding atmosphere is like an impressionistic X-ray. We are always conscious of the skeleton of this house of terror, even though we have peripheral impressions, like the chant of the Mexican woman which forms a background to a solo scene of Stella in her bedroom downstage.[10]

The memory-like, almost impressionistic quality of the play's visual environment intensified the subjectivity of Blanche's memories, '[her] reality,' in Kazan's words, 'becomes fantasy too.'[11]

Whereas the first production of *Streetcar* was designed by Mielziner and carried his artistic sensibility over to subsequent stage interpretations of this play, *Summer and Smoke*, when first produced on the arena stage in the Margo Jones Theatre in Dallas, Texas, had practically no scenery at all. When the production was transferred to Broadway, Mielziner was asked to design the play on a proscenium stage under the same direction of Margo Jones. This was the third Mielziner-Williams collaboration, and the playwright knew very well what kind of visual effects he could expect from the designer's scenery and lighting. Needless to say that the scenic components, described in the play's stage directions and implied in its actual action, underscore the form and the lyrical atmosphere of the play and rely on Mielziner's ability to design drama of poetic evocation in which memory and illusion sometimes supercede reality. According to Henderson, Williams wanted Mielziner to create a 'set with the least amount of literal realism,' as he also emphasized the importance of a, 'very moody and romantic sky.'[12] Mielziner's design for *Summer and Smoke* did emblematize the blue sky as a background to the skeletal outlines of the two houses, utilizing once more his principle of juxtaposing exteriors and interiors on the same set.

From this we can infer that, as in the process of staging and re-writing *A Streetcar Named Desire*, Mielziner's design concept for the production of *Summer and Smoke* had an effect on the playwright's shaping of the visual milieu of the play. In the production notes for *Summer and Smoke*, Williams writes that:

> there must be a great expanse of sky so that the entire action of the play takes place against it. This is true of interior as well as exterior scenes. But in fact there are no really interior scenes, for the walls are omitted or just barely suggested by certain necessary fragments such as might be needed to hang a picture or to contain a door frame.[13]

Summer and Smoke (1948).

It is noteworthy that the production notes were written in Rome, where Williams was vacationing at the time, and dated March 1948, a year after the first staging of the play took place in Dallas and a few months after Williams and Mielziner discussed the design concept for its Broadway production. While in Italy, Williams continued working on *Summer and Smoke*, which was due to open in October of the same year. Henderson writes that Williams, before leaving for Italy, asked Mielziner to send his production sketches to him abroad, reminding him how his sketches for *Streetcar* had previously stimulated his imagination and encouraged him to keep revising the play.

After the collaborations on *The Glass Menagerie*, *Streetcar*, and *Summer and Smoke*, as Smith rightly argues, '[the] development of the Mielziner-Williams style becomes fully apparent…[and] [t]he affinity between the two men's aesthetic expression seems to have taken visible shape.'[14] The New York production of *Summer and Smoke* did not, however, become a Broadway hit; one reason for this lukewarm critical audience reception was perhaps the lack of a strong directorial vision. Williams himself comments on, 'a rather mediocre job' of the director, who was 'not inspired, not vital, as Kazan would have been and as the play so dreadfully needed.'[15]

Mielziner and Kazan

Not only did *A Streetcar Named Desire* launch a rewarding even if painful artistic partnership between Williams and Kazan (who at the time was a young aspiring director from the Group Theatre), the production of *Streetcar* also became the inauguration of Kazan's collaborative relationships with Mielziner. This collaboration between the designer and the director led to a series of their successful collaborative experiences, with the next one being the acclaimed production of Arthur's Miller play *Death of a Salesman* in 1949.[16] Although Kazan was undoubtedly a director with a strong, uncompromising vision, Mielziner's design principles influenced if not shaped the director's interest in subjective realism and, later, overt theatricality on stage. In response to a movement away from the strict naturalistic theatre that prevailed on Broadway in the 1940s, Kazan writes: 'No one appreciates how much *A Streetcar Named Desire* did to open the avenue to a less literal approach toward the theatre. Because of *Streetcar* we had *Death of a Salesman*. Now we all hope people are ready for this.'[17]

As much as Mielziner's principle of simultaneity juxtaposing exterior and interior scenes through the use of transparency and complex lighting affected Kazan's painstakingly created *mise-en-scène(s)* in *Streetcar*, the design scheme for *Death of a Salesman* prompted the director to use on stage cinematic techniques that he had previously developed as a film director. Instead of changing locales from the present to the past and back to the present, Mielziner decided to establish the Lomans' house as a main set while all the other scenes occurring not in the house should be played on the forestage. Mielziner writes that this decision, which allowed the scenes to blend avoiding even the shortest break for

Death of a Salesman (1949).

physical changes on stage, 'was not just a visual one; it would set the style in direction and performance, as well as in design.'[18] As a result of this approach, the house itself became a skeleton, a continuation of a *Streetcar* and *Summer and Smoke* motif, and the fragmentary scenes required only the minimum of furniture and props merely to suggest the locale. The rest of the visual environment was achieved through the use of transparent backdrop and lighting. For instance:

> to show the Lomans' house when it was new, the backdrop disappeared into darkness with the lights off and another painted transparent curtain was dropped in front of the stage to show the tree-filled, sun-drenched suburban surroundings of earlier years.[19]

Mielziner's talent in juxtaposing exteriors and interiors on stage gave contemporary playwrights, Williams in particular, the opportunity to blend the contrasting worlds of present and past, reality and memory, truth and illusion without breaking, in the words of Williams himself, 'the fluid quality of the sequence scenes.'[20] To the extent that Mielziner's design vision influenced the direction of playwriting, the designer's ability to create various stage configurations inspired directors, especially Kazan, to explore the limits of stage theatricality, examining the application of cinematic techniques on stage, as in *Death of a Salesman*, as well as probing a different type of relationship between the actors and the audience, as in *Cat on a Hot Tin Roof*. In the latter production, a raked floor protruding into the audience beyond the proscenium eliminated the 'fourth wall' separation between the stage and the auditorium, thus producing a stronger involvement on the part of the audience.

Cat on a Hot Tin Roof was produced on Broadway in 1955 and became a third Mielziner-Kazan production and the second collaboration that included all three of the collaborators Williams, Mielziner and Kazan. Mielziner writes in his memoir that the idea of using a presentational set was born out of the first discussion between him and the director. Interestingly, the vulgar nature of Big Daddy's elephant joke became for both of them the deciding factor in the use of the presentational aesthetics creating the design for this production. Mielziner thought that, 'if the old man is going to tell this story let him work right down not to the footlights but out beyond,' which would clearly create a greater impact upon the audience.[21] This idea excited Kazan, who later wrote that both he and Mielziner realized that the play's, 'great merit was its brilliant rhetoric and its theatricality.'[22] The setting then became, 'a large, triangular platform, tipped toward the audience.'[23] The presentational nature of the setting in *Cat on a Hot Tin Roof* allowed Kazan to explore the combination of Stanislavsky-based internal acting and the explicit theatricality in the relationship between the actors and the audience:

> The play was both a series of eloquent speeches delivered straight to the audience and a series of eloquent pictorial compositions encoding some of its deepest meaning, both surrounded by constant noise and activity that was at the same time realistically detailed and overtly theatrical.[24]

Cat on a Hot Tin Roof (1955).

This particular interpretation of the style of the play significantly differed from Williams' original concept. He was less interested in open theatricality than in poetic evocation of his characters' emotional life on stage, a kind of poetic evocation that he and Mielziner had previously created in *The Glass Menagerie*, *Streetcar*, and *Summer and Smoke*.

Williams, Mielziner and Kazan

Whereas the artistic relationship between Mielziner and Kazan continued to be mutually influential and constructive during their next collaboration on *Sweet Bird of Youth* in 1959, Williams became increasingly discouraged by the direction the designer and the director were taking in relation to his dramatic works. A year before the production of *Cat*, Mielziner and Williams had already experienced a fallout during the pre-production process of *Camino Real*, which was also directed by Kazan but eventually designed by Lemuel Ayers. The next two productions, *Cat on a Hot Tin Roof* and *Sweet Bird of Youth*, became proof that Mielziner had outgrown the subjective realism of his previous collaborations with the playwright, which was compounded by Kazan's strong belief in the necessity of intensifying the theatricality of Williams' plays. This became especially evident in *Sweet Bird of Youth*. In this production, Mielziner combined the openness of the space he created in the *Cat on a Hot Tin Roof* with the design and lighting techniques he used in *Death of a Salesman* to maintain the continuous fluidity of action while shifting the locale. As in *Cat*, the centerpiece of the open set was a large raked bed, and using multiple projections, with the help of 'an expressive lighting code and the very minimum of furniture', he established a convincing set change.[25] 'As in *Cat*, the set contained no doors or windows. The actors mimed the opening of a door or looking out of a window when it was called for. A cyclorama at the rear of the stage allowed for the projection of shutters in the first scene and of palms, sea, and sky when the 'shutters' were 'opened', much as the blinds and the sky had been projected in *Cat*.'[26] The use of small transparent curtain-travellers that could be opened and closed by the actors to determine the time of the day or create a certain mood intensified the theatricality of the production. This overpowering theatricality of the stage language was a definite move away from Williams' subtle lyricism.[27]

While praising, 'a stunning performance [of the actors] and a colorful production', Mielziner was critical of the overall, 'lack of cohesion' in *Sweet Bird of Youth*. Was it in fact the weakness of the script itself, as Mielziner and Kazan were convinced, that prompted the designer and the director to rely on the, 'codes of lighting, space, movement, and gesture'[28] to propel the play's story-line, or the mutual interest of Mielziner and Kazan in unequivocal theatricality and abstraction on stage? In either case, it caused a lot of tension in the collaborative team during the pre-production negotiations, essentially resulting in a production that demonstrated the unprecedented significance of the visual language, which propelled but most likely weakened the play's story-line. The vision of Mielziner and Kazan overpowered the playwright's intentions during the collaborative process. This was a

Sweet Bird of Youth (1959).

relatively new phenomenon in the American dramatic theatre of the 1950s, which was not conducive to the further artistic relationship between Mielziner and Kazan, on one side, and Williams, on the other, but it arguably paved the way to later theatrical developments in which the role of images on stage became predominant.

In fact, in the theatrical experiments of Robert Wilson and Richard Foreman, performance has been dominated by a series of images and the narrative diminished or completely disappeared. As Bonnie Marranca comments on the works of these American avant-garde theatre artists: 'In the Theatre of Images the painterly and sculptural qualities of performance are stressed, transforming this theatre into a spatially-dominated one activated by sense impressions, as opposed to a time-dominated one ruled by linear narrative.'[29]

Although heralded as the master of the modern stage design who inspired succeeding generations of contemporary stage designers, Mielziner did not belong to the American avant-garde and his most successful design projects were accomplished on Broadway. His influence on Tennessee Williams and Elia Kazan, who he collaborated with during the several decades of the mid-twentieth century demonstrated, however, the significant role of the designer in shaping the vision of both the playwright and director, as well as ultimately developing theatrical aesthetics. This paramount importance of the designer's vision in the process of theatrical negotiations has its roots in late nineteenth- and early twentieth century stage explorations of both Gordon Craig and Adolphe Appia; it also foreshadows the late twentieth century emergence of a theatre artist as a designer-director and/or designer-playwright. What differentiates Mielziner's theatrical practice from that of Craig and Appia or late twentieth century theatre artists such as Richard Wilson and Richard Foreman is that Jo Mielziner worked closely with the playwrights and directors in the commercial setting of Broadway theatres.

Understanding and appreciating this role of the designer in any collaborative theatrical model is essential today, in the twenty-first century, as we look at the past practices in theatre to uncover various ideas and models that could help facilitate and prompt the theatrical developments of the future.

Notes

1. Kazan, E., *A Life*, New York: Knopf, 1988, p. 339.
2. Postlewait, T., 'Simultaneity in Modern Stage Design and Drama', *Journal of Dramatic Theory and Criticism*, 3, 1988, pp. 5–31.
3. Murphy, B., *Tennessee Williams and Elia Kazan: A Collaboration in the Theatre*, Cambridge: Cambridge UP, 1992, p. 164.
4. Henderson, M., *Mielziner: Master of Modern Stage Design*, New York: Back Stage Books, 2001.
5. Mielziner, J., *Designing for the Theatre: A Memoir and a Portfolio*, New York: Bramhall House, 1965, p. 124.
6. Henderson, M., *Mielziner...*, New York: Back Stage Books, 2001, p. 143.
7. Postlewait, 'Simultaneity...', *Journal of Dramatic Theory and Criticism*, 3, 1988, pp. 5–31, p. 22.

8. Murphy, pp. 22–3.
9. Henderson, p. 162.
10. Murphy, p. 27.
11. Ibid, p. 25.
12. Henderson, p. 166.
13. Williams, T., *Summer and Smoke*, 1948, p.569. Originally titled *Chart of Anatomy* in 1945 and then became *The Eccentricities of a Nightingale*, 1964. The play tells the story of a lonely, unmarried minister's daughter (Alma Winemiller) who is courted by her childhood love, a wild, undisciplined doctor (Dr. John Buchanan, Jr.). First performance at the Music Box Theatre, New York City, on 6 October 1948 in a production staged by Margo Jones and designed by Jo Mielziner.
14. Smith, H.W., 'Tennessee Williams and Jo Mielziner: The Memory Plays', *Theatre Survey*, 23, 1982, pp. 223–35, p. 233.
15. Hayman, R., *Tennessee Williams: Everyone Else is an Audience*, New Haven: Yale UP, 1993, p.126.
16. Mielziner-Kazan collaborations include the following productions: *A Streetcar Named Desire* (1947), *Death of a Salesman* (1949), *Cat on a Hot Tin Roof* (1955), *Sweet Bird of Youth* (1959), *After the Fall* (1963), and *But for Whom Charlie* (1964).
17. Devlin, A.J., (Ed.) *Conversations with Tennessee Williams*, Jackson: University Press of Mississippi, 1986, p. 33.
18. Mielziner, p. 26.
19. Henderson, p. 171.
20. *Summer and Smoke*, p. 570.
21. Henderson, p. 205.
22. Kazan, p. 542.
23. Ibid, p. 543.
24. Murphy, p. 126.
25. Ibid, p. 144.
26. Ibid, p. 144–145.
27. For the record: *Sweet Bird of Youth* became the last production involving all three Mielziner, Kazan and Williams and the last Williams' play directed by Kazan. Mielziner and Kazan, however, continued to work together. After *Sweet Bird of Youth*, they produced Arthur Miller's autobiographical play *After the Fall* (1963) and Sam Behrman's comedy *But for Whom Charlie* (1964). Mielziner also designed four more plays written by Williams: *Period of Adjustment* (1960), *The Milk Train Does Not Stop Here Anymore* (1963), *The Seven Descents of Myrtle* (1968), and *Outcry* (1972).
28. Mielziner, p. 202.
29. Marranca, Bonnie, Ed., *The Theatre of Images*, New York: Drama Book Specialists, 1977, p. xii.

Chapter 8

Problematics of Theatrical Negotiations: Directing, Scenography and State Ideology

Julia Listengarten

State Ideology and Cultural Assumptions

The investigation of the dynamic relationship between the theatre artist and the state in this chapter is based on the notion that theatre functions as a culturally- and socially-constructed product. As Susan Bennett argues in her book, *Theatre Audiences: A Theory of Production and Reception,* 'cultural assumptions affect performances, and performances rewrite cultural assumptions.'[1] In this reciprocal interplay of cultural assumptions and performances, the role of the artist as a citizen is instrumental. In fact, as much as cultural assumptions affect the artist's ideology and aesthetic, the artist's vision inevitably contributes to the reshaping of existing cultural assumptions or constructing new ones for the audience and thus for the community as a whole. Brecht, in particular, reacted against the notion of theatre as a social institution supported by and reflecting the dominant ideology. Instead, he called attention to the theatre's oppositional cultural practice, whose main purpose is to educate the audience by questioning existing assumptions constructed by the state. The artist, in this case, functions as an intermediary between the dominant ideology and community. The relationship that the artist has with the state, on one hand, and the community, on the other, is inevitably exacerbated during the periods of political instability and ideological propaganda: the artist experiences less freedom of expression yet is compelled to assume a greater responsibility for questioning or rewriting cultural assumptions as the state's ideological pressure begins to intensify. The early Soviet avant-garde is one of such periods that exemplify this inherent reciprocity existing between the notions of art and citizenship.

Through examining the dialogue between theatrical aesthetics and cultural assumptions, I will explore the complex position of a citizen artist in relation to the theatre career of Russian avant-garde stage director Alexander Tairov. Tairov's artistic direction at the Moscow Kamerny (Chamber) Theatre encompassed more than three decades including the aftermath of the 1917 Revolution and the transitional years of the twenties leading to the imposition of socialist realism by the Soviet government in 1934. Even though he was repeatedly accused of being apolitical at various points of his tenure at the Kamerny Theatre, one could argue that the aesthetic evolution of Tairov's theatre was in direct dialogue with the shifting Soviet ideology of the time. The aesthetic development of Tairov's theatre could roughly be divided into three phases – cubofuturism, constructivism, and structural realism – each reflecting a specific scenographic period in Tairov's position as an artist, as well as a particular strategy in his theatrical negotiations – whether intentional or not – with the state.[2]

Cultural assumptions affect performances: Tairov and Cubofuturism

Tairov began to explore the principles of cubofuturism on the stage of the Kamerny Theatre in his production of *Famira Kifared* (1916). 'Cubes and cones, large, densely colored, blue and black masses rose and fell along the steps of the stage,' announcing, in the words of Russian critic Efros, 'the birth of a new theatricality.'[3] Tairov's primary scenographer during this period was Alexandra Exter, whose costume and stage designs for *Famira Kifared* and even more significantly for *Salomé* (1917) and *Romeo and Juliet* (1921) defined the aesthetic of Tairov's theatre in the wake of the Bolshevik Revolution. According to John E. Bowlt, '[Exter]…managed to transcend the confines of the pictorial surface and to organize forms in their interaction with space… [I]t was precisely in *Famira* and *Salomé* that the old [stage] conventions were replaced by a kinetic resolution in which the actors and the scenery played equal parts.'[4] 'Exter's concentration on the "rhythmically organized space,"' continued the critic, 'pointed toward to her [future] constructivist creations, when she would build rather than decorate the stage.'[5] Exter's colourful costumes, demonstrating a variety of lines, shapes, and forms, as well as her multilevel sets, consisting of a multitude of stairs and piercing upward platforms, necessitated very definite and clear spatial arrangements on stage. Exter's cubofuturist costume and stage designs, therefore, undoubtedly affected Tairov's carefully constructed mise-en-scène(s). Contemporary critics commented on the graphic clarity and choreographic purity of the actors' performances in *Famira Kifared*, *Salomé*, and *Romeo and Juliet*, which in part resulted from severe spatial limitations and were necessary to offset the colourful turbulence and dexterity of Exter's sets.

Looking back at the history of the Moscow Kamerny Theatre, Tairov wrote later, in 1936:

> The revolution was destroying the old forms of life and we were destroying the old forms of art. It followed that we were in step with the revolution. This was, of course, an illusion but, at the same time, we sincerely believed ourselves to be revolutionaries.[6]

Was it a genuine statement, or in the attempt to save his theatre in the midst of purges and show trials, Tairov was compelled to link his cubofuturist experiments to the Revolution? What is certain, though, is that while remaining essentially apolitical, Tairov immediately embraced the post-revolutionary spirit to develop a spectacle-based theatre. But just as the spectacle-based theatre was supposed to be non-literary and propagandistic in nature in order to both artistically and politically engage a new type of the audience – peasants and workers, the Kamerny Theatre heavily relied on the classical repertoire. Indeed, one of the most significant aims of the post-revolutionary theatre, according to Meyerhold, head of Theatre Department at the Commissariat for Education, was to educate new proletarian spectators or politically indoctrinate the remaining old bourgeois audience. Contrary to Meyerhold's proclamation, Tairov's experiments with cubofuturist design forms in the late teens and early twenties continued to be elitist and somewhat intellectually abstruse.

Alexander Exter – Maquette, *Famira Kifared* (1916).

Alexander Exter – *Salome* (1917).

Thus, while the mixture of dynamism and turbulence embedded in Exter's designs did, in fact, reflect aesthetically the revolutionary fervour of the era, the cubofuturist scenography of the Kamerny Theatre was clearly not a sign of Tairov's acquiescence to the ideological pressure of the time. How then did the Kamerny Theatre survive those post-revolutionary years without becoming politically indoctrinated? The answer to this question may lie in the evolving condition of the state control in the early twenties. The state ideology was still in a process of defining itself in the early twenties; hence the state hegemony over the arts had not been fully established, allowing for a variety of avant-garde forms in the newly created Soviet culture.

Lacking any kind of propagandistic character, the Kamerny Theatre, instead, eagerly adopted the post-revolutionary romantic idealism. The romantic spirit of the post-revolutionary era in which idealism prevailed over reality permeated the aesthetics of Tairov's productions in the early twenties. This was especially manifested in the 1922 production of Racine's *Phèdre*. Designed by Alexander Vesnin, this production became one of the Kamerny Theatre's important transitional works from cubofuturism to constructivism.[7] Although not purely functional yet, the set was clearly subordinate to the actors' performances, unlike Exter's magnificently dexterous stage designs. The most significant element of Vesnin's set for *Phèdre* was the stage floor that was 'broken up into three planes patterned on a sloping, diagonal structure. Phèdre's first entry was made along this broken diagonal, very slowly... trailing a heavy purple cape which streamed out behind her.'[8] The structural simplicity of the set as well as the austere almost masculine lines of Vesnin's costume design underlined Koonen's portrayal of Phèdre as a strong, individualistic, passionate female in defiance of established social structure and moral codes. The austerity of the set and costumes in the production was in direct parallel with the tragic idealism of the main character, who sacrifices her life for not having conformed to the accepted ethical and social norms of her world.

Impacted by the post-revolutionary idealism and euphoria, Tairov's productions in turn began the process of reshaping cultural assumptions. Koonen's rendition of powerful women such as Salomé, Phèdre, and Antigone (in Tairov's 1927 production of Hasenclever's play) reveals the irreconcilable conflict of a lonely individual with the hostile masses and ultimately rejects the traditional patriarchal family structure as well as the principles of Soviet collectivism which began to be instituted in the late twenties. Significantly, Koonen's emphasis on the individualism of her tragic characters would soon go out of tune with the Party line. Post-revolutionary idealism and romantic euphoria did not last long, and 'romantic egoism,' in Spencer Golub's words, 'was replaced officially by comradeship predicated upon the assumption that "nobody is one, but one of."'[9] In his book *The Recurrence of Fate: Studies in Theatre History and Culture*, he posits, 'The subjective "I" was symptomatic of and conducive to bourgeois nostalgia and petty sentiment.'[10] By continuously creating spiritually strong, individualistic female characters, trapped in opposition to society, Koonen alluded to her increasing sense of alienation from the dehumanizing Soviet ideology and put herself, perhaps unwittingly, in opposition to the relentless machine of the Soviet government that

Alexander Vesnin – *Phèdre* (1922).

propagated collective faith in a politically-centralized and male-dominant patriarchy under Stalin. By the late twenties, the Soviet machine-like society and culture were headed toward total dehumanization, a process that transforms human beings into leaden masses.

Performances rewrite cultural assumptions: Tairov and Constructivism

There were still, however, a few years left before the state assumed its totalitarian function by reinforcing the dehumanizing ideology of Stalin's regime. One could argue that in the mid-twenties when constructivism became a major artistic force in design and architecture, Soviet avant-garde artists continued to enjoy relatively creative if not political freedom and Soviet theatre audiences had not yet been entirely turned into the dehumanized recipients of Communist propaganda.

Even though constructivism was not a state instituted movement, it did poeticize the power of machinery, which in pre-industrialized, mostly agricultural Russia had a political meaning. Moreover, in its initial programme, the first working group of constructivists that included Alexander Vesnin and the Stenberg brothers, who would later design a considerable number of the Kamerny Theatre productions, charged constructivism with the task to respond to 'the needs of building a socialist society'.[11] 'We should not reflect, depict, and interpret reality but should build practically and express the planned objectives of the newly active working class, the proletariat'.[12]

Lodder rightly asserts that 'It was...in the theatre, at the very beginning of the 1920s, that constructivist ideas of the interrelation of the environment with life – albeit hypothetical, but active and real – became first demonstrated and tested. The theatre acted as a micro-environment in which it was possible to explore spatial and material structures which could act as prototype components of a new, completely constructivist environment'.[13] The power of machinery was first clearly manifested on the stage of the Kamerny Theatre in Tairov's production of Charles Lecocq's operetta *Giroflé-Girofla* (1922), designed by Yakulov. Yakulov's design for this production immediately started a dialogue with other constructivist sets, designed by Lyubov Popova and Varvara Stepanova, which were mounted on the stage of Meyerhold's theatre at the same time. Worrall writes that 'Folding ladders, screens, revolving mirrors, trap doors and "acting accessories" [in *Giroflé-Girofla* were in fact] reminiscent of [1923] Meyerhold's production of *Tarelkin's Death*.'[14]

It was apparent that both Tairov and Meyerhold wholeheartedly welcomed and then embraced the new artistic movement in design and architecture. But it was not until another constructivist production *The Man Who Was Thursday*,[15] directed in 1923, that Tairov's constructivist approach to stage design became imbued with the overt critique of the capitalistic environment: Vesnin's stage constructions turned out to be a visual manifestation of the mechanized capitalistic society – a society that overpowers and ultimately crushes the individual. Worrall writes that 'one of the most interesting aspects of the production was the setting by Vesnin – a constructivist skeleton, the elements of which combined to

Georgii Yakulov – *Giroflé-Girofla* (1922).

Alexander Vesnin – *The Man Who Was Thursday* (1923).

suggest a modern urban landscape consisting of skyscrapers, oil derricks, pitheads, moving walkways, ironwork bridges and lift shafts.'[16] The central image of the production was thus a huge capitalistic city – a relentlessly exploiting, powerful machine – that turns human beings into identical mannequins, speaking in a 'standardized, monotonal fashion.'[17] This production signaled Tairov's realization that even though the use of machinery is necessary for building a new industrial world, the proliferation of technology may in turn lead to dehumanization of society. It is quite ironic that Tairov's vision of the Western capitalist world foreshadowed the Soviet reality of the immediate future: the soulless, dehumanizing totalitarian regime of the thirties. Indeed, Tairov and Vesnin's image of society crushing the individual could well be applied to the Soviet totalitarian government. Cultural assumptions were being questioned if not entirely rewritten.

Tairov in the Throes of State Ideology: Realism, Socialist Realism, Structural Realism

Although constructivism continued to prevail on stage and in architecture for a few more years, the ideological pressure towards realism in the mid-twenties slowly began to encroach upon Soviet artists. By proposing as early as 1923 the theatre slogan 'Back to Ostrovsky,' Lunacharsky, head of the Commissariat for Education, urged theatre practitioners and dramatists to fully explore and develop the principles of realism in order to 'truthfully' reflect contemporary Soviet life in the post-revolutionary era. 'Modern playwrights,' Lunacharsky declared, 'must observe the life around us sensitively, like Ostrovsky, and unifying profound theatrical…effect with precise, penetrating realism…must present a constructive and explanatory mirror-image of our times.'[18] The Kamerny Theatre production of Ostrovsky's *The Thunderstorm* in 1924 became Tairov's direct response to this slogan. This production also signified the beginning of Tairov's fruitful collaboration with the Stenberg brothers, a collaboration that defined his next period from mid-to-late twenties as structural realism. The period of structural realism became the last phase in Tairov's scenographic experimentations before the state imposition of socialist realism.

The term 'structural realism,' used by Tairov himself,[19] reflected a compromise of the Kamerny Theatre: the ardent desire to remain in tune with the spirit of the time as well as the necessity to pay close attention to the changing cultural and political environment in the country. 'Every epoch has its pathos. The pathos of modern times is simplicity,' stated Tairov.[20] The period of structural realism on the stage of the Kamerny Theatre was indicative of the director's interest in simplicity of form and style as well as his astute awareness of the increasing ideological pressure in the direction of socialist realism.

The simplicity and purity of form also fascinated the Stenberg brothers who designed nearly all of Tairov's productions of the mid-to-late twenties, namely: Ostrovsky's *The Thunderstorm* (1924); Shaw's *St. Joan* (1924); O'Neill's *The Hairy Ape* (1926), *Desire Under the Elms*, and *All God's Chillum Got Wings* (1929); another operetta by Lecocq, *Day and Night* (1926) and a new Soviet play *Natalya Tarpova* (1929) by the proletarian author

Sergei Semyonov. In their designs for the Kamerny Theatre, The Stenbergs, in Rudnitsky's words,

> bridled and tamed the Constructivist set. In their hands it lost the importunate mechanistic and fragmented quality, ceased flashing and flickering. The construction calmed down, quietened down and turned into a rigid framework that dictated an economical and clear sculptural form. This framework retained the ability to change, although metamorphoses were rarely executed and, as a rule, only during intervals and not in front of the audience. The place of action was designated honestly but sparingly. The space remained fundamentally unlived-in although its functions were not concealed: a house was a house, a street was a street, and the deck of a ship – the deck of a ship.[21]

In short, the space lost its playful characteristic of Tairov's earlier constructivist productions such as *Giroflé-Girofla* and *The Man Who Was Thursday* but gained the monumental quality, geometric austerity, and concreteness of detail. The complex and somewhat extravagant construction of the modern urban landscape designed by Vesnin for *The Man Who Was Thursday* was replaced by the simple geometrical outlines of a ship's deck, stockhole, Manhattan streets, prison cells, and so on, in *The Hairy Ape*. Indeed, rather than recreating a nightmarish feel of a mechanized capitalistic city through moving sets, mercilessly flickering lights, and unrelenting city sounds, the Stenbergs' designs would merely give a suggestion of high buildings that form a gloomy chasm of a soulless city.

These both ascetic and monumental qualities of the Stenbergs' structural realism presented, however, a danger of being too schematic and emotionally detached – incidentally one of the later characteristics of the socialist realist aesthetic – especially in its further scaled-down version by the designer Vadim Ryndin.[22] Ryndin collaborated with Tairov on a majority of Soviet plays, which Tairov directed in the thirties – the period that put the most exacerbating political pressure on the avant-garde artists. Under this increasing state control, Tairov was compelled to turn to the new Soviet repertoire which, in most cases, was propaganda-based, and thus, quite mediocre in nature. It was during this period that Tairov and Ryndin worked on Vishnevsky's *Optimistic Tragedy* (1934), a production unanimously hailed by the Soviet critics as a model of socialist realist theatre.

Paradoxically, this production became one of the pinnacles of Tairov's directorial success in the period that preceded and followed the state-imposed socialist realism. Arguably, it was Koonen's passionate portrayal of the central character of the commissar along with Ryndin's scenic design that helped the director to overcome the schematization of the majority of his previous works. In order to reflect the struggle between the Collective and the Individual in the play, as well as the universal conflicts between 'life and death…chaos and harmony… negation and affirmation',[23] Ryndin incorporated the notion of a whirlpool in his setting. In Worrall's words:

Vladimir Stenberg and Georgii Stenberg – *The Hairy Ape* (1926).

Vadim Ryndin – *Optimistic Tragedy* (1934).

Ryndin and Tairov wished to give palpable expression to three elements – Sky, Earth, Humanity. The circular setting with its central vortex [suggested] the elemental aspects of the struggle…It could also, with slight adjustments, take on the appearance of a warship, or become the endless road along which the regiments marched to immortality.[24]

Whether or not a model of socialist realist theatre, the production, on the one hand, continued the principles of structural realism developed by the Stenberg brothers; on the other hand, however, it was permeated with life's humanistic concerns despite the overtly propagandist content of the play itself. The scenic design that visually reinforced the dialectic nature of the political struggle subverted the ideological straightforwardness of the time. The audience was thus allowed, one more time, to be part – albeit a small one – of constructing cultural assumptions.

The Death of the Artist

The reciprocity between cultural assumptions and performances, the necessity of which is rightly suggested by Bennett in her book *Theatre Audiences*, soon, however, came to a terrifying halt. The ideology of Stalinist society smashed the humanistic ideals and beliefs of the post-revolutionary period and imposed the era of totalitarianism in which fear and obedience triumphantly manifested themselves. Various administrative committees and unions, such as the Supreme Committee for the Control of the Arts, reinforced a uniform ideological control over subject matter and style in the arts. The period of experimentation that allowed Tairov to develop the scenographic aesthetic of his theatre through cubofuturism, constructivism, and structural realism ended. Tairov's theatre, like many other artistic enterprises, could not adapt to the strict ideological and aesthetic formula and, though it survived severe political repressions and purges of the thirties, was closed by the government in 1949. The theatre was subsequently renamed the Pushkin Theatre, and the new artistic leadership hastily began to dismantle Tairov's legacy. Tairov died a year later in 1950.

While the state-sponsored stage propaganda disseminating the official doctrine destroys theatre as an artistic phenomenon, the state itself may not necessarily be detrimental in its influence on cultural production. The former annihilates any individual artistic expression through a theatrical production; the latter endorses the role of theatre as a culturally-constructed product and forces artists to establish a dialogue with current political conditions. Tairov's Kamerny Theatre, although largely apolitical in nature compared to that of Meyerhold, was clearly in dialogue with the spirit of the era, political climate, and the state hegemony at the early stages of Soviet culture. The fascinating scenographic evolution of Tairov's theatre from the romantic extravagancies of cubofuturist design to the austere geometrical lines of structural realism evidences a series of explicit as well as implicit negotiations that Tairov and his designers continued with the state as they occasionally succumbed to, but more often refused, political indoctrination.

Notes

1. Bennett, S., *Theatre Audiences: A Theory of Production and Reception,* London: Routledge, 1997, p. 2.
2. There is, however, at times no clear delineation between these phases as one could notice some overlapping of the visual principles between either cubofuturism and constructivism or constructivism and structural realism.
3. Rudnitsky, K., *Russian and Soviet Theatre: 1905–1932,* translated Roxane Permar, New York: Harry N. Abrams, 1988, p. 18.
4. Bowlt, J.E., 'The Construction of Caprice: The Russian Avant-Garde Onstage,' in *Theatre in Revolution: Russian Avant-Garde Stage Design, 1913–1935,* ed. Nancy Van Norman Baer, New York: Thames and Hudson, 1991, p. 64.
5. Ibid.
6. Worrall, N., *Modernism to Realism on the Soviet Stage: Tairov, Vakhtangov, Okhlopkov,* Cambridge: Cambridge University Press, 1989, p. 16.
7. Whereas Tairov's constructivist phase encompasses a few years in the mid-twenties and is mostly connected with his collaborations with Alexander Vesnin and Georgy Yakulov, his tackling of constructivist elements began in *Romeo and Juliet* (1921), designed by Exter. According to Nancy Baer, 'A brilliant metaphor for the tangled intrigues of Shakespeare's tragedy, [the set] created a three-dimensional, multileveled, cubofuturist environment but it remained a 'setting' rather than an active construction' *Theatre in Revolution*, p. 44.
8. Worrall, *Modernism to Realism*, p. 38.
9. Golub, S., *The Recurrence of Fate: Studies in Theatre History and Culture,* Iowa City: University of Iowa Press, 1994, p. 79.
10. Ibid.
11. Lodder, C., *Russian Constructivism,* New Haven: Yale University Press, 1983, p. 94.
12. Ibid., pp. 98–99.
13. Ibid., pp. 173–174.
14. Worrall, *Modernism to Realism*, p. 39.
15. *The Man Who Was Thursday* was based on a stage version of G. K. Chesterton's detective novel.
16. Worrall, *Modernism to Realism*, p. 39.
17. Ibid., p. 4.
18. Lunacharsky, *O teatre: sbornik statei* [On theatre: a collection of articles] (Leningrad: n.p., 1926), 5, quoted in Konstantin Rudnitsky, *Meyerhold the Director*, trans. George Petrov (Ann Arbor, Mich.: Ardis, 1981), p. 329.
19. Tairov also used the following terms such as 'neo-realism,' and 'concrete realism,' not to mention his famous 'synthetic theatre' which he coined at the beginning of his directing career and which meant the absolute fusion of 'dialogue, singing, dance, pantomime, [and] even elements of circus' in a single performance. Alexander Tairov, *Notes of a Director*, Coral Gables: University of Miami Press, 1969, p. 54.
20. Rudnitsky, *Russian and Soviet Theatre*, p. 195.
21. Ibid., p. 195.
22. This visual schematization and emotional detachment clearly contradicted Tairov's continued interest in creating the theatre of great passions and romantic ideals.
23. Worrall, *Modernism to Realism*, p. 60.
24. Ibid.

Chapter 9

Methodological Practices for Directing and Designing

Christine White

The role of the director in British Theatre changed quite radically over the last half of the twentieth century and the advancements in, and use of technology within the theatre, resulted in some changes in directorial practice. As these advances in technology changed, the emphasis of the process of theatre production, the prominence given to the director as sole 'auteur' of a piece of work, has become diminished. The members of the scenographic team are now more legitimately described as the 'auteurs' of a production. Another reason for this has been the changes in theatre practice, influenced both by European and Eastern European performance theories. These changes are evidenced later in the book by the discussions of various practices and relationships of directors and designers. In this section, I will explore the nature of these changes and influences, and discuss the theatre technology, which has offered more scope for the manipulation of the stage image, that is, the use of lighting.

The director of the late twentieth century and the early twenty-first century is no longer a specialist in every area, 'a man of the theatre'. S/he has begun to work more collaboratively with the other artists in the production team, in a much more democratic process of production. Now more than at any other time the director works as another member of the team, not only because s/he lacks knowledge but because the technology has allowed considerable flexiblity and the director's 'vision' can be translated into many forms, materials and theories. The contribution of scenography to these developments and changes in acting styles, of what is expected within a performance space, has transformed the way in which an actor uses that space.

The importance which Brecht placed on Caspar Neher's designs for a cohesive performance structure, (based on his sketches of/for the rehearsal process), and the relation of the actor to light, (which Appia recognized as important), has resulted in stage technologies and scenography emerging as a partner of the actor, and thus, a new aesthetic.

At the most basic level developments in technology have changed how we actually 'see' in the theatre. Lighting design, in particular, has affected the direction of a piece, and led to certain precepts in the actors/director's mind as to where on the stage is a good place to stand or be blocked.[1] The technological development of the lighting rig for theatre in the late twentieth century fundamentally affected the acting style of western performers. The importance of the actor's position on stage, prior to the middle of the twentieth century, had been determined by where that actor could be lit from. As a consequence of this, they were directed in relation to those instruments. Actors' entrances on the diagonal were lit by side lighting, which illuminated the sets and screens, whilst the strength of the down-stage position as the brightest part of the stage, was due to the proximity of the footlights and the throw of the follow spots, or limes. Modern technology has meant that the acting style can be a more intimate experience for actor and audience, as the technology allows the actor to be clearly seen anywhere on the stage from the auditorium. The lighting acts as a very strong medium for directing the audience's reception of the whole event, which has traditionally been the role of the director. As such, the lighting of the actor's work on stage has changed quite fundamentally not just with reference to a theory of performance but also as part of an aesthetic of the design and, therefore, the all-embracing scenography.

Lighting Methodology

Lighting can be defined as a deictic, as has been revealed through the discussion of aspects of scenography by using the theory of semiotics, however, its deictic qualities have become more apparent and useful in the theatre as the technologies used have also improved. Most of these new lighting technologies have been developed to aid their usefulness as deictic features.[2] (However, the manufacturer rarely considers this theory.) Consequently, the direction, focus and indexing of significant moments in a production has been transformed by these developments. The re-writing of recent developments in lighting technology must be rooted in its deictic quality and in the developing importance of scenography for the presentation of the commercial product. The commercial product of scenography can be clearly seen and in some cases can be referred to as simply packaging. However, the importance and effects that lighting can create can now be quantified as a necessary part of a top-quality production. As the technology of lighting has increased and become more and more specialist, so the expert has entered to take over this extremely influential and powerful role of directing the audience's attention on stage. The obvious power of lighting has also become recognized both by directors and the theatre industry. Where directors have designed their own lighting for theatre, they have had to have a lighting consultant to act as an interface between them and the equipment. For instance, directors such as Terry Hands in the UK take on the task of lighting their own productions, with the prerequisite lighting consultant. In addition, the theatre industry began to award the aesthetic of lighting. Twyla Tharp, as a director and lighting designer, received the first Olivier Award for lighting design in 1992. The link between her as not 'just' a lighting designer but a director, who undertook the lighting, has advertised the idea of the lighting designer as 'director' of the visual images, which can be presented to an audience. Directors understand the amount of control that is possible over the audience's viewing and, therefore, the audience's perception of the event, a position of control, which has evolved due to the advances made in the technology used to light productions.

For Adolphe Appia, the 'creative' light was a light that interpreted and expressed the inner rhythmic movement of the drama, its musicality. The development of lighting dimmers has enabled a vast range of possible transitions in terms of the movement of light through intensity. Sophisticated lighting equipment can fade on or off using instruments not only as groups of actors, but also as an isolated actor, or effect an emotional response, and lighting in the theatrical space has responded to changes in the choices of spaces of performance. With these technologies, simultaneous stages can be made to work due to the 'directing' of the lighting. In the late twentieth and early twenty-first century, we have begun to get closer to the 'über marionette'[3] that Gordon Craig wrote of, not due to the director as auteur but because lighting can pick people out and silhouette others, allowing the montage to become more sophisticated, with light used in an expressive sense rather than as a utility to seeing. Different locales can be located on the same stage and identified to the audience through light. As scenic design has begun to use architectonic forms, it has become necessary for lighting to sculpt the images presented and, in a greater sense, to affect the audience through symbolic design and, therefore, to become part of the dramatic performance text.

The complexity of theatre lighting is highlighted by Judith Greenwood:[4]

Lighting works on two levels: It can present one mood on stage which may produce a second complementary or contradictory mood in the audience, as when a garishly-bright lighting state, seemingly festive and indulgent, may provoke apprehension in an audience which senses rising hysteria beyond the lights' unreal edge…for light can induce in people common states of happiness or sadness as well as more complicated attitudes of resentment, conviviality, introspection or unreasonableness.[5]

The naked face can reflect the psychological course of events, appearing in quite another way than was possible in the unfocused, general lighting of the nineteenth century.

Over the last twenty years of the twentieth century, and with the development of digital technology, lighting design has become part of the scenography of stage production. In his article, 'A Scenography of Light', Brian Arnott describes both elements of light and movement as an integral part of *The Architect and the Emperor of Assyria* by Arrabal. The production he refers to was performed at The National Theatre of Great Britain in 1971. The play was directed by Victor Garcia and designed by Michel Launay, (Arnott describes him as also creating the scenography), he then refers to David Hersey as lighting designer. The title of his article suggests surprise at the malleable and flexible way in which lighting is not merely a single element to be later attached to a production, but is in fact an imperative for the scenography of the theatre production. He goes on to describe 'Garcia's basic scenographic outlook', rather than that of Launay or Hersey or the team. This example of a theatre production as early as 1971 illustrates the use of moving lights before the automated systems we now have available: 'the constant presence of the four black-clad mobile light operators who also worked on stage in full view of the audience throughout the performance.'[6] It also illustrates the belief that the creator of the visual images is Garcia the director and that the designers facilitate this.

The performance arena was defined by light, and light determined the method of performance:

The overriding visual image into which Garcia set these basic scenographic elements was both stark and disquieting. As the audience seated themselves, they looked into the open box and saw the dark back wall and wing spaces. Above, five electric pipes hung visibly. A long, highly polished metal floor stretching away from the audience was banded by bars of light emanating from two-hundred and fifty watt Reiche and Vogel beam projectors. These instruments were overslung four feet apart, about a foot off the floor on castered pipes that ran fence-like up and downstage just off the metal deck. The effect was vaguely reminiscent of an airport runway.[7]

The lighting instruments are not only placed to effect a look and style but in themselves become part of the scenography. 'This was Garcia's principal scenographic image, and the metaphor was that of the theatre itself – the naked, unadorned proscenium stage with its mirror-finish floor proclaiming the triumph of theatricality over illusionism'. In this production, we also have an example of lighting operators who are coached to achieve the desired effects.

> In accordance with general guidelines established by the designers, the lighting operators had to respond improvisationally to the movement and values of each scene from day to day. Adaptation to this format was made possible by the use of hand-held five-hundred-watt sources. These highly mobile instruments provided the experimental basis for that part of the lighting plot that was concerned with facial and focal emphasis for the actors. The lighting operators were also provided with other raw materials in the form of prisms and pulsating and rotating mirrors. The main body of the three-hundred odd instruments of the Old Vic rig, however, remained unavailable throughout the rehearsal period, and effects to be achieved from it had to be plotted on paper in the usual manner, then set aside until the technical run-throughs.[8]

The need for an improvisation period and a period of experiment for all the scenographic elements was not only integral to the process of production but also to the method of performance: the lighting designer as a performer, in the same relation to the composer of a score that is later to be played. This choice of production aesthetic did not emanate from a lack of technology but it was prescribed by the production style; a similar experience could not have been created by automated systems.

Ultimately, for the Garcia project, this method of production provided an organic platform for performance, allowing the actor's total freedom of movement 'without fear of not being lit. The movements of these instruments onstage toward center also tended to reduce the cavernous empty stage house to a space of more intimate dimensions.'[9] Again, the lighting was used as part of the scenography of the production. The most interesting and perhaps innovative technology was the use of a Polychromatron, which is a sound-activated device. It can convert audio signal into a power surge within a lighting circuit: 'Thus when the Emperor had cast off the parachute and switched to violently flailing the floor with a large piece of hide rolled like a wet towel, there was a pulsing burst of light in response to every smacking blow on the metallic stage.'[10] In addition, Hersey used a light curtain, and sodium, mercury and Compact Source Iodide specials. 'At floor level from the open wings and proscenium door areas, large wattage ellipsoidals, fresnels, and sky pans on castered stands had taken the place of the smaller hand-held sources formerly used in rehearsal experiments.' Along with these were numerous reflective surfaces, pulsating and rotating mirrors, the improvisation of rehearsals began to become controlled for the plotting period with 'the operators wearing transistorized earphones through which he directed all lighting sources that were not part of the console-controlled rig.'[11]

During the late 1980s and 1990s in the theatre, through the medium of light, the lighting designer as part of the scenographic team has become a director of the action. This fluid and almost symbiotic relationship of roles between the scenographic team is most clearly realized in this production, although not realized by Arnott. It is the lighting designer who conjures for the audience and directs our sight to the moment of importance. It is the lighting designer who frames the moment in a similar way to the film and television editor – 'the rolling follow-spots dollied in like TV cameras until they came to a stop only inches from each side of the actor's face.'[12] Arnott speaks of graphic lighting effects, by which I believe he means those that are a literal translation of the actual event presented: 'Another graphic lighting effect was achieved during the war scene. The stage went suddenly black while the sound effects' speakers delivered a fully dimensional battle score with voice-over harangue. Augmenting the noise of the gunfire, the follow spot operators shot tracers of light obliquely through the house.'[13] We need to redefine the performance in terms of the lighting technology.

There was a trend in theatre productions of the 1990s (other than those of the West End) towards low technology, where designer and director have no desire to hide the illusion, and lighting rigs have been totally open to the scrutiny of the spectator. This rather hackneyed but effective metaphor for the theatre originated as part of the aesthetic for studio spaces, where the mechanisms of performance are harder to hide. Gradually, the acceptance of this aesthetic has become a part of many theatre environments. However, if a spectator sees the equipment in some theatres, why not in all, and when does the designing of the position of the lighting rig apparatus become a piece of environmental design which is more intrinsic to the production than simply illuminating the stage? This 'environmental' use of lighting equipment was most effectively achieved by Jean Kalman for *Richard III* at the RNT.[14] In this production, Kalman placed rows of parcans either side of the stage, which formed the actual environment of the action. They metaphorically suggested battlements, searchlights and barbed wire by the use of the cabling and rigging apparatus. This was both scenographic and functional and we saw both the poetic and metaphorical statement of the objects as well as their more functional use to light the show.

Similarly, Rick Fisher created a rig of 40 par 38 lamps, some of which were also on pulleys, for Shared Experience's production of *The Bacchae* in 1989. The oppressive nature of the rig, amplified the oppressive nature of the production. Single lamps were lowered onto Bacchantes, spotlighting and literally closing in on the performers. Both the movement of the light and its changing quality as it came nearer a performer's face, or the floor, enhanced the atmosphere for the production, and the whole rig was a substantial part of the setting. As such the lighting was used as a mystic force.

Lighting, when used as in these examples, extends the palette of what is possible through the use of traditional units, in an innovative way. It also calls into question the 'innovations' which the manufactured goods can make and the possible dramatic affect they might have on the final product – the performance. As can be seen from these examples, these aesthetic changes are designed by the lighting designer and involve innovative use of units and apparatus rather than innovative specification by the manufacturer. The open-stage settings and changes in production aesthetic, which rely on concept and metaphor, have enabled lighting to perform within the scenographic context of productions. Through the use of a different aesthetic in *Assyria* by Arrabal, in *Richard III* with traditional units as a visual image and in *The Bacchae* with non-theatre lights as part of the scenic and kinetic, lighting has not only been used as a source to illuminate but as a form and a metaphor. In these examples, the actual units of light have formed part of the scenographic aesthetic.

The most obvious use of light as a scenic contributor is through projection and this technology was initially used to produce naturalistic effects. The kinetic stage was first produced through projection in 1640 by Athenasius Kircher and the use of projection instead of scenery was used by Edward Fitzball at the Adelphi in 1827 to present a ship. This image was projected onto a surface called union, a glazed calico.[15] Subsequently, complete sets of effects slides became available commercially and the beginnings of moving pictures at the end of the nineteenth century meant that moving slides and dissolves formed part of the optical host available for scenic design:

> I do not want to depress our scenic artists…but it sometimes seems to me that as stage lighting develops more and more the scenic artists will become superfluous. I grow more and more convinced that lighting has hitherto been in its infancy and that it is rapidly taking its place as by far the most important of all the ancillary arts of the Theatre.[16]

The importance of painted sets has subsequently diminished in the sense of naturalistic painted scenes, but also, now, with the development of new media. Whilst the kinetic use of light and projection are not new, the use of such effects for a non-naturalistic purpose is. Josef Svoboda experimented with the use of kinetic forms on stage: 'Svoboda has understood more than anyone else, how to employ projectors in order to create a kinetic stage in the rhythmic movement of drama.'[17] Late twentieth century lighting evolved beyond the presentation of moving 'filmic' scenes to a quality of light which contained metaphoric meaning within the production, the nature of which the audience must interpret. This change in aesthetic has been due, in part, to the popularity of open-stage settings, which have altered what can be achieved through lighting for a production. As a consequence, lighting can be used as a more expressive contributor to the scenographic aesthetic, and the style of modern theatre lighting has become sophisticated, and often emblematic, as it uses old and new technologies in a 'playful' and experimental way.

The importance of lighting has been contiguous with its use in both public and domestic life. In the home, we now fit dimmer switches in order to control the level of light in particular rooms, enabling us to change the mood of our environment, and we can programme lighting environments at home in the same way as one might light a scene for the stage. The revolution in the entertainment in clubs and bars, where lighting is one of the deciding factors for which club or bar to go to as it generates a particular experience, suggests that an audience is aware of the evocative nature of lighting, and light shows in these venues have popularized lighting and, in particular, lighting technology. Consequently, the audience is more aware of these aspects of production as the technologies have become more visible.

Whilst Adolphe Appia and Gordon Craig theorized the importance of light within the theatre and the late twentieth century provided the apparatus by which theories of lighting have been able to be applied, the twenty-first has enabled ever more sophisticated use of lighting. The technology that has been developed for lighting design has, however, not necessarily been determined by theories of plasticity but has been more orientated to theories of the market place, in particular the use of other entertainment equipment rather than the development of specific theatre equipment. Theatre practice in the UK and the US reveals many similarities of theatre production and the kinds of developments which have changed the aesthetic of lighting.

The Art of the designer is confined by the technology available and the technology is produced for a specific technical function. Many members of the profession feel they are often presented with new technology, and it is assumed that the technology leads the Art. However, no matter how exciting the technology, it is not until the imaginative skill of the lighting designer has taken hold of it that its full potential, intentional or otherwise may be fully realized. At the point when the designed lights are rigged, lighting designers require a high level of flexibility from luminaires, not to avoid making decisions on the drawing board, but in order to avoid imposing limitations on the design at this relatively early stage in the production. This technology is not determined by the spectacularly gratuitous, but needs to be viewed as an instrument of expression. Expression of the visual poetic interpreted from the literary text. The advances described above in terms of angles possible to the stage, the use of colour and projection mediums, comparisons of control equipment, the luminaires and sources, and the advent of computer-aided design, have all radically changed the nature of lighting for theatre. They offer specific tools for the lighting designer to use and have both created and reacted to the fundamental differences in theatre aesthetic which have occurred in British scenography, not least in terms of the role of the director and the nature of Text.

Directors and Texts

The separation of the role of the actor from that of the director was not consistently practised in the UK in the early twentieth century; many directors still took part in the plays they directed. Edward Gordon Craig's *The Art of the Theatre* (1911) became a rallying point for directors as Craig debated the concept of the theatre as an Art as opposed to an entertainment. From this period, the word 'Art' was increasingly used in connection with the stage, and a division between commercial theatre and art theatre became more apparent. Although, it is debatable whether the overall mastermind and single view controlling a production has ever been totally realized, Craig's publications contributed to the downfall of the actor-manager. This division between commercial theatre and art theatre again presupposes a distinction, which is based on nothing other than the commodification of that Art. It is a difficulty which has become insuperable due to the need for some patronage of the Arts in general and the dominance of a capitalist funding system based on market forces. These contradictions can be seen in the theory that the audience is a major creator of meaning, as this suggests that any art of the stage does not exist without them. The sense of the audience as the major creator of the mise-en-scène is discussed by Appia: 'Our eyes...determine the staging and always create it anew...we ourselves are the mise-en-scène, without us the work remains a written piece.'[18] This expression of the audience as creator of sense and, therefore, meaning voiced by Appia has become a central feature of recent theatre theory and practice. In practice, it has enabled the scenographic team to provide suggestions, symbols and references. In theoretical terms, it is crucial to an understanding of theatre theories, in particular deconstructionist patterns. The ideas of Appia and Craig have reinforced both the nature of the visual and the importance of the audience as viewer, and therefore creator of meaning in the stage space. The influence of the visual has become paramount, and thus, as this realization has seeped into mainstream production, the importance of the scenography has been given a sense of place.

In philosophy, psychology, and the like, we give such phenomena technical terms. This does not alter the fact that all could be reduced to the term 'to imagine', for all of them imply an image before their realization. These facts are well known, yet we do not utilize them in those phases of our existence where imagination could be of great service. This indifference distorts and lowers our scale of values; for, in order to evaluate, the object of evaluation must be understood or invoked by imaginaton...One wonders whether it is not urgent to admit imagination as a specific branch of academic instruction or, at least, to encourage it by pointing it out and conferring upon it a very high value.[19]

In one sense this is exactly what higher education attempts in the teaching of theatre and theatre design. Here, Appia foresees interest in audience reception by suggesting that it is recognized as a necessary part of the theatre experience.

The involvement of the audience in the theatre experience has also come to affect the separate role of the director as the manipulator of the art. In the former hypothesis of the audience as creator of meaning, the audience should be admitted free, for without them what else exists? The latter belief of the director as the manipulator of the art suggests that they have come to view genius in the form of the director's vision. The problem for many theatres has, however, been to get the audience to go to the theatre at all and this is where the use of technology has been successful in marketing the product, whether it is one supporting a director's vision or not.

The dominance of the Oxbridge trained director in the UK, who is rooted in an academic tradition of the literary text, and the subsequent diversification of training for the actor, has provided a break from an actor's theatre in the UK. The director's theatre had reached its height during the late 1970s and actors have tried to reassert their power. Some actors have begun to take directorial roles in an attempt to wrestle back some control from the authoritarian practice of some directors, for example Kenneth Branagh, Ian McKellen and Simon Callow, Callow writing particularly scathingly about the profession of director in the theatre.[20]

The demise of actor-manager, director and actor as the author of theatre, has occurred partly as the complexity of theatre production vis-à-vis scenographic images has been realized. Directors are no longer required to interpret the literary text and reveal some great insight. They now revise their role as being one which coordinates numerous messages to the audience beyond that which is laid down in any interpretation of the literary text. Independently, directors may have learnt to lace their productions with concepts that show their skill and cleverness but this approach has been mediated through the director, with the lighting designer, set designer and other designers, who form the scenographic team, in collaboration. As a consequence, the meaning of a given performance has been played out in the rehearsal room rather than prescribed by the literary text.

In the latter part of the twentieth century, directors used rehearsals to explore rather than define a production. For director Sam Mendes:

Going to the RSC at that stage in my career completely changed my perception of what it is that you do in rehearsal. It became about the collective consciousness of a lot of very intelligent, sensitive people, and the imaginative exploration of an empty space.[21]

This shift in understanding and aesthetic has changed the practice and production of theatre:

In the eighties, directors were getting too big for their boots. But now there is a new generation of directors who have tried to hark back to the Peter Brook experimental era and away from the empire building of Peter Hall, Trevor Nunn and John Dexter. They want something that is more studio based and unconventional and that also takes on board a great understanding of the actor's desires and their needs as human beings rather than as pawns in a master plan.[22]

It was not just actors who felt they were simply a part of the director's grand plan. Designers from all fields felt that the ideology of the director's vision was outmoded and egotistical. In Alison Chitty's production of *The Rose Tattoo*, which she designed and Peter Hall directed, her approach was to create 'moment drawings to express the tension and relationships in the text...Peter Hall is a strong advocate for naturalism and if it says it in the text he has to have it.'[23] Hall was not keen, therefore, on the idea of transparent walls, so Chitty designed in what she described as 'a heightened realism, extracted out of naturalism.'[24] However, in this example we have an illustration of the designer setting the performance aesthetic rather than the production being the result of 'the imaginative exploration of an empty space.'[25] Sam Mendes' ideal is always at the mercy of economics and working practice and the question must be raised as to 'who' is allowed to experiment? In the responses I have received from designers through the Society for West End Theatre, the lack of time for experimentation is continually highlighted. In large institutions it is no better, as the RNT and RSC have schedules tightly planned around the demanding repertoire system which defines when designs must be completed, irrespective of the process.

A further change in the directorial role is the signature, which is used to identify a piece of theatre. In the 1960s and 1970s literary texts were known by their author, the playwright, and dramatic texts were described either by the playwright, the producer, or the director. Generally, the naming of the product depended on which was the most famous name to use in relation to the production. Although in the case of Peter Brook's *A Midsummer Nights Dream*, one would expect Shakespeare to get top billing! In this case, however, it was the extraordinary nature of the production, most notably in terms of the scenography used. As Iain Mackintosh points out, the creator of the striking scenographic image, Sally Crabb, is rarely mentioned in relation to this production.[26]

In the 1980s and 1990s, there has been a more homogeneous tagging of the authors of the production, irrespective of whether that production has been a success or a failure. The employment structures have also altered this naming as directors, designers, lighting designers, choreographers and composers now work in teams to produce the work together, and are recognized as teams in the market place. As such, the individual's signature becomes less relevant to the means of production. Therefore, the scenographic team has become the auteur because of changes in the means of production; the specialist departments in the theatre; the importance of image to convey meaning; and the involvement of the audience as maker of meaning. These modes of production brought about by the changes in technology have facilitated a rise in the presence and significance of scenography as part of the new text: the performance text.

The making of images for the stage is recognized as highly significant and theatre departments have focused on the detail of production, rather than the broad stroke and potentially 'poor' theatre look of previous generations. For, if the audience is to make meanings of the experience called 'theatre', this form of presentation must naturally become more complex, layered and provocative. The sophistication of audience perception has in many ways provoked this complex signification. However, this can also be perverted in the market-place to mean ostentation rather than image for the audience to engage with. An example of this in the early 1990s was the subcontracting of specific areas of design in the set of *Sunset Boulevard* at The Adelphi Theatre, London. The attention to detail was hardly noticeable from the back of the stalls and the intricacies of the work could only be appreciated in photographs as seen in theatre design catalogues. In addition, it was photographed and reproduced in the programme, giving the audience a closer look at what their ticket money had been spent on. The detail on the part of, in this case, scenic artists provides a job but not a role within the creation of the theatre production and its process. The set became merchandise for the audience to wonder at. This practice differs little from the nineteenth century; it encourages the applause of the scenography as object and not subject. In effect, such precise detail becomes insignificant to an audience's appreciation or response to the performance text. The scenic art is part of the commodity and little else.

Directors and designers of the late twentieth century have tried to find an angle for modern drama, and for classical pieces in particular, in order to make the performance relevant to our time, but also, and perhaps more importantly, such practices have reinforced the perception of the scenographic team as the interpretative artists. 'The intellectual, by contrast, is interested in the road as an activity, but he cannot evaluate it because his imagination fails to show him the goal clearly; he has to wait for it. When the goal is reached, he evaluates the result but loses sight of the road that led to it.'[27] The evaluation of the process and the product through theory often imported from other art forms has a relevance to scenography and aspects of its production but not its poetic value within the context of a piece of performance. The methodological practices for directing and designing continue to develop within the contexts of interpretative artists engaging in creative relationships, some examples of which are outlined in the rest of this book.

Notes

1. Greenwood, J., unpublished interview with author 1984, and reference to Judith Greenwood, *Am I Lit Here? – An historical survey of the theory and practice of lighting the actor on stage, from the age of gas to the age of electricity*, M.A. thesis Leeds University, 1984.
2. Esslin, M., *The Field of Drama: how the signs of Drama create meaning on stage*, Methuen, 1988; Elam, K., *The Semiotics of Theatre and Drama*, London, New York: Methuen, 1980.
3. Craig, E.G., *On the Art of the Theatre*, London: Heinemann, 1911, p. 84.
4. Judith Greenwood, Associate Director, Cheek by Jowl.
5. Judith Greenwood, unpublished interview with author, 1982.
6. Arnott, B., 'A Scenography of Light, The Architect and the Emperor of Assyria', *The Drama Review*, Volume 17, no. 2 T58, June, 1973, p. 74.
7. Ibid.
8. Ibid.
9. Ibid., p. 75.
10. Ibid.
11. Ibid., p. 76.
12. Ibid., pp. 78–79.
13. Ibid., p. 76.
14. *Richard III*, RNT, 1990 for which Jean Kalman was awarded Olivier Award for Best Lighting Designer 1991.

15. Fitzball, E., *35 years of a dramatic authors life*, London: T.C. Newby, 1859.
16. Alan Parsons, *Daily Mail*, 18th August 1931, antedated by J.B. Fagan in 1919, in a paper given to the Insitution of Environmental Sciences.
17. Bergman, G., *Lighting in the Theatre*, Stockholm: Almqvist & Wiksell, 1977, p. 365.
18. Volbach, W.R., *Adolphe Appia, Prophet of the Modern Theatre: A Profile*, Wesleyan University Press, 1968, edited and translated by Richard C. Beacham, p. 103.
19. Appia, A., 'Mechanisation', Part 5, 1922, in W.R.Volbach, *Adolphe Appia, Essays, Scenarios, and Designs,* edited Richard C. Beacham, London: UMI Research Press, 1989, p. 364–5.
20. Callow, S., *Being an Actor*, London: Vintage, 2004.
21. Edwardes, J., 'Directors: the new generation', p. 211, in Theodore Shank, *Contemporary British Theatre*, London: Macmillan, 1994.
22. Ibid., p. 212.
23. Alison Chitty, unpublished interview with author, 1992.
24. Alison Chitty, unpublished interview with author, 1991.
25. Ibid.
26. Mackintosh, I., *Architecture Actor and Audience*, Routledge, 1992.
27. Volbach, W.R., *Adolphe Appia, Essays, Scenarios, and Designs,* edited Richard C. Beacham, London: UMI Research Press, 1989, p. 365.

Chapter 10

The Digital Platform as a Communication Tool

Adele Keeley

For a costume designer, the design process is about identifying a problem, gathering research and using the creative process to solve it. The designer's job is to work collaboratively with the director to find solutions to the questions posed in a script. This chapter discusses research into the implications that computers can have when used as part of this design process. By drawing on observations from a case study and extracting anecdotal evidence from interviews and personal reflection, I describe the communication process of design using the digital platform. As part of this study I have considered research by Delahoy,[1] who discusses this subject but offers limited practical instances. In this, my research, I present examples to support my theories and discuss the impact this has both practically and artistically.

A costume illustration is visual shorthand communicating what a designer may struggle to say in words. The costume design has many functions and, as Delahoy writes, 'inform[s] and connect[s] directors, performers and makers.'[2] However, these individuals can often translate different things from an illustration. As part of a wider piece of research to test the effectiveness of digital costume design, a case study was established to explore this notion across a series of theatre productions. The main body of the research explored the communication of costume design through digital representation. The case study involved designing costumes for three productions, working with different directors, actors and production personnel within the same setting and similar timeframe. This framework enabled me to triangulate findings and compare outcomes both creatively and technically.

As part of the design development process, I used mood boards as the main method to visually communicate my conceptual ideas to the directors. This visual discourse consisted of art and costume imagery collected in response to the scripts. This mode of collating images, whether created digitally or not, is often used by a designer to suggest ideas to the director when discussing visual outcomes for the play. Using the computer as an integral part of this process, I edited images and collaged them, using Adobe Photoshop, to create 'moodscapes'. These were then presented on a laptop screen at initial production meetings in a series of digital slides. Delahoy suggests that 'the ability of CAD [computer aided design] to collate and merge diverse imagery could result in a clearer pinpointing of visual concepts.'[3] I would agree with this point as, in the context of this case study, I found that the use of digitally-presented mood boards aided in the clear visual communication of my ideas. As one director commented: 'They were an excellent tool for me to focus in more depth.'[4]

The first production I designed, in the case study, was *Tender* by Abi Morgan. For this production the mood boards were presented in a series of digital scrapbook-style pages.

This intentional 'design look' was chosen to evoke the emotion of the production. Creating a basic template, I scanned in pictures from magazines and catalogues to create a collage of ideas. To add to this sketchbook feel, I scanned in a metal spiral which was placed down the side of the page. This feature, I felt, reinforced the mood I was trying to generate but also subconsciously by using this analogue image in a digital environment I was, perhaps, reinforcing the notion that I was presenting a 'digital sketchbook'. This could suggest that the computer screen as a digital space can be made atmospheric in a manner that, normally, may only be accepted in an analogue display. The final pages presented a contemporary look which stayed in keeping with the style of the script. During the process of creating the mood boards my creative approach was assisted by the computer. By using a combination of learnt digital techniques and a few happy accidents the computer opened up opportunities which I may not have considered otherwise.

I presented my ideas for the second production, *La Ronde* by Arthur Schnitzler, in a similar way. However, these visuals aids demonstrated a more formulaic layout, a decision prompted by two major contributors. The first was in response to the script, which had a regimented pace to it. The second was as a consequence of my first telephone call with the director. Ascertaining her personality, I noted that she was uncertain of my abilities at first and made it clear that she wanted the production to have an accurate period feel. I sensed that she required designs that would be easy to understand and have clarity. Responding to this when creating the mood boards, I gained her trust by demonstrating my knowledge and design abilities in the visuals I created. In fact, I observed when showing the digital mood boards at the production meeting that her confidence in me was greatly enhanced.

In the next stage of the design process, I hand drew images and enhanced them in Adobe Photoshop. Sketching the characters first by hand helped me focus on their personalities and assisted my costume design choices. The characters' figures were also hand-drawn; these were then scanned into the computer, rescaled and merged with the face. In the past I have noticed that my drawing skills have been hindered by restricting sketches to a certain page dimension. By adopting this technique I could draw the elements for each design, such as the face and body, on separate and, in some cases, different-sized paper. By taking this approach for *La Ronde* I was able to scan and rescale the images and position them together in Adobe Photoshop. Once the costume drawings were merged, I touched up the images and erased any unwanted lines. This mixed-media approach shows real potential for costume design and offers possibilities not available to designers who do not use digital media.

The next stage was to print out multiple copies of one figure. This allowed me to try out various design options for each of the characters. When discussing her designs for *Twelfth Night,* theatre designer Claire Lyth comments: 'By creating a body for each scene digitally it was possible to re-design the costumes as ideas progressed, without starting again each time.'[5] Figure 2 demonstrates how I have used the same body shape to test four different design options. By using this digital technique I found I was able to try various options quickly and respond more freely to the director's comments without fear of ruining the original image.

Mood board created for the production of *Tender*. Here is an example of how images from magazines and fashion catalogues have been digitally collaged to communicate initial ideas for the character.

Development sketches for the production of *La Ronde* showing how the same pose can be used to try out different design options. Adele Keeley, 2007.

Costume illustration for the production of *La Ronde* showing the same body shape to communicate the layers of a costume. Adele Keeley 2007.

The director's vision for this production required some of the actors to perform in underwear, therefore the communication of undergarments became an essential element of the costume designs. By illustrating a basic image for each character, I was able to copy and paste the body shape for each layer of the costume. By using this kind of layering system a designer can use the virtual platform to dress the character, showing the director far in advance of the dress parade the different stages of the character's state of dress.

The approach for the third production, *Mary Barton* by Emma Reeves and Andrew Louden, was quite different. The script was being adapted from a classic novel and it was incomplete for the first meeting. I had originally planned to present all development work for the three productions on my laptop. However, with little time to prepare for the first meeting, I only had time to collect together some photocopied images. Though disappointed at first that I could not continue with my planned mode of presentation, I used this as an opportunity to observe the director's reaction. Louden, the director for *Mary Barton,* was unfazed by the analogue presentation of my initial design ideas.[6] Also, I observed that the costumes were discussed alongside the set design rather than reserved for the second part of the meeting, which had been the case in the meetings for both *Tender* and *La Ronde*. Perhaps this could have been down to the nature of the director, who adopted an all-inclusive attitude, or that, in the previous meetings, the other production members felt alienated from the process as the images were being presented on-screen, primarily facing the director. This observation opens up a larger debate about the psychology of computers and the response they receive from different individuals.[7] In this instance, I could not be sure if the production team felt excluded or that it hindered their interaction in the meetings, but a theory can be drawn from this which may have a bearing on how a costume designer might use the digital platform when presenting their ideas.

Keen to communicate to the director the mood and atmosphere in my rendering style, I adopted a technique, though digital, which replicated that of painting. Using digital drawing equipment the technique echoed the action of drawing by hand. Figure 4 shows how the image is built-up in layers. This is achieved by using a low opacity setting on the brush tool. I used visual references to assist me in the image-development and looked at paintings and costume drawings to help get the period look. To aid the communication of fabric, texture and pattern were scanned into the computer and added to the designs.

Overall, I did not observe any significant difference in the response from the directors. In general I found that, as long as the final product fulfilled its function as a communication tool, it is of little interest to the viewer how the designs were created. This was not surprising. I can recognize that a costume designer must choose the media which best suits their ability to communicate effectively. When asking the directors of *La Ronde* and *Tender* how they felt about viewing the design development mood boards on screen, their reactions were similar. One commented: 'I feel fine about it however, I do like something tangible. I tend to have them around me when I'm working things out'.[8] This reaction is interesting as it refers to the director working on the script outside of the design meeting. When practising in the analogue domain, I would not normally give the director a copy of

A series of images showing the development of a costume illustration for *Mary Barton* using a digital sketching technique.

MARY BARTON
ACT 2

Mary Barton   Adele Keeley

Costume illustration for *Mary Barton*.
Adele Keeley 2007.

the design development ideas as these would be stored in an analogue-based sketchbook. In this instance, I was able to print out the screen-presented mood boards and leave a copy with the director, thus adding to their own visual research. Additionally, I was able to e-mail the presentation boards and final designs, enabling them to be viewed on screen. The digital platform allowed images to be used in multiple ways and, when appropriate, multiple copies could be printed.

The case study allowed for a great deal of exploration, not only into the communication of ideas between the designer and the director but also the implication on the realized costume. The final designs for these three productions were finally printed and presented to the wardrobe department and actors at the first rehearsal. One question raised from this study could be: is there mileage in producing designs in digital format only? This would provide the wardrobe supervisor with the same options to switch off layers to reveal underclothing and perhaps construction ideas. As a consequence, there are environmental or cost benefits for not printing a digital costume design. Another area for further study, perhaps, is an analysis of whether a design which remains virtual is realized effectively?

My research opened up the opportunity for me to interact with theatre practitioners in a way that I had not previously considered. Though my research focused mainly on the analysis of the digital platform, I also observed the nuances of the relationships within a theatre production team. In particular, by working with three different directors simultaneously, I have observed how the personality of a director can influence the approach taken when designing costumes. Adapting the style of illustration or the mode of displaying visual information can be influenced greatly by the relationship that a designer develops with each individual director. Though in this instance it did not change the media I used, it did influence the clarity of line, depiction of historical accuracy and the layout of the concept and design pages.

Using digital media when developing ideas and integrating it at the conceptual and realization stage of the process has scope for further investigation. This could include looking into the psychological response of the viewer when the digital approach is used or whether or not the digital tool can further aid visual communication by introduction of a 3D element. How useful would it be for a director to see digital representations of characters virtually evolve as their ideas develop, and could the process of digital drawing impact on design solutions?

This research presents ideas and approaches to promote the digital platform as an option for costume designers. Methods have been highlighted which could save time, offering the designer more flexibility in their working practice. Various artistic representations have been presented, encouraging the notion that different styles can be created through digital representation. Though hand-rendered techniques will continue to be used, I have found that the digital platform is emerging as a valuable tool for costume designers to communicate their ideas with directors.

Notes

1. Delahoy, J., *Digital Scenography: Costume Design*, MA Thesis, Nottingham Trent University, 2004.
2. Ibid.
3. Ibid.
4. Tillet, J., unpublished interview with author, 26th July, 2007.
5. Lyth, C., in Ruthven, P., and Burnett, K., 2002,(Eds.), *2D>3D: Design for Theatre and Performance*, London: The Society of British Theatre Designers.
6. Loudon, A., unpublished interview with author, 23rd August, 2007.
7. See also: Robbins, C., 2002, 'Theatre Designers and Computers', *Theatre Design and Technology*, Fall, 30-37; Reeves, J., 2006, Digital Media and Costume Design: Learning and Teaching Strategies, The Arts Institute at Bournemouth, 'Costume Symposium 2006: Promoting Research in Costume and Performance, Bournemouth', 19–20 July 2006. Bournemouth: Arts Institute Bournemouth; Ularu, N., 1999, 'Using the Computer with Rendering,' *Theatre Design and Technology*, Summer, 65–7.
8. Kimberley, C., unpublished interview with author, 28 July, 2007.

Part III

Metaphors, Meta-Theatre and Methodologies

Within the context of metaphor many explorations of what theatre does can be found. The constant conflict and dissonance caused by at once being metaphoric and mimetic enables theatre to profit from this shape-shifting, to at once be real and also spectacular.

In this next section of *Directors & Designers*, Christine White starts with a proposition for spectacle itself and sets out to reclaim what is often categorized as populist and frivolous with value and meaning. Ewa Wąchocka investigates models of reality in European theatre of the twentieth century. She alludes to perceptions of realism but also the nature of theatre and 'theatricalness'. Scott Dahl gives us an account of the director and designer relationship with particular reference to the country and period in his account of the metaphoric creative practice of Moredecai Gorelik and Elia Kazan. This chapter offers a different perspective from that given in the earlier 'Performing Partners' section of this book. Harry Feiner takes us through an exploration of designing space and a full discussion of shape, volume and perspective and part of the designer's methodological practice. Gregory Sporton writes of how design works within Dance contexts and offers us a methodology of where dance and how dance can be used as a medium of theatrical exploration. He compares the use of bodies as a part of scenography and the function of design.

Chapter 11

The Seductive Scene or Reclaiming Spectacle

Christine White

The popular critical use of the word 'spectacle', in theatre criticism in the 1980s and early 1990s, was misguided, and not representative of the nature of spectacle in the theatre. Whilst 'spectacle' was often used to describe the gratuitous use of technology and/or performances, to highlight the self-conscious and self-reflexive nature of theatre, such a description was limited, as it viewed these affects as having added little in terms of meaning to such productions. The implied lack of integrity suggested by the term spectacle ignored the fact that such self-reflexive work was part of a separate genre which in the West End theatre in the UK during the late 1980s and 1990s was a part of, what may be termed historically, a postmodern aesthetic. Spectacle required a response from the spectator, as part of the planned event and as the expression of the 'theatricality' of theatre. However, this term has, towards the end of the century and in the early years of the twenty-first century, blurred the nature of spectacle, as theatricality and spectacle do not necessarily mean the same thing. The self-conscious and self-reflexive are not necessarily spectacular. In popular criticism, theatricality is a recognition of the practice of theatre, whereas spectacle is an invitation to lose oneself in the event and be affected by the presentation; one is self-conscious, the other requires the spectator to abandon their critical faculties. This use of spectacle, to describe a form which is soporific and inert, is inaccurate but was prevalent in the late twentieth century.

In 1993, David Edgar made the observation that there was a dearth of freelance writers commissioned by theatre companies to write new works. However, in the 1980s and 1990s many theatre companies were using a variety of processes to produce new work, including devising and writing through workshops. These production processes changed the theatre writer's profession and Edgar suggested such processes erased the writer from the production of theatre.[1] However, what he was articulating was yet another change in the way theatre was made.

One of the most pertinent changes to the process was the technique of devising, and the performance style of, physical theatre. However, the scenographic and the physical should not be seen as opposite practices, as such a perception equates scenographic theatre to a means of production related to financial largesse rather than to the efficacy of what is presented. Nor does this binary presentation of the two forms take into account the emotional impact of physical theatre and the size and spectacle possible. The work of Mike Alfreds on *Arabian Nights,*[2] and the subsequent use of physical theatre techniques for *Nicholas Nickleby*[3] and *Les Miserables,*[4] illustrates this; the last, an example of the conflation more clearly relating to the scenographic, not just the means of technological production but to the contribution of the physical in terms of an ensemble company, and thus to the spectacle. These examples all used designed space and had a scenographic content. While *Arabian Nights* as a precursor of the physical theatre style, which has since been adopted in the West End, had a minimum amount of inanimate objects, the environment was still designed as a scenographic whole to evoke a particular style of production and have an emotional impact on the spectator. This technique was used again in *A Woman in Black*,[5] where, at the beginning of the play, the act of storytelling is used to present the tale. The techniques used are similar to those used by Shared Experience, where objects changed their significance dependent on the context of the story. In *A Woman in Black*, it was only later in the play that we actually went to the actual house where the murder occurred. The spectator spent the first part of the play watching two actors recount the tale in a dressing room with a coat rail and a costume basket. This aesthetic enabled the spectator to 'see' the image created by the actors, who were creating the inanimate; the lights, costume and environment held the actors' activity in suspension in order that it was experienced by the spectator. The later revelation of the scene from beyond our initial imagination, provoked by the story told by the actors, engaged the spectator in the spectacular.

Efficacy of Spectacle

The efficacy of spectacle is based on its ability to manipulate our emotions and, thus, our emotional attachment to, and de-tachment from, theatrical events. An attempt to find a register to discuss the affects of particular theatre experiences is difficult, especially when the nature of the event can be so varied. The effect of spectacle and the spectacular cannot be defined without first trying to determine what we mean by spectacle, and what we use the word 'spectacle' to describe. Spectacle as defined by the dictionary can mean 'strange and interesting', 'an impressive, grand or dramatic show', 'designed to impress', 'magnificent' and 'important'. The word 'grand' suggests large, and the use of 'dramatic' refers to a sense of the 'striking' or 'effective', that which has some kind of 'emotional impact' or is 'performed in a flamboyant way'. A theatre performance may be striking, or large, and have an emotional impact on the audience, or a variety of these attributes and all, or some, of these features may constitute spectacle. However, the specific spectacular moment need not be large or flamboyant, but it frequently does have emotional impact on the spectator. The emotional impact of a performance, or a moment of performance, is the most tangible response that the audience has to an event. The impact of the emotional reaction a spectator might have to the spectacle determines the spectator's attachment to the event, and a lack of emotional impact will induce an attitude of detachment on the part of the spectator.

In describing the customers of a theatre event I have used the term spectator, and I will use audience to describe customers who are less involved with the visual impact of a production. For example, in this sense, an audience would be present at an orchestral concert, whereas the events of theatre are to be viewed strictly in conjunction with what is heard, and the efficacy of what is heard is related to what is seen – the process is visual. What is seen is often spectacular, or spectacle theatre, although whole performances need not fit into the category 'spectacle' but may shift between spectacle and non-spectacle. These fluctuations require the customer to oscillate between being a spectator and being an audience member. The efficacy of the spectacular on the spectator is a very individualistic moment; whilst the audience listen they often give a unified reaction. 'While audience homogeneity would seem to be most likely, it is worth remembering the vulnerability of that united response. That audiences generally concur as to what is a good play and what is bad merely evidences aesthetic codes as culturally determined.'[6] The customer has to become a spectator by allowing themselves to see an element of the theatre performance or the performance as a whole as striking or dramatic. Alternatively, the customers might not find the piece spectacular and so remain as part of the audience, passive; they are not involved in the events, as involvement requires some emotional activity, they are observers. The spectacular, whether it is a moment or a whole performance, is specifically 'designed' to have an emotional impact and to be dramatic. In this respect, it uses methods of evoking such reactions in the spectator. More crudely, the makers of theatre know what will work, or can make an educated guess as to what will produce the desired reaction in the customer. The makers are all working, as actors do, in the knowledge of how to evoke in the individual particular responses, and, as with actors, some of the makers of theatre are more subtle than others at concealing the mechanism for provoking reaction in the spectator. The techniques of acting, as with the techniques of production, can be crude cliché or an art form. The lighting and stagecraft of the last twenty years of the twentieth century have been used to 'heighten the theatrical experience for the audience.'[7] However, it would be inaccurate to see this heightening as purely gratuitous. Bob Crowley notes some of the early problems which occurred with the sudden explosion of stagecraft:

> I think what also happened is that in the 80s designers had the responsibility for turning rather dodgy musicals into pieces of theatre. These musicals weren't inherently theatrical and they depended for their lifeblood on the designer, because nothing else was happening. What's happened since has probably been a bit of a backlash…I was worried that all we'd done in the 80s was to replace one boring set of clichés with another set.[8]

This highlights the need to determine the nature of the theatre event, clarifying that which is spectacle, and that which is technological. The use of the term spectacle to describe technology, which is not integrated into a theatre production corrupts, the use of the word spectacle and does not accurately describe the experience. Technology is a means to an end and spectacle is the end effect created; as such they are very different from one to another. To speak of technology as being spectacular is inaccurate in terms of what spectacle actually means and what the technology is able to achieve. A customer's attachment to or detachment from the event is determined by the choices which theatre-makers elect to follow in producing theatre. Such production processes suggest manipulation on the part of the theatre-makers, which is a part of their skill. When the technology, and therefore the means of production, is revealed and not integrated into an event, it is not only badly designed within the context of the event but removes the potential for the spectacular to be experienced. The efficacy of the technology to produce an emotional response in the audience is only possible if the technology is combined with other features of the production and creates a cohesive signal to the audience. There is no excitement in watching a lift going up and down unless the lift is in the context of other activity within the performance, or if it is set within a landscape where it is given a context. The technology which moves the lift is of no interest whatsoever, therefore technology must not be linked with ideas of spectacle, and the spectacular must be reviewed in the context of the theatre event.

Theatre, which is flamboyantly manipulative, has frequently been judged as a lesser form of art, not because anyone can produce these works – anyone cannot – but because the production does not disguise the means of manipulation. Puccini was regarded as a populist composer and in many 'serious musical circles the subject of Puccini was held to be no less than taboo...His art was dismissed as *kitsch*'.[9] He directly manipulates the listener's emotional response through the dramatic use of music. Puccini aimed at *Gesamkuntswerk*: 'He insisted for example on the utmost clarity of verbal enunciation and on lighting effects following closely the musical changes and being regulated "with a most attentive ear".[10] He knew exactly what worked emotionally in terms of the libretti and the score for his operas, even to the point of how the curtain rose or fell.

The effect of *Aida* at Earls Court, London, one of many extravagant events staged there in the late 1980s, which at varying moments exhibited spectacular effects, cannot be discounted as an art form simply by calling it 'spectacle'. The word 'spectacle' in popular criticism has been used to suggest that the work is limited in its relation to human being's experience, but the effect of spectacle is to illicit an emotional response from the spectator. It is the difficulty in describing that response that critics have avoided. Louis Arnaud Reid expresses this difficulty thus: 'The thoughts which are expressed to me by a piece of music which I love are not too indefinite to be put into words but on the contrary too definite. And so I find, in every attempt to express such thoughts, that something is right, but at the same time something is unsatisfying in all of them.'[11] Human beings have often recorded the emotional affects of theatre but those effects have rarely been accorded status. Our emotions and feelings have been given lower status than our intellect. The means to manipulate the intellect has, since the Enlightenment, been considered to be literature and literary texts; works of art which take the form of the visual or ethereal have manipulated our emotions. A visceral response to the visual is very difficult to articulate, and our lack of articulation compounds the problem and the status of spectacle. We, therefore, have an art form, which is hard to describe, which appeals to our emotions and manipulates them, and if we give in to this phenomenon, we are not in control of our emotions, we are out of control. One fundamental problem for spectacle as a whole event or as individual moments is that it requires us to lose self-control. This concern about the way in which theatre worked in the last part of the twentieth century is expressed by Bob Crowley:

I think there's a basic puritanism. I think Oliver Cromwell has a lot to answer for, and when he closed the theatres something seeped really deeply into the English psyche. It's beginning to loosen up, but its taken the 1980s, when we were beaten over the head by design. You couldn't open a magazine without reading that its got to be black or its got to be chrome. It became an onslaught in the 80s, which I think has just loosened the corsets a bit.[12]

Throughout the 1980s and 1990s in West End theatre in London ideas of 'spectacle', and theatre which is spectacular, could be linked to the changes in the production processes, and the process of production includes a number of complex concepts. Firstly, the nature of production has taken processes from other industries, such as mass production, which have inevitably affected the manufacture of the product. Secondly, the product has then been marketed as popular theatre and, therefore, mass culture, both of which require definition as to what is 'popular' and what is distinguished as part of 'mass culture', as the control for what is popular in any market is related to how it is marketed. For the theatre industry, such popularity is not necessarily affected by the intrinsic efficacy of the theatre performance. The use of spectacle or components of what we may term spectacle are inter-linked with the financial expenditure to produce a marketable product and are not necessarily considered as part of the efficacious nature of the product. In short, theatre critics discuss the use of certain techniques of production which involve technology and neglect the efficacious nature of the spectacle presented. The reclaiming of the word 'spectacle' as a non-pejorative term to describe theatre which is striking, dramatic and emotionally compelling is an important part of the ownership of the art form, as it helps distinguish the work from the process, and its possible manipulation by the market. If mass culture refers to a created commodity made for profit then, to a certain extent, the audience expect to be manipulated and exploited emotionally,[13] as mass culture and spectacle are linked as both use techniques of manipulation. However, for the theatre industry in the UK, the dissemination of the product is not to a mass audience in the same sense as it is for other forms of communication. The link between the production of spectacle in the context of theatre with a mass culture (which is deemed to be of 'low quality'), and which manipulates our emotions, highlights the prejudice of an intellectual elite against such a culture.

The emotional content of the theatre product, and the involvement of the spectators in that emotion, has, as part of mass culture theory, been denigrated as feminine:

[O]ne major reason for the critical dismissal of mass culture arises from its allegedly 'feminine' qualities. For example, mass culture, like the cinema or the soap opera, is denigrated because it is sentimental and plays on our emotions. Hence, it can be dismissed because it evokes reactions associated with the feminine.[14]

This would explain the suspicion and negative criticism that has always surrounded the presentation of spectacle.

If mass culture is a threat to high culture and the avant-garde, then the result will be as MacDonald pessimistically suggested, that the good culture is driven out by the bad culture because the latter is more easily understood and is also enjoyable.[15] This explains some of David Edgar's fears. The simplicity with which mass culture is viewed is explained by this feminist analysis of popular culture. Modleski argues that 'our ways of thinking and feeling about mass culture are so intricately bound up with notions of the feminine that the need for a feminist critique becomes obvious at every level of the debate.'[16] The feminist critique of mass culture suggests that women are responsible for mass culture and men are identified with high culture and art. The effect of the implicit criticism of the theatre writing of the last twenty years of the twentieth century illustrates the abhorrence of spectacle, a part of mass culture and the means to create it, and this underlying principle of the feminine nature of emotional, rather than masculine intellectual theatre.

The more commercial the operation of theatre production, the more controlling its market and the more manipulated the product potentially becomes. The product becomes a repetition of elements which have worked before for this market. The variety of produced theatre styles in the UK would not suggest a standardization or an homogenized popular culture and so mass culture theory must be rather carefully considered in relation to the theatre product. However, the clarification of the theatre product, which is specifically profit led, must take into account the changed dynamic of theatre production across all genres. Theatre has achieved a form of mass communication through the new production processes, which have changed its nature. The technology has made transfers not only within a country possible, for example to the West End, but the new production processes have enabled the same production to be transported around the world and re-mounted. These identikit productions do not require specific performers to bring a new interpretation but require the repetition of the successful event for the paying audience. The success of the product enables an extended life for it: the globalization of the theatre product. More pertinent to current funding for UK theatre is the 'potential' for standardization with this method of production. It is also true for theatre, as Strinati points out in the case of mass culture, that producers can, 'at times make use of standardised formats, this is not unique to it *(mass culture)* but can equally be found in elite culture'[17] and these standardized production techniques become part of an accepted practice.

As central funding cuts in the United Kingdom challenge theatre companies to remain in production, the nature of the product, the theatre production, becomes a commodity for consumption, which will attract the largest audience. In the late twentieth century, the intellectual arbiters of taste and theatre critics have not affected people's tastes. This is illustrated by the continuation by popular demand of productions which have been very negatively reviewed. Strinati suggests this is due to the wide variety of mass culture which is available and the dismissal of intellectuals and critics as gate-keepers for the definition of pleasure associated with theatre products. Distinctions between popular culture, art, mass culture, high culture and folk culture become blurred and have to be redrawn, almost for each product. Ultimately, all of these distinctions must take into account shifting power relations and taste which are at stake when making these distinctions. Political ideologies are at the centre of these discussions, not just of production but also of consumption. The idea of the soporific mass, passively manipulated, is as inaccurate as the active critical participant within theatre audiences. 'Populism has clearly figured in the ideologies of the producers of popular culture as a way of justifying what they produce – "giving people what they want" – and it can equally be an ideology of audiences.'[18] Culturally, the production rarely challenges society, as this would alter the market dynamic. So popular theatre can be dismissed as manipulative, feminized performance which feeds a capitalist habit, and is produced by technology, which is taking over our society, but more pertinent is the dismissal of a theatre which produces these reactions in the élite. The relationship of critics to the theatre product and, in particular, the definition of this as either feminine or masculine, raises a more complex topic of criticism for the theatre than there is time to discuss here. However, I think it is worth noting that spectacle falls into a potentially dangerous and easily-dismissed area, as Modleski suggests is true for other areas of our culture. The need for a feminist critique of theatre is indeed a fruitful area for research. In respect of my argument, I feel it helps to illustrate the way in which many aspects of the feminine in human behaviour are trivialized and the scenographic is one of them.

Theatre which can manipulate the spectator must be recognized as being successful in its purpose. The techniques of theatre production are accentuated through spectacle, as it utilizes all production methods available to affect the audience. In the late twentieth century theatre, one of the methods by which the emotional, dramatic and flamboyant could be achieved was through the technology of scenographic components, however, the technology of change and transformation has always been a part of the theatre event. In Medieval theatre, trap doors and flying pieces were used; the Renaissance and Baroque theatre effected changes which were dramatic and flamboyant in their own right and the subsequent applause for the 'means of production' is best illustrated through the work of Inigo Jones. His work encompassed the role of director, designer, architect and production manager and, through the means of production, he conflicted with the writer of the literary text on his journey towards the performance text. Jones pre-interpreted the literary text and packaged it for the consumption of the Court. Jones' use of scenographic elements to 'produce' the narrative of the text, meant that the Stuart Masques were interpreted literally by Jones into scenographic components and, as he was architect, designer and engineer of the masques, it was his vision which directed the audience's reception of them. The masques and their content were used allegorically for the kinds of virtues which the King wished to encourage at Court, such as Platonic truth. These virtues were then realized in the harmonious use of spectacular visions. The Court society was confirmed in its wisdom and strength by the theatre. These intentions and the text itself clearly affected the masques' production, as Orgel and Strong point out: 'Illusionistic machinery for the dramatic stage first comes fully into its own, logically enough, when the drama becomes not only overtly philosophical but directly Platonic.'[19] The pre-interpreted metaphoric set is one which fits easily into the late twentieth century aesthetic:

There's a text and it's delivered, but it is not evaluated and not coloured and not interpreted either, it's just there. Then there's noise, and that's there too and is also not interpreted. I regard this as important. It's a democratic concept of theatre. Interpretation is the work of the spectator and is not to take place on the stage. The spectator must not be absolved from his work. That's consumerism…capitalist theatre.[20]

In this way Jones did not expect the spectator to work at the sense making process, however, a great deal of what he presented was allegorical and, as such, required the spectator to work towards the meaning of the poetic presented. This contradiction between pre-interpretation and the poetic of scenography is very pertinent to the efficacy of theatre production and defines the work that becomes reified:

If the curtain goes up, its a play about anarchy, the stage is at a ridiculous angle, the walls are falling in and there's a pile of masonry on the set, you think well so what? We might as well all go home. All you've done is to give the audience a metaphor for what's about to take place.[21]

The taste of what makes good theatre very much depends on how one views the process of production. As set design has evolved into an activity that no longer requires just a background, the scenographic team endeavour to present a poetic, which is as affecting as the literary text. A belief that new technologies are used in productions simply because one can use such technologies ignores the way in which productions are 'designed'. However, the use of technology to present a metaphor for the experience that will unfold for the spectator is an apparent aesthetic which developed in the theatre of the late twentieth century in the UK.

It is the success of the poetic which has helped reify scenography. An example of a cohesive scenographic presentation which can be praised for its inherent poetic and damned for its simplicity is the RNT production of *An Inspector Calls*.[22] The play itself deals with the hypocrisy of the Edwardian middle-classes and through the course of the play we see their deeds revealed, which culminates in their downfall, shame, and bankruptcy. The scenography for this production embodied these themes. The open stage of the Olivier Theatre had at its centre a quarter-sized Edwardian house, which stood on a hydraulic mechanism; the rest of the stage was a cobbled street with potholes and puddles. A false proscenium arch had been created which was swagged with tattered red velvet. Outside of the proscenium was a red GPO telephone box. The opening of the play took place in the house. The spectator saw the comfortable family, whilst outside in the street the poor working classes peered in at their wealth. This extended metaphor culminated in the literal collapse of the house, which rocked forward dispensing the china and glass and other worldly goods of the Birling household. Now on the street, it became apparent that the older members of the family were going to have difficulty coping with their changed circumstances and society, whilst the younger members, who owned up to their hypocrisy, were more able to adapt. The scenography of this production exploded the myth of this play as a rather dusty drawing-room drama and it was the production which was reified, not the literary text of Priestley. One interpretation of this production and its reception by the audience is that this presentation enabled a better concentration on the politics of the piece as it was continually before us, encapsulated as a poetic in the scenography. This can be countered by the concern that the use of scenography in this instance patronized the audience because of its simplicity and, rather, distanced the spectator from the politics of the piece. It is hard to prove one result over another, but the aesthetic presented was particular to British theatre at the time.

This representation of a concept can result in the success of the production of a play that needed a face-lift. The excitement around this production was due to the use of the scenographic and its subsequent transfer was advertised as such. In *Post-War British Theatre Criticism*, John Elsom discusses the first effects of the production of *The Inspector Calls* by J.B. Priestley. The play was first produced in 1945 in Moscow. When it was first produced in Britain, at The Old Vic in 1946, it was criticized for being a slight play or an over-polemical one; either way it was thought to be an unlikely fantasy. 'Can the Birlings stand for that complacent world of 1912, tottering blindly to its fall?' J.C.Trewin wrote: 'It is an indication of the play's lack of theatrical truth that its author was obliged to put it into an Edwardian scene and costume.' Stephen Potter of the *New Statesman* wrote, 'the best coup de théâtre of the year.'[23] Visually, this metaphor was encapsulated in the scenography and it was the pithy extract of Priestley's text. The RNT production extended the play beyond the period piece, as a set text for examinations and placed it in the 1990s as a deconstructed truth for the spectator to see, quite literally. The efficacy of the spectacle was to reinforce the idea of the Birling's downfall. The spectacle was not without emotion, or critical awareness of the relation of the scenography to the literary text. If the legs on which the Birling household toppled had been manually dislocated, it would not have changed the result, but the use of technical means when seen by the spectator can leave scenography open to the criticism of the gratuitous and gimmicky, which may further the sale of the performance. Even though the resonance of the use of technology to create the image comes after the production has been deemed a success.

Alison Chitty referred to the 'lift and tilt' school of design, best illustrated by Richard Hudson, which Chitty sees as a trend and fashion in design. 'Visual values becoming exploded for spectacle. In this sense the result is over-designed under-scripted work.'[24] Now that the production team take an equal interest and responsibility for the presentation or concept of a production, the scenographic team have to find out what they want to say. The use of allegory and metaphor becomes relevant to their working practice and the student of scenography is asked to think about a production in these terms. The radical aesthetic of the Royal Court in which, as Jocelyn Herbert described, it is 'more interesting to evoke the mood of the play in a less naturalistic, less heavily decorative way, and let the play speak for itself',[25] has been a starting point for the change in aesthetic, but rather than the play speak for itself, scenography has provided another voice. The pre-interpreted performance can then be judged by the spectator. This method of production lends itself well to literary texts which are produced again and again. The production processes of the RSC, for example, which involve staging the same literary texts for production, require re-interpretation. The interest in the performance becomes in what so-and-so will do with, for example, *A Midsummer Night's Dream*. As most theatres in the UK use established literary texts as the main proportion of their work, the need for re-interpretation is an imperative of production. The practice of re-working texts through the scenography presented impacts on all theatre as a method of using stagecraft, lighting and technology.

Having accepted that scenographic components can have an emotional impact on an audience, critics have felt that an excess of such emotions may be detrimental to the theatre as a form and the more frivolous manipulation of the spectator will give the art of theatre a bad name. Alternative forms of performance that abhor the use of technology to create spectacle deny its meaning and potency. Although this meaning is perhaps not universal, it must certainly obtain some strands of familiarity for the spectator, as aspects of productions are recognizable as the triggers which produce specific responses in the spectator of a global theatre product.

Notes

1. David Edgar, 'New State of Play', *The Guardian*, 1st March, 1993.
2. *Arabian Nights*, Shared Experience, London, 1978.
3. *Nicholas Nickleby*, RSC at the Aldwych, London, 1982.
4. *Les Miserables*, The Palace Theatre, London, 1985.
5. *A Woman in Black*, opened Fortune Theatre, London, 1990.
6. S. Bennett, 1994, *Theatre Audiences A theory of production and reception*, London: Routledge, p. 165.
7. Ibid., p. 119.
8. RNT, *Platform Papers: 4. Designers*, Bob Crowley, Jocelyn Herbert, John Napier, 1993, p. 19–20.
9. Carner, M., *Puccini A Critical Biography*, London: Gerald Duckworth & Co. Ltd., 1958, p. ix.
10. This is from *Puccini: Interprete di se stesso* by Luigi Ricci, Milan 1954. The book is a record of first hand observations made by Puccini during rehearsals. Ricci assisted Puccini in the supervision and production of his operas. Carner, 1958, p. 256.
11. Reid, L.A., *Meaning in the Arts*, Muirhead Library of Philosophy, London: Allen & Unwin, 1969, p. 198.
12. RNT, *Platform Papers: 4 Designers*, Bob Crowley, Jocelyn Herbert, John Napier, 1993, p. 18.
13. Strinati, D., *An Introduction to Theories of Popular Culture*, London: Routledge, 1995, p. 12.
14. Ibid, p. 47.
15. MacDonald, D., 'A theory of mass culture', in B. Rosenberg and D. White (Eds) *Mass Culture*, Glencoe: Free Press, 1957.
16. Modleski, T., 'Feminity as mas(s)querade: a feminist approach to mass culture', in C. MacCabe (Ed.), *High Theory/Low Culture*, Manchester: Manchester University Press, 1986, p. 38.
17. Strinati, D., *An Introduction to Theories of Popular Culture*, London: Routledge, 1995, p. 41.
18. Ang, I., *Watching Dallas*, London: Routledge, 1989; Strinati,1995, p. 257.

19. Orgel, S. and Strong, R., *The Theatre of the Stuart Court*, Volume 1, Sotheby Park Bernet: University of California Press, 1973, p. 10.
20. Heiner Muller and Oliver Ortolani, 'Die Form entseht aus dem Maskieren', *Theater*, 1985, translated by E. Wright, 1989, in *Post-Modern Brecht: a representation*, London: Routledge.
21. RNT, *Platform Papers: 4 Designers*, 1993, p. 18.
22. RNT Production Olivier Theatre July–August 1993, Director Stephen Daldry, Designer Ian McNeil, Lighting Designer Rick Fisher.
23. All review quotes in Elsom, J., *Post-War British Theatre Criticism*, London: Routledge & Kegan Paul, 1980.
24. Christine White, unpublished interview with Alison Chitty, 1992.
25. RNT, *Platform Papers: 4 Designers*, 1993, p. 1.

Chapter 12

Metatheatre: A Discourse on Contemporary Staging

Ewa Wąchocka

The reform of theatre in the twentieth century is rooted in the conviction of a symptomatic paradox, hidden in the aesthetic assumptions of realist theatre, and reducing the doctrine of realism on stage ad absurdum. The main prerequisite of that doctrine was being 'true to life' or even 'becoming life' as naturalism had it, yet what was postulated was to be implemented via the sphere of stage performance where a fictitious world is created. Meanwhile, in theatre the only real things that exist are the materials, objects, and persons/actors, to whom extended meanings have been attributed. The realist theatre wanted to reduce fiction to reality, and to hide from spectators the reality, serving as material for the creation of a fictitious world.

No wonder, then, that the reform of theatre, like numerous later experiments in theatre, aimed at emphasizing in the performance the semantic procedures executed on reality; it also aimed at abolishing the, previously strictly delineated, division between stage and spectators. It is also clear that the issue of relations between theatre and reality will be deeply reflected in the playwriting, making itself profoundly pronounced especially in the plays dealing with metatheatre reflections. Although one cannot underestimate the influence exerted on drama by novel staging practices, exposing among others the 'play with text', playwriting itself, to a much larger extent, started to impose conditions upon theatre, delineating the directions for new quests. In the twentieth century, playwrights often refused to be obedient to theatre as a definite social institution, as an aesthetic environment with clearly defined principles of spectacular values and credibility, as well as a binding set of conventions of presentation. The measure of those changes, in fact, is the correlation between contemporary staging and the playwriting developing in parallel. In the theatre of the twentieth century tradition, opposing the primacy of author and literary fiction, the plays themselves are often most efficient in expressing the dissension to the latter.

One cannot leave out of account the conviction that, characteristic for modern consciousness, the multitude of information and the flood of signs which result in the diminishing of meaning, fictionalizing of various areas of social life, simultaneously, in artistic and literary creation, result in making unimportant the traditional ways of rendering reality and creating plots. Gerald Graff wrote: 'Irony and scepticism towards the traditional claims of art regarding truth, seriousness and the depth of "meaning" started to penetrate into art.' The artist, refusing to treat art as 'seriously' as it had been customary so far, uses art itself as an instrument which annihilates its traditional pretences and which shows the helplessness and weakness of art and language.'[1] Similar to the general situation in communication, a crack is also conspicuous in the language used in art, a break-up between the sign (or text) and the signified, between sign and meaning, between text and reality. The effort in criticism taken by Jacques Derrida, resulting in the rejection of representation,[2] has been used as a key for interpretation, to prove the separation of objects from words (or signs) and being aware of that delineates the nature of creation in the present day. As a result, art increased its interest in itself, which usually is manifested during the periods of breaking with the existing tradition, and which takes the form of getting interested in its own tools for cognition, as well as means and opportunities of articulation.

In drama, the self-reflection, perhaps more than at any time previously, applies simultaneously to theatre and to drama, which is 'performed' in theatre. One can even risk a statement that intensification of the reflection leads to the impairment of one of the ways of understanding metatheatre – described some 40 years ago by Lionel Abel – as reflecting the concept of the world as theatre.[3] Metatheatre, departs from the observation of theatricalness inscribed into our lives, proposing instead a discourse of the main topic, which is the art of theatre: its identity, its standing in the contemporary world, the means of expression and the perception proper to it. The reason for that is, undoubtedly, the degradation of theatrical illusion, resulting from a crisis of the categories of representation. The less perfect the representation, understood in the spirit of *mimesis*, the more playwrights focus upon the means of representation, which is theatre, the more intense the liking for demonstration of the techniques of symbolizing reality by means of reality proper for theatre. Thus, anticipating the deconstructive efforts of stage directors, the texts meant for the stage transgress the traditional mechanisms of dramatic fictitiousness and evoke the crisis of literary representation. As Luigi Pirandello or Stanisław Ignacy Witkiewicz shattered the principles of stage naturalism and verisimilitude, as the founders of the Theatre of the Absurd led to wrecking the canonical structures of action and characters, considering the stage to be a place that is specific and abstract at the same time, contemporary playwrights also rejected the principle of the organic development of structure, covering for the lack of continuity and fragmentation of the theatrical picture of the world. Such a decomposition of the existing patterns turns utterance into discourse about the rules of shaping utterances, and the limitations it is subject to.

The metatheatrical character is, here, of a more narrow scope; it is not, unlike what Richard Hornby[4] wrote in his book *Drama, Metadrama, and Perception*, an almost ever-present feature of drama, but is also different from what has been described in the studies by Robert Nelson or Tadeusz Kowzan, for example.[5] Thus, it is not going to be identified with one of its manifestations, namely with theatre in theatre. It is a form of self-reference of the dramatic text, thanks to which theatre 'speaks' about itself, it may be considered an approach parallel to contemporary staging strategies. This may surely be the way to interpret the unconventional operations performed on the tissue of drama in the plays by Polish authors Tadeusz Różewicz and Bogusław Schaeffer. The revealing of the self-referring nature of creativity leads (in both playwrights) to a multiplied and multi-layer play with theatre, but whilst Różewicz exposes old rules of genres and conventions to criticism, Schaeffer attempts to develop upon the possibilities of 'pure' theatre as a means of communication.

The 'subcutaneous' dialogue with the conventions, always present in the playwriting by Różewicz, openly appears in *Akt przerywany* (*The Interrupted Act*), in which the analysis methodically deals with the limitations of traditional realistic techniques. That is why drama as a literary genre and as a substance for creation poses for him not only a problem to be solved in the play but, most of all, demands fundamental theoretical pondering. Drama, due to the reversal of the process of moving towards the structuralizing of forms, ceased to be a stable construction, forcing its discipline, yet sure and durable; instead, its constituents underwent a substantial decomposing. Różewicz's experimental play turns around the usual order of production and perception of a work of art: in the place of the intended comedy, entitled in fact *Akt przerywany* (*The Interrupted Act*), an essay or theoretical and polemical comments of the author have been substituted, in short a confession of the author regarding the process of creating a play. The project for shaping situations on stage which emerges here irresistibly poses the question about presentation in theatre, if the most desired means for it are the possibilities lying in silence and abstaining from action. The joke about a fly flittering over sugar cubes is not without irony or deeper meaning, and is used to testify to the limitations. Not only does the joke have such a purpose, it also proves to be in vain to present the experiences of the Girl (Dziewczyna) or to show all the implications of the behaviour of the Housewife (Gospodyni) – exactly because of the sense of realism that we are used to. The realism of Różewicz attempts to break with or go around the aesthetic principles established – those of representation, of rendering the world in objective forms, assimilated socially, of the predetermined sense of purpose of the work. This is inevitably connected with the rejection of the approved ways of representation, the literary ones, referring to the conventionalized patterns, as those of staging. Freed from the ballast of staging and expression, drama would be fulfilled in an almost wordless presence of a protagonist on stage; in the existence outside the models usually organizing their existence; in silence.

The existing languages prove of little value to express what has not been done or spoken, yet what comprises all the real wealth of human affairs? However, giving up the updating of established rules means a serious reduction of the gists and meanings of the drama, which is successively described by the author in the notes, exemplifying the reasoning and the idea of the not-written-comedy by a handful of study-scenes. The incomplete character of that play leads, in fact, to contesting the system of theatre based on ready and complete texts, a system according to which the task of a playwright is to deliver a literary, composed and prepared product. On the other hand, joining the two types of discourse, critical discourse with parts of the play, appears to anticipate a definite theatre situation. It suggests, namely, that the performance is to be composed directly on stage, with improvisation of actions characteristic for that process, rehearsing various variants, accompanied with elements of discussion. Departing from the assumed order, play-spectacle has been underlined by isolating consecutive versions of the play – for example, sketches of the same scene in various poetics – by multiplying the possibilities of developing the play, which is meant to trigger the perceptive activity of the recipients. Multiplying and juxtaposing the expressions thus removes both the idea that stood at the start and the final implementation of the idea in favour of potential and trial transformations.

Yet something more important lies behind it: the concern towards the easy repetition of ready sets of signs detached from primeval meanings and thus destined to the mystified ways of expression. Or, in other words, the attempt of defining anew the relation between the conventional and literal meaning of signs in theatre. There is also a trace of the eternal contradiction, as in the *Six Characters in Search of an Author* by Pirandello, between life, endlessly capacious in meanings and impossible to be exhausted in art; life which, as Maurice Merleau-Ponty wrote, 'needs yet to be expressed and thought over applying partial perspectives, unable to render it in its totality';[6] therefore, contradiction between that and form, which provides means of expression but also restrains and immobilizes.

The process of turning the existing reality into the fictitious one, shown in *The Interrupted Act,* in which the world to be described is confronted and re-conciliated with the order of literature, of theatre, is allowed to follow from the inside of the complex mechanism of staging. A similar thing takes place in *Przyrost naturalny* (*Birth Rate*): here the questioning of existing conventions as well as formulating notional and aesthetic foundations for a different dramatic-theatrical practice becomes a sort of subject of investigations.[7] Only that, even more than in the *Act,* the possibility of making a play fades as the play depicts the decomposition that creative plans are subject to even before they materialize. In *Birth Rate* the action consists of activities connected with writing the script: the history of the material maturing and turning concrete from the original concept; of accumulation and destruction of the material; of repeated rehearsals and conflicts going on in the mind of the artist – all get presented with specific dramatization. The constructed play turns into the history of the play, in which the difficulties of staging the idea, the possibilities of choosing situations and themes, of discovering words and images, the giving up of some elements of plot, interrupting the description of the play, all have the function of traditional elements of plot. As a result, the writing of a play appears as an act of restricting, of 'closing' the intentional piece, which opens towards various solutions.

Yet it is the incidents connected with making the utterance real, or in fact the impossibilities of making things real, that explain the incoherence of the world image that is proper for modern culture, and also for modern theatre. The drama emerges from the discrepancies between the idea and the themes, which are resistant, and between the work of imagination and the language; it shows the conflict between consciousness and action. Surely, the writing experiment undertaken in both plays undermines the acknowledged criteria of writing for the stage, blossoming with results which are in an unfinished, 'draft' version, according to those criteria. However, neither *The Interrupted Act* nor *Birth Rate* (which have in common the search for new, alternative, solutions for drama and theatre) present a coherent, univocal proposal or, what is more, a theoretical programme. The process of deconstructing the constituents of a drama that has been described should, rather, aim at, 'creating a form which would not have been representation, yet which would make a field for incessant mediation between drama and reality'.[8]

Such dilemmas seem strange to Schaeffer, although his playwriting demonstratively reaches beyond the borders of traditional theatre. Rendering of reality appears to have lost the power of focusing imagination: what is presented is a game, the topic of which is itself; only indirectly would it indicate objects and phenomena that it portrays. The principle of acting in theatre, duplicated or even multiplied in its course, is the basic motive in his constructing of plays. The acting, most often, takes place simply in the theatre or, at times, a space which openly imitates the conventionality of a stage in theatre (as in *Tutam*), and is associated with a place for public appearance: lecture (*Seans* – The Séance), a TV programme (*Razem* – Together). In *Aktor* (The Actor) the 'real' situations and dialogues copy sequences from scripts of plays in which the main protagonist used to act, acts nowadays (at rehearsals) or will act, while both layouts intertwine to such an extent that they both appear to totally lose their relative identity. In *Tutam* the whole sense of acting and its theatrical value result from multiplying the combinations provided by the two situations in which the action takes place ('tu' here and 'tam', there, hence the title) and the four protagonists, performed by pairs of actors. In *Gdyby* (If), we have a simultaneous intertwining of three copies of one and the same institution: an exclusive school, where each of the four actors (two women and two men) personifies as many as three protagonists. More conventional solutions have also been applied, when a character turns into a different protagonist every time they appear on stage (Cham in *The Actor*, Multiindywiduum in *Rondo* – The Roundabout) or when the protagonists pretend to their partners that they are somebody else than in reality, which makes their previous actions conventional. The Mirror-like or box-like composition, albeit being related to the observation of contemporary culture abundant with endless reflections and repetitions, is first of all a testimony of striving towards 'pure' theatre. As has openly been said in *The Actor,* 'the substance of theatre should…simply be theatre itself'.[9]

The world that gets shaped in such a way has strictly defined borders of its identity: it is mainly a reality of the stage. The protagonists, whatever they are and whom they personify, are fully aware of their illusory existence, which comes true during the performance:

SHE: Come on, let's have a better exchange, but not with those people present.
HE: Remember, we are in the theatre and perform for people.[10]

They are, then, according to June Schlueter, metafictional characters, as their fictitiousness is not only disclosed by the author but also implemented in the way they function.[11] A metafictional character extracts and manifests the dual nature characteristic for any protagonist of drama, that is, the fact that it is, simultaneously, a protagonist taking part in the action and an actor. This duality means that a metafictional character 'possesses two distinct fictive identities, between which we are forced to distinguish, accepting one of the fictive identities as "real" and the other as "fictive".[12] In Schaeffer, the fictitiousness clearly dominates. As 'real' his characters possess a sort of identity, but they simultaneously lack it as they are, in fact, not governed by any visible motivations. As 'fictive' characters they, with ostentatious openness, perform their games 'for' the audience, not hiding their being interested in the signs of acceptance or disapproval expressed by the audience.

The activities of actors, much more those of actors than those of protagonists, hardly make any reference to the world outside the stage: fiction gives way to metafiction, hidden in the remnants of plots, treated rather as pretext to develop the improvisations of actors, whereas the multiplication of foregrounds and backgrounds (as in *Próby* – Rehearsals, *Kaczo, Tutam*) leads to a spontaneous generation of 'worlds' on stage. What lies behind it is presupposing that fiction is not capable of describing reality in the same way as reality cannot be locked in the canons governing fiction. Hence the 'action' in his plays consists of travesties, overstatements, stereotypes, and anti-stereotypes which destroy the former. The mechanism of multiplication is best rendered in the theatre of Schaeffer by the situation of 'writing on stage'. Either the improvisation meant to arrive at a scenario of actions turns out to be just the implementation of a scenario already approved (the epilogue of *Kaczo*), or just the other way round – the actors compose ('write') a project of a situation which they act out at the moment, that is, being strict, they act that they do something which they act just now (ad infinitum). Thus, what gets revealed is the bilateral and procedural approach of all scripts or scores, to the fluctuating, not formed substance of reality before it finally makes up the shape of the performance. A reprise or modification of the structure does not purport to be a communiqué about the world; it is a message about the theatre itself: its nature, language, and possibilities of expression. A strict junction of 'scenario' and 'improvised' action, reaching as far as the mutual interchangeability, is the expression of the formula of theatre, which, with narcissistic fancy, demonstrates its own creative abilities, wanting to evoke an illusion of its self-sufficiency.

However, a significant dichotomy may be noted in the relation between theatre and reality. To cut a long story short, it is the dissonance between theatre as the art utilizing the power of 'pure' theatricalness, backing the immediate character of the act of creation, creating directly out of the material available from reality, and the theatre which, after all, still uses literature. The constructing of situations which show the participation of actors in creating the performance are meant to make the impression of the performance not being ready, so that the audience would consider the spectacle in which they participate as an autonomous being, capable of emerging without previous instructions of the playwright. So mystified, a theatre 'without author' would be a theatre liberated, in an institutional and an aesthetic sense, from literature, a theatre which instead would expose its inherent attribute: the simultaneousness of the act of creation and the act of reception. Schaeffer builds complex metatheatre arrangements in order to exemplify typical situations and the state of consciousness of contemporary repertoire theatre, with the inevitable conflict of arguments on both sides. It also seems to project, often in a parodistic convention, the staging practice that aims at rendering performance independent of the literary forms of representation, or treating the text of drama in a pretty factual way. The theatre that Schaeffer proposes is, in fact, incapable of escaping from the written text, in the way that *commedia dell'arte*, to which the author makes a clear reference, could not exist without a scenario.

The presented attempt at departing from a theatre based upon literature may only be possible through making reference to that theatre, by uncovering its tricks and catches, by questioning the constructive and semantic possibilities, by criticizing and objectifying language – so as to achieve, in consequence, a compromised acceptance of the relations with literature, already under different conditions. The plays of Schaeffer, written in the context of theatre that has grown together with playwriting, expose and classify its system of creation and rules of communication. These rules reveal the reality of code entangled in various parallel structures, in the surroundings of which it has to appear. His theatre keeps its distance from the 'pressure of systems' which turn the meanings of utterances into schemes, as well as from mechanical productions of conventions demanded in order to move within the field of probabilities which are opened by the play of conventions and the transgressing of them; in the world of constantly unmasking which goes on between reality and convention.

The avant-gardes of the twentieth century undermined the shape of European theatre, present since the Renaissance until naturalism and symbolism, where theatre treated a performance as a representation of a different reality, either as its imitation or its symbol. The disintegration of the union built upon those principles is simultaneously connected with a change in perception and in cognition. As theatre functioned before as a model of reality, the audience, in the opinion of Erika Fischer-Lichte, watched and listened in order to understand the presented model.[13] One may assume that the members of the audience did not differ substantially in their understanding of the performance if they were able to recognize it as a model and read it through a reference to the represented, objective reality. In contemporary performance it can be seen particularly clearly that the questioning of representation brings anew the issue of agreement regarding theatre and its reception – for example, through an attempt at departing from convention, through multiplied metatheatrical games, through getting rid of the 'world'. The emphasis on theatricality allows the destruction of one, shared, reference system (to be demonstrated). Instead there may be as many realities, as the individual recipients are able to create, relying on their own perceptions. Today's playwriting, as well as staging, exposes the lack of continuity and fragmentation of the image of the world rendered in theatre, whereas it also leaves it mainly to the recipient to establish a rule arranging the presented reality. In this way it provokes the recipient to be more active, as he/she obtains something like a Cortazar-like 'model kit', to assemble his/her own variant of the work of art. Using similar procedures, the producers and playwrights attempt to render the experience of the world contemporary, as the world had lost the status of objective reality a long time ago. In that sense, as Manfred Schmeling wrote, 'metatheatre may have an imminent hermeneutic function, consisting of pointing out what is a part of tradition already gone, and of making recipients aware of the evolution taking place.'[14]

Notes

1. Graff, G., *Mit przełomu postmodernistycznego.*(*The myth of post-modern turning-point*), in: *Nowa proza amerykańska. Szkice krytyczne.* Selected, edited and provided with introduction by Z. Lewicki, Warszawa: Czytelnik, 1983, pp. 59, 56.
2. Derrida, J., 'Structure, Sign and Play in the Discourse of the Human Sciences', R. Macksey and E. Donato (Eds.), *The Structuralist Controversy: the Languages of Criticism and the Sciences of Man*, Baltimore and London: John Hopkins UP, 1975.
3. Abel, L., *Metatheatre. A New View of Dramatic Form*, New York: Hill & Wang, 1963.
4. Hornby, R., *Drama, Metadrama, and Perception,* London and Toronto: Associated University Presses, 1986.
5. Nelson, R.J., *Play within a Play: The Dramatist's Conception of his Art: Shakespeare to Anouilh,* New Haven, Yale University Press, 1958; T. Kowzan, 'Teatr w teatrze czyli o dialektyce iluzji scenicznej' (Theatre in theatre, or on the dialectic of stage illusion), in *Dialog* 1971, No. 4.
6. Merleau-Ponty, M., 'Postrzeganie, ekspresja, sztuka' (Perception,expression,art), translated, E. Bieńkowska, in: *Proza świata. Eseje o mowie.* Selected, edited and provided with introduction by S. Cichowicz, Warszawa: Czytelnik, 1976, pp. 187–188.
7. Głowiński, M., 'Powieść jako metodologia powieści' (Novel as methodology of novel), in: *Porządek, chaos, znaczenie. Szkice o powieści współczesnej,* Warszawa: PIW, 1968, pp. 93–100.
8. Filipowicz, H., *A Laboratory of Impure Forms: The Plays of Tadeusz Różewicz,* New York, London: Greenwood Press, 1991, p. 91.
9. Schaeffer, B., *Utwory sceniczne I,* Salzburg: Collsch Edition, 1992, p. 110.
10. Schaeffer, B., *Tutam,* in: *Utwory sceniczne I,* Salzburg: Collsch Edition, 1992, p. 307.
11. Schlueter, J., *Metafictional Characters in Modern Drama,* New York: Columbia University Press, 1979, pp. 13–17.
12. Ibid., p. 14.
13. Fischer-Lichte, E.,'From Theatre to Theatricality – How to Construct Reality', *Theatre Research International* 1995, vol. 20, 2, pp. 102–103.
14. Schmeling, M., *Métathéâtre et intertexte. Aspects du théâtre dans le theatre*, Paris: Lettres Modernes, 1982, pp. 8–9.

Chapter 13

A Metaphorical Mise-en-Scène: Elia Kazan and Max Gorelik at
The Group Theatre

Scott Dahl

Outsiders within the Group

In 1930 a theatrical collective formed in New York City and adopted the name The Group Theatre. They lived and worked together for ten years producing 24 Broadway productions. They are remembered for the socio-political content of their productions and the important figures that sprang from their ranks. Amongst them was Elia Kazan, the most heralded American Director on stage and screen through the 1940s, 50s and early 60s. He began directing at the Group Theatre at the age of 23.

Another less known figure, who came of age at the Group Theatre was the designer Mordecai 'Max' Gorelik. Max Gorelik designed 11 Group settings. Lee Strasberg, the most important Group figure, only directed nine Group productions. Only six members of the Group were involved in more productions than Gorelik. Of the dozens of individuals involved with the Group during their decade together, Gorelik's importance in the Group's legacy is little known.

Both Kazan and Gorelik emigrated to the United States at a young age, Kazan from Istanbul, Turkey, at the age of 4 in 1913 and Max Gorelik from Shchedrin, Russia, shortly after his birth in 1899. Their status as immigrants took form in many aspects of their lives. They both shared a hunger for success and a need to prove themselves worthy in the eyes of their entrepreneurial parents. A competitor of Gorelik said he was the type who would steal a loaf of bread simply because he was hungry. Gorelik responded, 'That's a good reason!'[1] Both men shared an independent spirit, a feeling that they were different from their peers. They worked toward a singularly unique and personal form to express their artistic work. They wished to be accepted, but as a unique voice. Thus, both men hated and embraced the role of outsider. Kazan felt, as an artist, that he should be judged by, 'his depth, not his breadth.'[2] Kazan also stated, 'Why be good at everything? No artist is. That's for gossip columnists.'[3] The playwright, Robert Ardrey, understood the difficult role of professional theatrical artists. According to Ardrey:

> A dramatist is a specialist, in a sense, in human nature. In another sense, however, he is a specialist in nothing, and therefore a generalist…the most suspect of creatures in the view of the modern, specialized human animal.[4]

The 1930s were a confusing and fervent decade in America for artists devoted to depicting human nature in their work whilst balancing a need for financial security and the respect of doubting families. However, the 1930s presented young artists with a crossroads of models to live by: follow a failed capitalist set of values at home or a seemingly idealistic socialist set of values from abroad. The 'foreign' values they embraced in their work were significant artistic choices at the time. These decisions would become life-altering in the politically-conservative decades to come.

Unlike Kazan, Gorelik never joined the Communist Party, but he did spend much of his early career working with the smaller politically-oriented workers' theatres. Both men were passionate radicals by any standard. Their mutual interests overlapped at an important time in both of their careers. It was also fortunate that the short career of Robert Ardrey produced two plays at this time for them to collaborate on. Ardrey shared a similar outlook on life to the Group members. He later stated:

> Much of what we have experienced in the last terrifying half century has simply been what happens, no more, no less, when human energies become preoccupied with the building of social institutions upon false assumptions concerning man's inner nature.[5]

Even Ardrey was an outsider: an anthropologist, observing human nature at arm's length. They were all fortunate to find a producing organization devoted to exposing society's false assumptions and, true to form, the Group was most successful when sticking to their principles, even though they abandoned them fairly often, but never found commercial or critical success when doing so.

Elia Kazan: Combining the external and the internal

Kazan noted early on how unique his thoughts on directing were; he wrote: 'Only I knew both sides of the problem of stage art, the external and the internal. How arrogant I was in those years!'[6] It was he who would, for the first time, combine the external image of the mise-en-scène with the internal emotions of the actors, so that even a deaf man in the audience could sense the 'human event in all its complexities and subtleties.'[7]

Group directors felt directing was mostly a matter of coaching actors. The Group directors created what Kazan referred to as 'spontaneous, surprising and true inner experiences' on stage[8] but Kazan wanted to go beyond what he saw from Strasberg and Clurman. He dreamed of a day when he would have the opportunity to combine the, 'shaping of scenes and the manipulation of the positions and movements of actors,' with the Group's Method.[9]

Kazan first credited Yale directing Professor Alexander Dean for his introduction to directing as an art of 'position, picture and movement.'[10] Dean thought this was important to young directors as stage positions need to tell the story of the scene and the relationship of the characters. From Dean, Kazan first learned that behaviour, feeling and conflict could be suggested through the visual stage picture of actors in a setting. Kazan instinctively felt a director's need to communicate through rhythm, speed and grace. He clearly recognized the importance of his own sense of warm and cool spaces on stage, how to use strong downstage movements, and to allow weaker moments to move up and off stage. He treated actors not only as the emotional and oral storytellers they are but also as a vehicle of visual expression. Yet, in the early 1930s Kazan would leave these lessons at the back of his mind as he found himself knee-deep in the Group's developing emphasis on the emotional and psychological training of the actor. However, they were never lost to him and would soon re-surface as important ingredients in his own personal approach to directing, tested for the first time on the settings of Max Gorelik and in the plays of Robert Ardrey.

The mise-en-scène of the Kazan-Gorelik productions are extremely evocative. Gorelik borrowed from Brecht the concept that the ordinary must appear new and surprising, and that everyday life should be re-examined. However, Gorelik was quick to point out that shock for its own sake should be avoided. He felt shock was the 'besetting sin' of yesterday's Expressionism, Surrealism, and Absurdism. Kazan's staging was never as obvious as those 'sinful' modernists. It was well-crafted, dynamic, communicative and deeply psychological. The strong visual angles, contrasting asymmetrical groupings of actors and use of shadow, mass and highlights created a subtle form of communication to Kazan's productions, which set him apart from his contemporaries in America.

Max Gorelik: Metaphor within the Method

Max Gorelik developed a detailed theory of metaphorical stage design throughout his decade-long association with the Group. Not only did Kazan work with Gorelik at a time when his ideas were solidifying, he had for years known Gorelik's work as a Group actor. The evidence suggests Kazan's use of actors and setting in creating dynamic stage pictures and mise-en-scène was greatly influenced by his working relationship with Gorelik. The significance of these collaborations has been long overlooked and their results are too important to ignore. These collaborations are important to our understanding of the work of these two significant theatre practitioners and invaluable to our understanding of the Director-Designer relationship.

In general, Gorelik's place within the Group is little known or misunderstood. The depth of meaning executed in the scenography of the Group is rarely documented. Lee Strasberg was among the few who later acknowledged the importance of staging in Group Theatre productions:

A lot of aspects of the Group are misunderstood. The Group set a style, not a fixed style, but a certain basic approach to the treatment of reality on stage not only in acting but also in production. Max Gorelik and to some extent Boris Aronson, of course, were very instrumental in that aspect of the work. Especially Max, who had ideas of his own and who could contribute what he had to offer. He was really in a sense the Group Designer.

He had as much to do with creating the vision of the play on stage as any of us, and his role and that of design generally in the Group has not had enough attention paid to it.[11]

The actor Ruth Nelson added, of Gorelik: 'He was totally our designer...his sets spoke the very sense and feeling we had of our own work.'[12] Gorelik seemed to phrase the growing sense of production process both he, Kazan and other Group members were creating: 'The Group Theatre has perfected its ensemble approach and is moving onward. They are creating toward a true synthesis of script, directing, acting, and setting.'[13]

Gorelik is historically referred to as a Group associate; however, he was unanimously elected a member of the Group by the acting ensemble in 1934. The directors later denied him membership, which caused a three-year split from the Group, after designing five of their first seven productions. He was for at least two seasons contractually given the right of first refusal to design Group productions. In 1938 he was on the collective's weekly payroll whether he designed a show or not.[14] The Group enjoyed their most complete and satisfactory productions with Gorelik setting the scene.

As Kazan forgot early lessons while being captivated by the Group's almost religious exploration of truth on stage, so did Gorelik. Gorelik was academically trained as an illustrator and his use of iconography and strong sense of imagery showed itself in his first professional work, designing settings for vaudeville shows. Broadway producers shouted, 'Nut stuff! When we start doing burlesque we'll give you a call.'[15] Gorelik's use of a little known Russian Jewish style he termed 'Hassidic Grotesque' for his Yiddish Theatre designs also alienated him from the mainstream. Lee Simonson termed his and fellow designer Boris Aronson's work as 'full of Russian dogma. Totally inapplicable to the American stage.'[16] This was nothing but professional jealousy and intimidation of younger designers encroaching on the established designer's territory. Yet it solidified Gorelik's reliance on his own beliefs, much as Kazan would rely on his own isolation at times and both men were often stung by the ridicule of those they admired.

In fact, Gorelik's work was particularly 'American'. He designed mostly new American plays about American socio-economic conditions. More importantly to his process, Gorelik's sense of design was based on his association with the Group ensemble. He studied the movement of the actors and the inherent action of their characters. He understood and embraced the training of the Group and their devotion to the physical as well as vocal and interpretive aspects of acting. Gorelik often said he learned more about scenery watching actors than by studying colour, light, and construction. After all, did not Stanislavsky say he could get more use of one good chair than all the intricate staging of the world?

Gorelik asked questions that needed answers: How will the actors move? When might the stage picture be most important to the audience? Will there be subtleties in the acting to overpower or to accentuate? Is there a texture to the performance that should be attributed to the set as well? Is the playing space to be ample or condensed? Should actors be pronounced by their environment or blend into it?[17] They are obvious questions, yes; however, they are all too often ignored. Gorelik discussed these issues with his director, or in the case of the

Group's *Golden Boy* and *Men In White,* with the Assistant Director Elia Kazan. Clurman allowed Kazan to work with designers on their designs, sketching out detailed staging to give them a sense of the space their blocking would require.

Although it would take seven years in the Group for Kazan to direct, he had performed in nine Group Productions, as an actor and stage manager, and he had the opportunity to observe Gorelik's work first hand. Gorelik avoided absolute realism. He developed a theory of design he termed the 'Scenic Imagination', which had at its core a visual metaphor, and detail was used only as necessary. Although Social Realism or Naturalism may best explain Gorelik's approach, some compared his sense of minimalism to Epic Theatre. Even Erwin Piscator wrote to Gorelik that one day theirs and Brecht's name would be synonymous with Epic Theatre,[18] however, Gorelik seems to have escaped the limelight of history.

A popular topic at the time, many artists felt that an understanding of Freudian psychology was necessary to the theatrical artist, Kazan and Gorelik included. In particular, Gorelik studied Freud's Gestalt psychology and the phenomenon of attention. He simplified the concept into the study of 'Contact and Confluent' attention.[19] Contact attention describes human behaviour that takes immediate notice, which may be accepting or resentful (as Gorelik noticed), or sometimes where rejection is more immediate than acceptance. In contrast, Gorelik described 'Confluent' attention as a gulping of data during which an audience is overwhelmed by new information and, therefore, associates them to things already known. There is no time for acceptance of new ideas and your intent as a visual artist may be lost on an unknowing audience. Gorelik utilized these concepts in his attempt to reach his audience effectively. Gorelik merely anticipated the expectations of the audience for visual meaning in what they observe. No one familiar with the theatre on a regular basis could argue this point. Most importantly, Gorelik was convinced the best order of acceptance was a subtle one; otherwise the risk of confusing or even insulting the audience was possible, as so many modern abstract artists do. Even Brecht was less effective away from his loyal audience following for just such reasons. It was Gorelik's process that made him unique, not a visual agenda, and photographs of Gorelik's work prove a broad range of resulting designs, despite a consistent and theoretical basis.

Robert Ardrey: A personal journey through the nature of man

The Group Theatre was formed, in part, to provide a forum for new plays by American playwrights about American social conditions. But it also provided a place of experimentation. Playwrights such as John Howard Lawson, Clifford Odets, and Robert Ardrey wrote realistic psychological and sociological plots, yet at times used prose to create a poetic atmosphere. The poetic intensity usually developed as the play neared its climax. Thus, designers of these shows had to provide for both natures of the dialogue by providing a design to appear both realistic and abstract, typically transforming as the plot unraveled. Gorelik never veered far enough from realism as to risk losing an audience's attention and their acceptance early in a show. Yet his sense of proportion and restrained use of detail allowed an audience to unwittingly find themselves in the midst of many an unrealistic third act.

Robert Ardrey was one of the most unique playwrights of his day. A native of Chicago, Ardrey was trained in the Natural Sciences at the University of Chicago and for two years lectured on anthropology at Chicago's Century of Progress Exposition. It seems likely that such a man would write about human relations and our search for meaning, but it is odd that he would choose playwriting as an avenue to explore these interests. A man of science, Ardrey had tolerance for artists as well. A student of human nature, he spoke of his 'weakness for lights and shadows, for mystery and irony and situation and adventure, for the rude joke or the great story.'[20] Ardrey's title character from his play *Casey Jones* is merely a creative extension, a realization, of observations present in his many anthropology texts, such as, his 1961 *African Genesis: A Personal Investigation into the Animal Origins and Nature of Man.*

Thus, the young Elia Kazan found himself teamed up with a cantankerous left-wing activist production designer and an academic social theorist to collaborate on his first two Broadway productions. An odd trio, one might say, but according to Kazan, the three meshed immediately. Ardrey thought Clurman was too 'New York' for his plays and urged him to allow Kazan to direct.[21] In fact, in 1937 Kazan stated of Ardrey: 'I felt more at home with Bob than I did with my fellow Group members. I'm not sure I belong with these people anymore.'[22] Kazan was more than pleased to cast outsiders, as most Group actors were performing in *Golden Boy* and Kazan was solidifying his own artistic sensibilities and collaborating with strong outside personalities for the first time. The influence of these productions on his later career should not be ignored. What the collaborators shared was an obsession with understanding human behaviour through their own artistic process.

Gorelik quoted Mark Twain to emphasize the importance of the search for accuracy in one's work: 'The difference between the right word and the word that is almost right is the difference between lightning and the lightning-bug.'[23]

The Group Approach

While Kazan was an outsider amongst the actors, he quickly became an insider with the directors. By the re-organization of 1937, Kazan was an influential member of the Group leadership and, aside from the original directors, only Kazan designed multiple Group productions. Bobby Lewis was the only other to direct a Group Production. Max Gorelik designed all three of Kazan's Group productions: 1938's *Casey Jones,* 1939's *Quiet City* and 1940's *Thunder Rock*. Robert Ardrey wrote both *Casey Jones* and *Thunder Rock,* which were two of the most artistically acclaimed Group productions and the most widely regarded set designs of Gorelik's career. The production images are outstanding and this alone makes them historically significant. Yet the 1939 Kazan-Gorelik collaboration on Irwin Shaw's *Quiet City* adds important background to the Kazan-Gorelik relationship. It was produced as an experiment in Epic Techniques. Gorelik was in fact the first American proponent of

Epic Theatre and had worked with Bertolt Brecht as early as 1933. Both Kazan and Gorelik spoke German, a skill that made Gorelik Brecht's interpreter at the Theatre Union in 1933.

Gorelik pondered why so many directors see an intense acting sequence in rehearsal go irrevocably dead the moment it is surrounded by a setting. He stated:

> There is something about the way The Group functions which tends to eliminate these mistakes instead of leaving the door wide open to them. . .the play's statement can not be made properly if it has not already been made clear to the whole personnel – the dramatist, the director, the actors, the scene and costume designers, the technicians, and the business and publicity directors. Only a permanent company is equipped, by its nature, to know how decisive this sort of cooperation becomes in the theatre. And in the long run only a permanent company is able to develop such cooperation effectively.[24]

While many preached of organic, synthesized executions, few produced them. Renowned designers such as Robert Edmond Jones, Donald Oenslager and Cleon Throckmorton found it difficult to work within the Group's collective mentality. Only Gorelik and Aronson found success within the Group as designers. European designers were considered scenographers, influencing every aspect of a production. American designers were often considered troublesome and meddling for practising similar approaches. In the commercial theatre most decisions are based on hunches instead of thought, and decisions tend to be based on proven precedents or hysterical demands. Gorelik spoke of a Broadway theatre where success was considered unconscious and incomprehensible. Producers shied away from defining a play's statement and cringed when a director, designer, or actor attempted such a definition. This mysticism is nothing but poor planning. Productions without clarity of intent have no real unity, no agreed viewpoint. They are accidental in their direction. Even with a standardized, conventional set, uncertainty remained until opening night. In the end, the set usually does not relate to the script or the actors. It was Gorelik's experience that the permanent company of the Group Theatre could eliminate these problems.[25]

Both Kazan and Gorelik worked their way up through the ranks of permanent companies: Kazan with the Group and Gorelik at the Provincetown Playhouse. They understood a collective approach and the value of hands-on experience and the relationship between Kazan and Gorelik was well established before Kazan came into his own as a director. However, Kazan makes few specific references to Gorelik in his books. Yet the process by which Kazan became aware of his own creative process as a director seems to have important connections to the strong visually-metaphorical settings Gorelik designed for the Group.

While Gorelik felt that a designer's application of a strong visual metaphor should be a universal technique, Kazan on the other hand saw it as a personal vision. His art was his own creation and he felt that an audience would appreciate it based on that consideration alone. Yet Kazan cannot stand alone from his collaborators. Anyone familiar with theatrical collaboration can attest to the misplaced arrogance of that remark and, yet, it was Kazan's artistic arrogance that fuelled the passion that made him a master of his craft, an attribute less accepted in designers than directors.

Gorelik's work at the Group can best be seen in his designs for *Success Story* in 1932, (glass and Formica walls moved between poetry and realism, their proportions mocking the 'motorcar sleekness' so many advertising executives built around them); *Men In White* in 1933 (a large institution with dark polished features looming over the many scenes below, contrasting the white garb, glittering instruments and intimacy of the operating room); *Golden Boy* in 1937 (its well-known scenes and simple sets incomplete without seeing the effect created with cyclorama and triangular ground cloth representing the naked brutality of a boxing ring); *Casey Jones* in 1938 (its famous locomotive, only half of the metaphor, incomplete without comparing it with the cramped boarding house basement which represented the tomb of Casey's retirement), and *Thunder Rock* in 1939 (cylindrical tower walls and raked stage pouring ghostly stories down the floor boards of a solitary flame flickering in a storm). All of these settings contributed significantly to the meaning of their productions. The final two were directed by Elia Kazan, written by Robert Ardrey, and are the subject of this analysis.

Robert Ardrey's *Casey Jones* was presented on 19 February 1938. A critical success, it failed financially in an otherwise-successful season that featured only one other production: *Golden Boy*. After the Group's reorganization, Gorelik was invited back to design both shows. It was the Group's seventh season together. While some Group members had left, new colleagues had been introduced. *Casey Jones* featured an almost entirely outside cast. The 'outsider' was now a leader. Many longstanding members now resented Kazan's authority. Unfortunately, Kazan found their Hollywood lead, Charles Bickford, 'hostile and invariably suspicious' of the young director.[26] Clurman's and Stella Adler's meddling with the actors also undercut his authority. This was Kazan's first large-scale commercial directing assignment. Overwhelmed by the politics of it all and unable to rely on the Group's usual psychological approach to rehearsals, Kazan perhaps relied more heavily on a visual approach to directing than he might have otherwise. This did not affect Kazan's relationship with Gorelik and Ardrey, as the three would collaborate on another Ardrey play in 1939.

The message of *Casey Jones* was that men become dependent on the self-meaning they get from their work in life, therefore, men are captured by the modern machines they work with. This was Gorelik's best example of stylized realism and an obvious statement that a set should make a point. The staging was an active participant. It was vivid to say the least. Gorelik designed his *Casey Jones* set as a metaphor of its tragic hero, Casey the railroad engineer. His world was his locomotive; on it he felt like a king. The throne-like locomotive of Casey had exciting visual beauty and impact. Casey's black velour-covered locomotive was designed in forced perspective, Meyerhold's active angle of the oblique, to accentuate Casey's driving persona. Its praise dominated the critical reviews.

However, as memorable as the locomotive was, it was its contrast to the other scenes that created the overall metaphor. The old grimy engineer was out of place everywhere but aboard his machine. After being forced to retire by the railroad company, Mrs. McGuiness' boarding house would become the tomb of his retirement.

The Locomotive was constructed by William Kellam and painted by Bergman Studios.

The basement tomb of Casey's retirement.

The boarding house featured a steep and narrow set of stairs. Casey had to duck under beams and move clumsily about the furniture. He became the metaphorical locomotive within the confines of the room. His griminess was contrasted to the white washed walls, white curtains, and neat green felt of a pool table. Gorelik somehow knew either would be incomplete without the other:

> Theatre is entering on a long struggle to maintain its integrity and freedom of thought, to hold on to its sacred duty of clarifying life. In an effort to remain clear in judgment, it will reach its greatest moral sensitivity, its most scientific accuracy, its most stirring imagination.[27]

Theatre is as difficult and precise as engineering. Norman Bel Geddes described it as 'exciting a stage setting as I have ever seen.'[28] The scenes acted as foils to one another; they emphasized each other by contrast. The actors interacted with a very physically demanding set. This created a visceral effect for them as well as the audience, whilst the visual effect reinforced the metaphor. The psychological 'truth' of this room as Casey's tomb made up for the fact that it consisted of little more than a back wall, stairs, and furniture. It was minimal yet not 'unrealistic'. The effect was that the audience accepted it as realistic, consciously or not.

At the conclusion of the play, Casey is going blind, and yet he insists on running his train. He is loyal to the company when he retires, refusing his pension, stating: 'The company owes me nothing',[29] but, just before the curtain closes, Casey collapses, realizing he has been a slave to the railroad all his life. This is the personal failure of one man. Ardrey provides no last-minute attack on the economic system, but the question must be asked: what to do with one man whose usefulness is over? Does he go onto the scrap heap? Their machines often overshadow men. Sometimes they are a metaphorical 'political machine' and sometimes a real life monster. We must throw ourselves into their powerful gears or find assurance within their well-oiled mechanism. The industrial world offers the same dangerous attraction as the apple and the snake. Ardrey's *Casey Jones* is an example of a schoolboy whose dream to be a train engineer gets twisted with the realities of life. Casey Jones is an individual; there is no attempt to force organized labour issues or attacks on the capitalist system. Because of this, *Casey Jones* almost succeeds as a fine play despite its obvious caricatures. Most critics gave fine reviews to the production; the staging was highly acclaimed and the extremely flamboyant setting stated the point more effectively than the play itself. Some attributed this to Gorelik's political beliefs: *Theatre Arts Monthly* noted Gorelik's move 'further leftward and propagandistic. Realism has now been lifted right out of itself that it may become a more potent factor in the solution of social problems.'[30] Whether this was a fair statement or not, none could argue this set moved quickly and directly at the audience. Its message and metaphor concerned the retirement of an old cog in the machine more than a dissection of social barriers. Unfortunately, *Casey Jones* was a box-office failure. This was foreseen but the play continued both for the actor's employment and for Kazan's directing debut. This is the first example of Kazan combining the external and internal to create a mise-en-scène that inherently communicated his ideas of what a stage picture should be.

Another Kazan, Gorelik and Robert Ardrey collaboration would begin the Group's ninth and last season together. *Thunder Rock* opened on 14 November 1939 at the Mansfield Theatre. Gorelik had now designed five out of seven Group productions since the re-organization. Elia Kazan directed a cast of eleven and took from *Thunder Rock* an interesting observation: the cast of a show should share the same basic quality as the playwright.[31] Unfortunately, for the financial success of the production, the Group's ensemble did not resemble the mid-western quality of 'cornstalk' Ardrey.

Gorelik designed a single setting for the three acts of *Thunder Rock*: a lighthouse on Thunder Rock in northern Lake Michigan, where a ship has wrecked almost a century before. The passengers are re-born in the mind of the lighthouse-keeper. The play develops against a background of war, although the references are vague and scattered. Harold Clurman began directing the show but, after a nervous breakdown, the task was taken over by Kazan. Kazan was a newer, younger Group member and some older members resented his directing opportunities. He had also left the Communist Party and was resented by some for this defection. Kazan thought the scenic design was Gorelik's most effective to date. His opening-night telegram read: 'You're the finest designer in our theatre and I'm even getting to like your personality. In fact I'm proud to call you a friend.'[32] Kazan had reason for praise. Their only other collaboration was Ardrey's *Casey Jones* and both were acclaimed for their work.

The two plays *Casey* Jones and *Thunder Rock* may be Gorelik's most successful designs. The circular interior included a raked floor, ramped toward the audience. The actors experimented with the one-inch-to-the-foot slope before the final set was constructed. The actors showed hesitation at first, but from the moment the setting arrived they were unanimous in the belief that it actually helped their performance. The tower stairs disappear upward into shadows toward the light chamber above. Half way up they stop at a circular rail, reinforcing the cylindrical shape. The lighthouse was to represent a tower of light and hope. Gorelik's metaphor was a flickering flame, struggling to stay alight in a storm.

The stairs have a platform that leads to the second floor of the lighthouse, into the keeper's adjacent house. Below the stairs is a door to the first floor of the house. The water of the lake is visible outside the entrance door, stage left, and the entire tower was surrounded by a cyclorama. A few props are dispersed around the ground floor: a bookshelf, table, desk, bench, locker, one comfortable chair and a ghost's unending supply of cigarettes. As the ghosts appeared, the tower was silhouetted against the cyclorama, lit as sky and clouds. Michael Gordon, given credit for a fine execution of the lighting, an important feature of the design, was one of the few lighting designers credited in Group productions.[33] John Anderson stated: 'Mr. Kazan's direction is strongly accented and fluent, and makes picturesque use of Mr. Gorelik's fascinating setting.'[34] Robert Rice of the *Telegraph* stated: 'Mordecai Gorelik, a much-too-little seen scenic designer, has designed a spectacular set of the lighthouse interior that ranks as a genuine masterpiece of scenic art.'[35] Others termed it eerie, inspiring, grand, and extraordinarily theatrical. Donald Kirkley of the *Baltimore Morning Sun* added: 'Mordecai Gorelik's setting is a triumph in realism filtered through the brush of a genuine artist.'[36]

Gorelik art with the required lighting. Costumes designed by Paul Morrison, constructed by Helena Pons. William Kellam constructed the set, and Center Studios painted it.

Despite the splendid reception of the directing and the production design, few found the same level of satisfaction with the play itself. John Mason Brown said the playwright 'should stop relying upon Mr. Gorelik to do his most impressive playwriting for him.'[37] Too many saw it as all thunder and no rock. While the Group had lost their novelty after a decade of productions, the struggle against tyranny was still in vogue. The opening scene is the last summer before the Second World War. There is an atmosphere of coming events the characters are either unaware of, or indifferent to. The ghosts are mostly pathetic characters clinging to a world gone by as is the primary living character, Charleston, played by Luther Adler. The confusion of the characters is what The Group actors disliked. Perhaps they saw some sense of themselves being portrayed, as they were all, no doubt, contemplating the death of their own institution.

Clurman was not entirely impressed with the script but had long since reasoned script quality sometimes had to be sacrificed for continuous activity, especially in light of The Group's total reliance on contemporary scripts. The critics' response was almost predictable. The Group had delivered another fine production of a play that failed to conclude itself clearly and dramatically. The play's opening reviews in Baltimore were better than the mild reviews it received in New York. Other playwrights wrote letters of acclaim to the press. While its acceptance was only marginally improved, it was a major success in London the following year. *Thunder Rock* was a fine example of the fight for world peace within the dramatic circle. The play forecast the coming of World War II, but only vaguely debated the morality of the United States' involvement. With a clear backdrop of war behind it, *Thunder Rock* spread through Britain as an inspiration to its citizens after the fall of France. The American critic, George Jean Nathan was less inspired, he commented: 'It succeeded in curing me almost instantaneously of my insomnia.'[38]

Unfortunately, the unfocused theme was lost in the somewhat trite relationship of the lighthouse-keeper and the ghosts. In the opening scene a friend, Streeter, is off to China to fight the Japanese. Charleston remains behind, indifferent and content to keep the lighthouse in a lonely and solitary comfort. The Communist Party clique within the Group had no passion for the play as it was. They felt it was not strong enough in its stance. The critics didn't fault The Group or the author for this, as no one in the country had been able to clearly suggest what role the United States should take in the war. It was perceived that the author's opinion at the end of the play was that America should not get involved in the conflict. A decade earlier John Reed had been quoted as saying: 'Great things are ahead, worth living for and dying for.'[39] Many Group members would have been content to let *Thunder Rock* die as their youthful enthusiasm for a challenge was gone, their passion less quickly offered. Yet the Group was acclaimed for doing a play with such a political statement. The acting was generally approved of; in fact, the critics felt their attitude was back in order. It seems, though, that the Group felt differently. Perhaps it showed in performance. Despite the fact that many of the cast were long standing Group members – Roman Bohnen, Luther Adler, Morris Carnovsky, Art Smith, Lee J. Cobb, Ruth Nelson, and Frances Farmer – *Thunder Rock* did little to cure the Group's ills.

The moral debate was lost on its audience as viewers tried to find meaning in the sometimes silly sub-plots of the ghost characters, such as an already-dead father-to-be awaiting the eternal birth of his child in an off-stage room. While life and death are important themes to consider, derision for him from an upstanding caregiver for having already fostered away nine previous children confuses the intent. Meanwhile, the very purpose and source of the ghosts is merely poked at between the dead Captain Joshua, played by Morris Carnovsky, and the lighthouse-keeper, as if they are intentionally keeping all important information from the their naive passengers. There are threats from the keeper to vanquish the ghosts from his mind and yet he suggests to his replacement at the end of the play to read the ship-wreck's memorial plaque and to think about the passengers, as if they occupy the rock and haunt any occupant. Unfortunately, the purpose of the ghosts is vague and non-conclusive, mostly because the keeper leaves, still indifferent. The audience waits for mysterious revelation but gets a sombre discussion in its stead. The false impression of the importance of these moments was perhaps aided by a stunning visual production. Kazan placed the actors among the shadowy entrances, circular stairs and interesting levels to paint very dynamic stage pictures. He had to rely on his visual instincts, as a veteran Group cast was defensive and unsupportive of their director. Morris Carnovsky was especially disagreeable; as with *Casey Jones*, perhaps the actors' unwillingness to pursue their usual psychological adventures in rehearsal made Kazan rely on his visual instincts all the more.

While the Group is often labelled experimental, their process could not be farther from that. They began as young and idealistic, but quickly developed into seasoned professional collaborators with a host of established professionals, including the leading producers and designers of the day. It is important to recognize this to give proper credit to experimentation when it did happen. Such is the case with two Group Productions: William Saroyan's *My Heart's In The Highlands,* and *Quiet City* by Irwin Shaw, a writer befriended by Group members in Hollywood. The only other non-original director to stage a Group production, Bobby Lewis, received tremendous acclaim for his Broadway directorial debut. On the heels of this success, the Group staged *Quiet City,* directed by Kazan. Aaron Copeland wrote what Kazan called a 'beautiful' musical score.[40] The large cast featured almost every original Group member. *Quiet City* was scheduled to play six Sunday evening previews. It survived only two on 16 and 23 April 1939 at the Belasco Theatre, where the Group was staging Shaw's *The Gentle People*. It was then withdrawn for revision, but never again saw the light of day. Rarely do relationships between collaborators survive failure, but Kazan, Gorelik and Ardrey's did. Months later Ardrey requested the same team for *Thunder Rock*.

Max Gorelik's scenic design featured a mixture of Epic techniques and metaphorical imagery. This was a run of four out of five productions credited to Gorelik since the re-organization. He was in favour of the Group doing experimental work, even for limited runs, and the Group was experiencing a degree of success. After the resignation of Lee Strasberg and the re-organization of the Group hierarchy, they were home again in Clurman's vision. They were noted by the critics for taking such artistic chances and coming through with respectable results.

The play had a mixture of realism and fantasy, which got only a realistic approach from Kazan and the Group actors. The theme surrounded the troubles of the middle-class, their shame of their own desires, and their troubled conscience. *The Gentle People* set crowded the Belasco wing space. For *Quiet City*, Gorelik designed three acting areas: one upstage centre, and one at each off-stage area, downstage of the proscenium. The stage-right platform led up to a bench seat and a telephone. The stage-left levels led down to a telephone. Atop the upstage levels were what Gorelik labelled in his sketches 'large plaques', representing skyscrapers. They were no doubt created as a series of flats in forced perspective. Actors were able to enter from behind and around the shapes. A projection screen hung over the stage just off-center to stage left. Images of New York relevant to the scenes below faded in and out throughout the play. While no production photos survive, it is important to consider the simplicity and large graphic imagery described as the *Quiet City* staging. While Kazan certainly approached his later film career with financial success in mind, his pictures incorporated the Epic traditions of extreme contrast in light and shadow and striking visual imagery often associated with German Expressionistic cinema. Kazan's great contribution to film directing was to incorporate these visual traditions of the avant-garde to unique American psychological themes and plots, all of which had begun in his directing work at the Group.

Elia Kazan went on to a controversial career of fortune and fame. Gorelik, having designed few Broadway productions after his Group days, began a career of teaching and writing. Decades later, Kazan would act as a reference for Gorelik's attempts to return to Broadway as a director. Yet potential meetings in their retirement years went unmet by Kazan's seeming lack of interest, although they did share occasional correspondence.

While the importance of their early collaborations on Kazan's career is now conjectured, no one can argue the clarity of their intent. In the words of Alexander Tairov, theatrical productions should be 'true from the point of view of theatre art – because they are in harmony with the reality of the material.'[41] Kazan and Gorelik collaborated to create a theatre in harmony with their reality, a mutual interest in visually evocative and socially meaningful theatre and they were fortunate to find a playwright who created plays that lent themselves to the visual as well as the social agenda of the two. To quote Ardrey: 'The animal nature of the human conscience demands images.'[42] After blowing the dust of obscurity off the aged black and white photographs, the results are undeniable. What becomes clear is the influence of one young designer on the work of another young director. Still photographs from the films of Kazan's career clearly show the lessons of this early collaboration.

Notes

1. Gorelik, M., Diary notes about Cleon Throckmorton, Special Collections, Morris Library, Southern Illinois University, Carbondale, 1927.
2. Kazan, E., *A Life*, New York: Knopf, 1988, p. 151.
3. Ibid., p. 151.

Kazan's film *On the Waterfront*.

4. Ardrey, R., *African Genesis*, New York: Antheneum, 1973, p. 14.
5. Ibid., p. 156.
6. Kazan, p. 90.
7. Ibid.
8. Ibid.
9. Ibid.
10. Ibid., p. 49.
11. Chinoy, H. K., 'Reunion, A Self-Portrait of the Group Theatre', *Educational Theatre Journal* 28.4, 1976, pp. 550–1.
12. Ibid.
13. Gorelik, M., 'I Design for the Group Theatre', *Theatre Arts Monthly*, pp. 180–6.
14. Gorelik Collection, Personal Correspondence with Sheryl Crawford and agreement on Green Masions letterhead, 6 August 1933. Personal correspondence with Harold Clurman and Elia Kazan, agreement on Group Theatre letterhead, 15th February 1939, Special Collections, Morris Library, Southern Illinois University, Carbondale.
15. Ibid.
16. Ibid.
17. Gorelik, M., 'The Scenic Imagination: Still Evolving', *Players Press*, No. 43.2, pp. 22–7.
18. Piscator, E., Signed Photograph, Special Collections, Morris Library SIU, Carbondale.
19. Gorelik, 'The Scenic Imagination…', pp. 22–7.
20. Ardrey, p. 15.
21. Kazan, p. 168.
22. Ibid., p. 182.
23. Gorelik, 'The Scenic Imagination…', pp. 22–7.
24. Gorelik, 'I Design…', pp. 180–6.
25. Ibid.
26. Kazan, p. 168.
27. Hewitt, B., and Gorelik, M., *The High School Thespian*, November 1941.
28. Bel Geddes, Norman, telegram of 1938, in the Special Collections, Morris Library, SIU, Carbondale.
29. Ardrey, R., *Casey Jones*.
30. Gorelik, 'I Design…', pp. 180–6.
31. Kazan, p. 182.
32. Kazan, E., telegram of 1939, in the Special Collections, Morris Library, SIU, Carbondale.
33. Paul Morrison designed the costumes, constructed by Helena Pons; William Kellam constructed the set, and Center Studios painted it.
34. Anderson, J., Review, November 1939.
35. Rice, R., Review, Telegram, November 16th 1939.
36. Kirkley, D., Review, *Baltimore Morning Sun*, November 3rd 1939.
37. Brown, J.M., Review, *New York Post*, November 11th 1939.
38. Nathan, G. J., Review, *Newsweek*, November 27th 1939.
39. Reed, J., *Ten Days That Shook the World*, 1st Edition, Penguin Classics, 1919.
40. Kazan, p. 181.
41. Rudnitsky, K., *Russian and Soviet Theatre*, London: Thames and Hudson, 1988.
42. Ardrey, p. 351.

Chapter 14

Ideational Conflict and Resolution in the Design Process: Positive Outcomes from Negative Relationships

Harry Feiner

In memory of Ralph G. Allen: artist, scholar and the best of friends.

…to extract from fashion whatever element it may contain of poetry within history, to distil the eternal from the transitory…

…the ephemeral, the fugitive, the contingent, the half of art whose other half is the eternal and the immutable…

This transitory, fugitive element, whose metamorphoses are so rapid, must on no account be despised or dispensed with. By neglecting it, you cannot fail to tumble into the abyss of an abstract and indeterminate beauty…

The duality of art is a fatal consequence of the duality of man

From The Painter of Modern Life, Baudelaire[1]

I have always felt that one of the defining qualities of any art form is its ability to convey a sense of 'being': an awareness of the ineffable sensation human beings experience when we perceive the consciousness of our selves. Thus our 'place' is intuited between a universe of our beliefs, and the vagaries of our empirical perceptions. It exists between the inevitability of (our own) time's end and our feebly-perceived sense of the vastness of the infinite. What I believe sustains such sentiments are the rich ambiguities inherent in the various forms of art and the skilful manipulation of those contradictions by artists. One's own era always believes itself the most capable of endeavouring to capture the experience of 'modern life', or being in the present. It is an endeavour the theatre is perfectly equipped to accomplish with its veridical juxtaposition of the 'ephemeral', 'fugitive' and 'transitory', with the 'eternal and immutable.'

Human thought seems to be nourished in such sensibilities by the constant atmosphere of conflict and opposition in our thinking and everyday experience. The pre-Socratic contradiction embedded in the Greek idea of 'the one and the many'[2] embodies the dialectic between the eternal and the mutable, belief and empiricism, and so many of the 'dualities' that pervade most aspects of our thought and action. Its development into the antagonistic world-views of Platonic idealism and Aristotle's (qualified) empirical materialism is 'natural', in the sense that it is our nature to organize experience, as defined by such contrarian concepts. It is no accident that the basic structure of drama is organized around the clash of protagonists and antagonists, mimicking the archetype of divergence and conflict that we can observe in almost every component of our lives. The pervasiveness of such antagonisms and the ambivalence associated with such a 'symmetric'[3] sense of truths, may be a 'fundamental aspect of the dynamics of cognition,'[4] suggesting, 'that reciprocality (or trade-off) may be a feature of all intellectual life, reflecting the irreducibly ambivalent operations of the processes of cognition themselves.'[5] So, although directors and designers clearly deal with space and the practicalities of composition within the domain of theatre sets, my interest here is in exploring how spatial composition in the theatre might replicate elemental archetypes of perception, and what those perceptual processes may do to support the diverse texture of experience that the theatre provides for us.

Of course, I am biased in believing that the theatre is paramount in its capability for sustaining the copious ambiguities of dualism. The theatre nurtures an attendant sense of 'being' that derives from the abstract formulations of the elusiveness of experience, into a suggestion of time and place. It is not just the theatre's incorporation of many arts and disciplines into an endlessly malleable and fugitive form, but also the constant variability with which perceiver and the perceived exchange positions and adjust their attitudes and perceptions (both in regard to one another and the space they share) for an evening's immersion into a performance's own autonomous verisimilitude. I believe the success of achieving a sense of that verisimilitude is not based on the photographic resemblance of objects or vistas, or the three-dimensional duplication of such objects and their spatial relationships, but of how the 'feeling' of perception in the theatre is a heightened metaphorical cipher of acuity. A key facet of this delicate manoeuvre of perception is the arrangement of the theatre's different constituent parts, of the physical production, space and associated visual elements of design.

I have previously written that my own preference for expressing the ambiguity of conflict and contradiction in theatre space is most fully realized in the interplay of the concepts of the *Real* and the *Ideal*.[6] The 'real' expresses our predilection to believe the world understood through the 'sensa' of empirical experience. The 'Ideal' understands experience as an imperfect expression of a universal structure that we believe exists; we cannot see it explicitly, but we rationalize its presence through the constructs of reason. Both concepts simultaneously maintain a tenacious hold on our ability to formulate a 'picture' of experience. 'Being', the awareness of ourselves and the sensation of the texture of consciousness, is perceived from the phenomenal framework that juxtaposes such dualisms within the construction of art. Perhaps it is the perception of 'being' that makes humans create art; that bittersweet awareness of the parallel existence of time's infinity and our limited habitation of the space it transgresses, which the theatre mimics so movingly in the act of performance. Space is a crucial element of such a sensibility and creating a vehicle to convey the sense of such feelings is what directors and designers intuitively do when addressing the needs of performance. The physical 'resemblance' of a mise-en-scène to a recognized or imagined place is not as important in creating a semblance of the 'act of being', as the mental processes of sensation and emotion invoked by the experience of perception. The director and designer map a journey between cognitive states that allow us to replicate the experiential sensations of Time's characteristics through imagistic transference. It is this 'back and forth' of potential perceptions, replicating how we comprehend and our thought mechanisms, that permit us to experience so vividly in the theatre. The skilful manipulation of such cognitive variants can emphasize which aspects of experience best seem to advance the awareness of a project's unique intent.

The director and designer formulate and resolve the contradictions and ambiguities within the conceits inherent in the use of performance space. This is generally not a conscious effort: as with most visual artists (as well as all types of artists), I believe these concerns are primarily addressed intuitively. They may also be processed in a combination of sub-conscious and intellectual processes, but collective sentiments feel like they are always approached as a tangent; they have the quality of a continuous, 'sub rosa' universality attached to the process of producing a work of art. That process is directed toward the end of producing 'compositions', the ability to shape the look of individual moments on stage as well as the progression and fluidity with which the staging can create the 'pictures' that are comprised of costumed actors in the space of a setting that has been (momentarily) defined in a certain aspect by light.

The theatre has always had a kind of identity problem in this regard; is it pictorial, a 'picture', set off by the proscenium's frame, or an architectural volume of space, containing masses (including performers), like any volumetric architectural interior? Because regardless of whether or not a setting is meant to evoke the outdoors, an interior space or an abstraction, it takes place primarily inside the volumetric hub of an auditorium's stage. In the pictorial, performers seem 'plastered' against a background; in the architectural, they are primarily oriented to the floor as the primary symbol of spatial expression. Design uses all three Cartesian axes formulated through the horizontal (floor) plane and the vertical (picture) plane, in conjunction with the dimensional aspects of time. By concentrating more of the compositional prestige in either the vertical or horizontal plane, the design may maintain a bent towards being more pictorial or architectural, thereby supporting the potential impact of all the possible meanings connoted by the association of that particular visual formula for the piece being presented. Is this tendency to shape the stage picture between the pictorial and the architectural a sign of some fundamental aspect of our humanity that is part and parcel of our nature? Is it a manifestation of the classic dualism that seems to have always preoccupied human thought and predominated so manifestly in the modes of expression we have used to express our sense of our own existence?

The 'vertical' is an equivalent for what I have called the pictorial. It displays a tendency toward using the Cartesian vertical plane, or the frontal plane of projection, as the principal organizing directive in composition. In the theatre, the pictorial can be imagined as a compression of the space between the most upstage element (often a backdrop) into the most downstage plane.

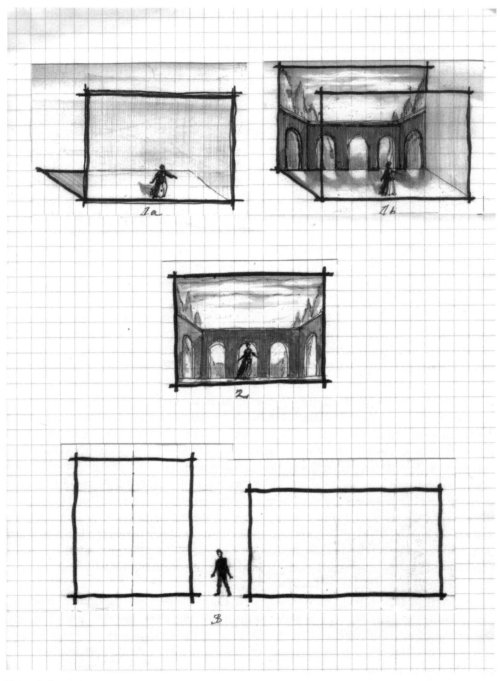

Figures 1–3.

This imaginary downstage 'picture' plane, situated at the proscenium or the edge of the stage space closest to the audience, is a symbolic equivalent for the stage 'as a painting'; such a setting is metaphorically disposed of as if elicited on a flat surface, as shown in Figure 2 above.

In Illusionistic painting, this 'compression', or confusion happens 'naturally', because the sense of depth is not actual but virtually indicated on the plane of the painting itself, which occupies the vertical plane.[7] In such a system, the elements of the design become flattened as a frontal view and the impact of the actual depth between elements is negated or minimized.

We seem to have a tendency to want to see things frontally. Is this because we have an innate desire towards experiencing life with the clarity of the Ideal and its pleasing qualities of balance and stability? The pictorial type of composition seems simpler in that it is based, in a pure sense, on the contrast of shapes, or positive objects, on a ground, or negative space. It has the appeal of the Gestalt paradigm for the prevalence of the regular and the equally proportioned. The pull of the Ideal seems so innately strong that to be a realist we have 'to force' ourselves to give up what may be perceived as unrealistic ideas and adopt cynical notions in conflict with what we would rather believe things are like. We seem to 'adopt' ideals naturally, but we need to be dissuaded by realistic observations to abandon them. The frontal plane seems to advocate for many idealized qualities. It tends toward a strongly-centred symmetry, where the weights of composition are distributed in a way that locks balance by means of a 'closed'[8] compositional system emphasizing stability. The vertical has a greater ability to sustain the immobility of the Ideal, emphasizing its quality of stasis through a stable system that is more independent of the fugitive characteristics of Time. To be at rest is to emulate a presence at the centre of a hierarchal system that is pleasing in its clear, obvious structural relationships and groupings.

The notion of a parallel to a Gestalt paradigm of organization is appealing. There are many theories of perception, and they all may help explain some aspect of how we visualize experiential phenomena, but the tendencies to organize objects and space in a manner that parallels expression of the Ideal seems to be predicted by many Gestalt precepts.[9] Gestalt theory notes the propensity for the human mind to function innately along certain perceptual guidelines. The desire to experience 'wholeness' and 'satisfaction' in 'balance' and 'completeness' are powerful dispositions that may make us both 'group' elements in the act of creating visually and also be disposed to see the same constructed groupings as part of the perceptual experience of cognition. The proclivity toward 'simplicity' or 'pattern recognition', for example, may impact on the way in which designers and directors formulate compositions for theatrical space as well as the way in which the audience perceives what is presented to them. Whether the perceptual frameworks we are biased toward 'setting' experience in, or not, 'blinds' us, misses an important point; in a visual medium the artist has the opportunity to control the impact of their material through the manipulation of such bias in the processes of perception.

The greater the vertical in the orientation of the frontal plane, the more 'free' objects in a composition seem to be from the humanizing pull of gravity. A lack of concentration on the floor of a space (the plane of depth) not only pushes the composition more toward the frontal plane, it also makes the objects of the composition (which are principally the performers) 'float' more. Thus, greater freedom from the powerful anti-idealizing force of gravity (a constant reminder of our physical limitations) is analogous to the tendency of 'closed' compositional devices to create a sense of superseding the movement seen in the perambulation of Time. The impression is created of a composition that stands 'outside' of the transient limitations of mortal existence, a necessity for transmitting the transcendent qualities of the Ideal.

The more vertical the proportions of the frontal plane, the more the verticality seems to be able to support divisions into multiple panels, each with its own central focus. As a result, the vertically-oriented frontal plane lends itself well to bipolar and tripartite divisions, like the multiple panels of many Medieval and Renaissance altarpieces and architectural painting. These panels create compositions of manifold centres in reflective balance, as they each make up a symmetrically-balanced mini-composition within the symmetry of the whole.

When such compositional techniques are used on stage, they tend to 'freeze' or lock space, with the geometrical connections they superimpose on the vista. This type of overriding stability and stasis is typical of 'closed' compositions, because one of the principal ways we experience Time is through the change of bodies' relationships in space.

'Framing' helps to sustain the vertical mode of composition, whether through the emphasis of the proscenium or the inclusion of framing elements as part of the setting. The prominence of a frame in the view of the stage promotes the 'frontality' of the vertical plane as the principal organizing factor. The less horizontal the ratio of the frame, the less significance to the composition of the floor's horizontal plane, which is at odds with the vertical, both literally (through its perpendicularity) and conceptually in what it connotes. As shown in Figure 4.

The effect of the framed field of view to concentrate attention on a selected visual area directs further focus on the importance of a strong centre to the composition. The frame seems to command a central concentration. This is perhaps made clearer by imagining a space without a frame. Unbounded, the stage can have no measurable centre. No stage space is unlimited, but choices can be made to play down the clear, structural delimitation of the frontal plane so that cognizance of its perceptual presence attenuates. This is shown by comparing Figure 4, with Figure 3. I shall refer more to this point later.

The use of strong peripheral limits supplied by a physical framing device relates stage compositions to one of the quintessential paradigms of frontal organizational, linear perspective. In contrast to its use on the flat surface of painting, perspective has a compound relationship to the stage, inherently contradictory, and indicative of the complexities of stage composition in general. Those complexities arise from the fact that in addition to mixing sculptural, painting, architectural, fashion, decorative, graphic, multi-media and light disciplines, theatrical design also merges actual three-dimensional space with

Figures 4–6.

illusionistic devices to purport virtual contexts of space. Like the frontality of the vertical plane, perspective tends toward provoking heavily-centred compositions, particularly when a single vanishing point is used, as in Figure 5. This is especially true in the traditional Italianate perspective format for the stage, which depends on a series of receding surrogate 'proscenium' frames, thereby heavily reinforcing the frame's centralizing power. Although the use of perspective devices is supposed to convince the viewer of the limitless extension of space, its ability to do so contains the contradiction of achieving its effects on a flat projected 'picture' plane of geometrical constructions that mitigate the perceptual sense of extension in the horizontal plane. Even though a traditional perspective vista onstage displaces a relatively large depth of space from the proscenium to the backdrop (or end of the space) it has the psychological sense of being compressed into the frontal plane of pictorial composition because, regardless of where audience members are viewing from, it demands to be read that way. Paradoxically, because perspective can be a symbol of infinite space, the series of framing elements keep the sense of the composition from spreading out in the horizontal plane for several reasons. First of all, the lateral sides of the scenery frames limit its flat expansion. Secondly, the traditional wing and border format sets up a rhythmic encroachment of the horizontal plane, both visual and architectural, moving in towards the centre of the series of rectangles created by the portal frames. That series of frames geometrically focuses on the centre through the suggestive presence of its diagonals, which recede into the depth of the stage's vertical picture plane rather than spreading horizontally, as in Figure 6.

Once more this biases the composition to be developed around the centre, visually and psychologically. Lastly, as mentioned before, the construction of the perspective around a vanishing point tends to make it weighted toward central organization. Though this seems like a self-evident observation for conventional single-point perspective, even the two-point perspective associated with the Baroque's 'scena per angolo' tends to proportion the emphasis of its multiple viewpoints equally around the centre.

If the frontality of the vertical plane makes it more prone to centralized, closed compositional tendencies, then the horizontal, architectural plane (often called the 'plane of action') is more suitable for emphasizing the expansive scope of decentralized composition. Here we have the world seen 'sideways'[10] through the picture plane, in its true depth, rather than being compressed into the pictorial vertical plane. As one would imagine, such a schematic opposition connotes and provokes many antithetical qualities to its rival visual component. This is the plane we actually move in, a simulacrum for action, and what should be the principle orientation of thought for theatrical design. It has a physicality anchored in time that contrasts with the potential of the vertical to liberate itself from terrestrial concerns.

Although we move primarily in the horizontal, perhaps the vertical is the more appropriate realm of idealization, imagination and dream. Here the experiential nature of human existence is prominent; the constraints and quotidian concerns of our obligations to gravity are pre-eminent as the objects of composition are anchored to the ground. One of the horizontal's prospective connotations is equality; it is on this 'levelled' stage that men strive and fully exercise their fundamental potential for the antagonistic tendencies essential to dramatic construction and so vital to the human psyche.

In the theatre, the floor, the greatest corresponding visual symbol of the horizontal architectural plane, becomes a dynamic compositional element. The more the audience sees of the floor, the less capable a composition is of dominating in the vertical realm. The devices that raise the floor plane into greater prominence, such as the use of rakes on the stage or the steeper elevation of pitch for the audience seating, increase awareness of the horizontal plane. With that increased awareness comes a sense of a greater gravitational dependence of the performers. They are seen 'in' the floor plane, which naturally diminishes the compositional strength of the pictorial plane, as shown in Figure 7.

However, it can also create a feeling of visual frisson, for as the floor plane is raised higher into the audience's view, the vertical and horizontal plane approach a tendency to merge, illustrating one of the chief contradictions inherent in design for the theatre: the pictorial and the architectural both maintain distinct identities while perceptually also combining into other partial variants.

The horizontal is 'open', with less potential anchorage from the strength of central verticals in general, and their overbearing organizational centrality in particular. It is less prone to strong symmetrical centrality that heightens the aspect of frozen balance detached from time. The horizontal can stress 'linearity', and therefore Time's dominance, because the relationship of space to time is obvious in the architectural plane. We all instinctively 'know' that it takes a certain amount of time to cross a span, and we tend to think of such spans horizontally. 'Action' is associated with crossing through space; it is animated by the space necessary to 'do'. Distances that exist between elements purely in the vertical plane can have a supernatural quality, emphasizing the attribute of vertical release rather than horizontal pull. See Figure 8.

The performers are tied to the audience in the architectural plane, where they share the same basic physical orientation. This is especially true when the director and designer choose to de-emphasize the proscenium or other framing elements in the composition, as in Figure 9.

The horizontal aspect of space can then be thought of as not only being expansive from side to side, but can also facilitate a front-to-back sense of openness by using the thrust capabilities of theatrical space. Metaphorically similar to the virtual effect of Baroque foreshortening, the subjects are literally projected into the midst of the audience's space, another assault on the vertical plane of composition. The openness of the floor plane allows for the turbulent flow of earthbound eccentricity. It unleashes the full panoply of life devoid of any ideal construction of decorum. Rather than objects emanating an energy that keeps them hovering free, or centrally stabilized, they are pulled and pushed along by the endless scope of the horizontal expanse. In the horizontal plane, all is ephemeral. Its 'being' is in the fugitive present, tumbling along its transitory trajectory toward the realization of the action.

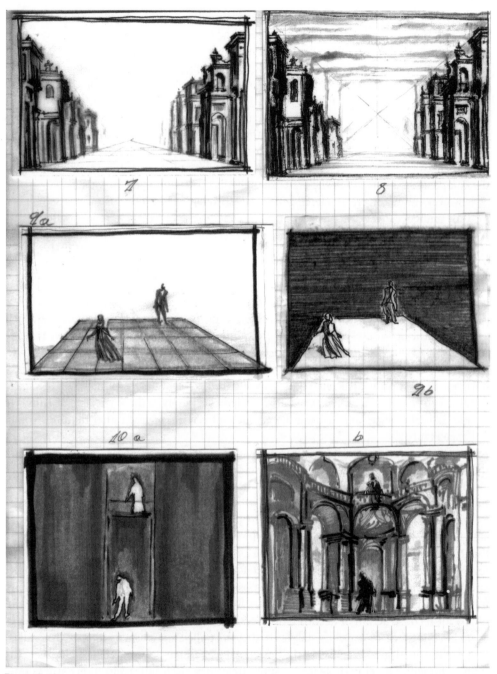

Figures 7–10.

It is where our primitive, biological, visceral senses predominate, rather than our rational, intellectual understanding.

Thus far, I have described some of the general differences in the compositional attributes of the pictorial vertical plane and the architectural horizontal plane. They are organizational paradigms, which taken together define a spatial 'modus operandi' prescribing a chief part of the purview of the director and designer's scope of interaction. They form a classic dualism, emulating our awareness of consciousness as a tendency to conceive of the expression of our perception of experience through seemingly contradictory concepts. In fact, their complementary engagement and ambiguous overlap is necessary to convey the intricacy of life's truths, as visual theatre composition does not exist solely in one of these two planes but in the tension that exists between the two modes of expression. The theatre simultaneously engages the human desire to step away and view experience in a pure objective manner, while actively drawing us into participation and subjective immersion in the moment.

The director and designer must skilfully manipulate the stage picture to approximate what they perceive to be the best relationship between verticality and horizontality. That relationship has many variables, depending on the sensibility of the project at hand, the given auditorium space, and the artists' feeling for conveying what will most amplify empathy for human experience and, therefore, the truth of that experience. Furthermore, the constant give and take between the planes of composition is a natural means for creating the visual variety necessary for an evening's performance. Skilfully manipulated, such juxtapositions of compositional structure can also achieve variety through the rhythmic patterns of the changing stage picture, not only maintaining interest through the course of a 'two hours trespass of our stage', but also creating a semblance of progression in time with visual cadences.

The preceding characterizations of these two modes of composition I have been describing concentrated mostly on their attributes in isolation, as if they could exist in a pure state without reference to the other. This is not only highly improbable but also undesirable; such purity might eliminate all the rich connotations of contrast and ambiguity to be derived from the lifelike entanglement of the different modes. Perhaps the purest expression of the pictorial is in the traditional Musical-comedy format, especially in the 'in-one' scenes in which a truncated downstage area is played against a backdrop located in the shallow space near the stage's apron. Such an example does not usually allow the elevation of the performers themselves into the vertical plane, which is one of the vertical's strongest images. On the other hand, an ascetic stage arrangement, which uses only the stage floor against an almost non-existent or neutral (absorbent black) ground, may be the best example of a purely architectural composition (although it may have little or no architecture per se). See Figure 10.

As pointed out before, such designs usually call attention to the floor as the most important visual element and 'plane of action'. Often a rake is used to enhance the prominence of the floor. Although the use of a rake places emphasis on the horizontal plane, and further ties the performers to a sense of gravity the more the horizontal spreads out, a rake also raises the floor plane (and the most upstage objects) into the picture plane, injecting a paradoxical tinge of verticality.

I have mentioned earlier the tendency to centralize compositions and the intrinsic magnetism of balance, symmetry and centricity to 'please the eye'. Certainly, the centre of any visual form has a powerful perceptual hold on our psyche and, in the case of stage position, that attraction seems all the more important. Although some of that power can be attributed to the practical aspects of maximizing visibility for the theatre audience, some of it must also come from the psychological power of the centre position and its implicit connotations.[11] Is the tendency to centralize cognitive visual schema prejudiced by any of our human neurological or receptive structures? Do we naturally mirror our own left-right symmetry (the cognitive amalgamation that naturally happens between the slightly disparate images perceived by our two separate eyes) when we express through idealized forms? We always seem to want to 'find' the centre, or 'balance' our view when looking up or straight ahead. Interestingly enough, the same tendency does not seem to predominate when we are looking down at the floor plane. Perhaps the compositional role of the director and designer can be thought of as the potential to create central nodes, or complexes of elements. The designer would then need to allow for the kinds of groupings, series of relationships, and locations of groups the designer and director instinctively feel the project requires. The designer then provides a type of 'chessboard' suited for certain types of conceptions in the arrangements of the 'pieces'. The main pieces, or elements, are the performers of course. They act as flexible sculptural parts, capable of being re-positioned bodies in space. They can fit into the board in numerous ways allowing for great variety, but the particular board (or setting) created for a particular production also predetermines a cluster of possible arrangements that will be most effective. What style will the board be? Will it be flat? Raked? Broken into raised levels? Separated along the rows? The columns? Will it stress the diagonal? Will it be made into a scaffold of stairs and balconies?

The vertical gains a great deal of prominence from elevation, so emphasis is naturally drawn into the frontal plane on stage with the use of elevating elements like stairs and platforms, even though those raised levels almost always move into the horizontal depth of the stage, as in Figure 11.

The most purely vertical use of height on stage would come from scaffolding or elevated structures close to the down stage vicinity that use height with a minimum of depth. This is because compositional approaches that depend more on the position of the performer are substantially more engaged in the process of the theatre. Such approaches rely on a model of scenography that is not visually independent of the performer. Of course, a stage environment could exist both as a successful visually independent piece as well as a space that gains its greatest imagistic efficacy from the presence of the performer. Perhaps the best work as both, encompassing yet another duality (and a poignant expression of temporality) in the legitimacy of the composition, both with and without the compositional impact of performers. The theatre setting absent of performers, empty after a presentation or waiting to be populated again, is a moving symbolic manifestation of the theatre's relationship with Time.

There are other means of emphasizing the vertical and its qualities (without suspending performers in the location of the picture plane, which is after all not an everyday necessity for most production schemes). The placement and suspension of major elements (or 'fragments') above the floor level creates the potential for vertical 'connections' to performers placed below. Any such compositional arrangement joins the performer to the power of the vertical, regardless of their proximity to the floor, for when the eye is drawn up it pushes the composition into the frontal plane. See Figure 12.

Simple backgrounds tend to stress frontal arrangements, especially when they are planned to create contrast with the performers and objects in front of those backgrounds.

Such backgrounds create a classic 'object-ground' relationship despite the separation between the planes, foreground and back. Such a relationship propels the verticality of the composition, compressing its sense of definitive three-dimensional depth into a metaphorically incongruous arrangement of two or more planes existing independently, as well as perceptually being squeezed into one level. Many kinds of backgrounds can operate in this manner. The simplest and purest example is a relatively flat surface, (both dimensionally and in the pictorial aspects of colour and shape), that performers and other objects stand out against. The ground can operate in a similar way, even if it has significant depth and dimension, if it has some sort of unifying theme that gives it a sense of continuity. Here, again, is another example of one of the ways in which theatre design has a great scope of impact; such a 'ground' can exist at many points 'between' the states of absolute flatness or depth. Depending on many factors, like the position of the performers, the lighting and the viewing angle, the variation of the visual potential in theatre is multifaceted.

An example of a 'ground' that is not flat is what we designate as a surround. It encircles the performers on all visible sides in a manner that visually integrates the enclosing stage. It has the depth of the stage space and is broken into multiple parts, but because it has some sort of overall motif (usually a singular treatment of surfaces that combines colour, materials, pattern or texture) it visually fuses its disparate parts with the scheme of a consistent background.

The 'surround' mimics the fluid reversal of spatial perception (between vertical and horizontal formats) familiar from the observation of paintings, but it is a mirror image of such a reversal. It is a dimensional space masquerading as a plane rather than a picture (conceived as a flat plane) that pretends to be dimensional space through the use of perspective.

Perhaps one of the reasons traditional wing and border perspective simulates the impression of a ground is that the underlying orthogonal structure of the illusion acts like a surround. Its substructure is an overall grid (like the classic tiled Serlian floor) on which the perspective shapes are developed and placed. The same might be said to be true of the decreasing increments of the portals usually associated with perspective; the proportional

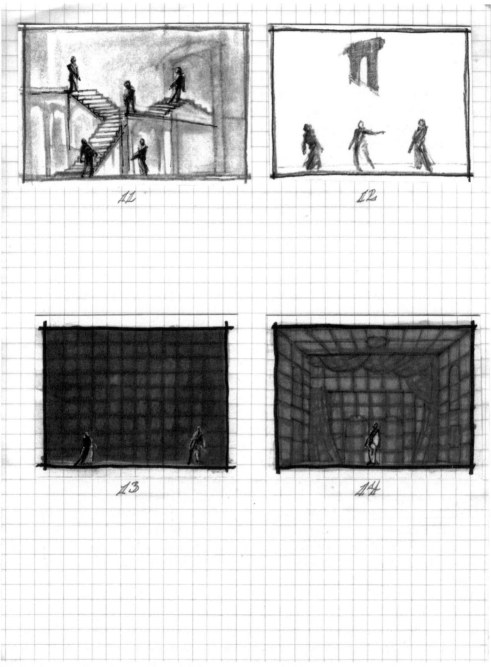

Figures 11–14.

Figures 15–16.

rhythm of the repetition of these elements sets up an 'all-over' grid that acts as a ground for the figures of the performers. See Figure 15.

Modern lighting also contributes to facilitating grounds because it both melds background elements together and picks out foreground objects (like performers) and perceptually 'projects' them forward. The stage designer has many techniques to use toward accomplishing this task. There are many devices that can homogenize backgrounds by subduing contrast. Edges can be softened, value differences reduced and colour variations harmonized. These can either make the background coalesce into a 'ground' or push it back, becoming a non-linear device for enhancing perspective depth and distance. The fact that such devices can potentially stress both the horizontal and vertical simultaneously (going back in depth and fusing as a ground to the frontal plane) again helps account for the dynamism possible in the visual characteristics of the theatre. The combination of types or modes of organizing space mimics pictorial art's conundrum of indicating depth and distance on a flat plane. That conundrum seems elemental to our perceptual sensibilities and desires because it combines these two seemingly antithetical systems into a perceptual whole in which both are indispensable.

The diagonal vector is the most powerful spatial relationship in the horizontal plane. Just as greater height-separation seems to increase the frisson between objects in the vertical plane, greater distance and depth displacement seems to provide for strong magnetism in the horizontal. The potential contained in spatial attraction and repulsion seems to gain power from increased distance between inevitabilities.[12] Having performers diagonally opposite each other not only has them apart from stage left to stage right, but also simultaneously maximizes separation in depth from downstage to upstage. The strength of the diagonal is amplified when it crosses the centre.

This phenomena is derived partially from the extended length of the vector the closer it comes to the true diagonal of the horizontal space, but there is also a part of it that comes from intersecting that centre of the compositional view, as if power was derived from the conflict with another point of great visual magnetism. Providing the possibility of elevating one end of a diagonal, with platforms or ramps increases its power by lengthening it as well as raising it partially into the vertical plane. Without any height difference, some figures visually intersect each other and lose the animate force of their separation. Once again, increased visual power can come from being in multiple planes simultaneously.

The actor or other performer is a dynamic, mobile centre that takes the focus with him, depending on where on the stage he is placed, what groups he is a part of and how he is related to the other visual aspects, objects and ground, of the design. Performers serve as 'landmarks' in a fluctuating compositional system because, regardless of whether or not a particular design is more 'open' or more 'closed', stage composition is truly 'finished' by the placement of the performers. This can be a momentary phenomenon, as performers usually occupy a particular arrangement briefly. Making stage compositions comprises configurations that are fluid or sequential. Composition in the theatre is built up, moment by moment, rhythmically. The director uses the stage's vertical and horizontal potentials to compose from beat to beat around centres, either demanded by the existing form or by avoiding implicit centrality directly and arranging around it, or moving between both. In a more 'closed' or vertical approach (and it does not have to be purely vertical to be closed) the stability of the composition is completed by the performer, as if a space had been left in a painting to be filled for the moment.

Regardless of whether or not the structural configuration of the scenography has been constituted as closed, locked or fixed on stage, it is unlikely to hold only one compositional possibility of completion. The disposition of the stage to be a composite of symmetrical perceptual formats allows (and in some sense demands) the complexity of multiple solutions succeeding each other in complicit contradiction and paradoxical support.

The 'open' system needs objects or performers to momentarily give weight and organization to an instant of composition. These instances are adaptable and unstable in regard to each other. They fluctuate, their own mobile centres of organization repositioning throughout the open space of the setting's metaphorical horizontality. This 'disunity' of reality and its unlimited multiplicity of potential centres is disturbing, possessing the instability of experiential life rather than the power of the mind's organizational biases. The notion of 'modernity', a sense of the immediacy of the moment tending to do without the distance of history to frame experience, makes the present seem fragmented and disparate.[13] Here I need to mention a parallel to the later-nineteenth century's tendency toward pictorial representations of reality as haphazard moments in the flow of time's chaotic course. Like the practices of the Impressionists and Post-Impressionists, such works are made to seem arbitrary and 'artless', trying to capture the chaos of the everyday by a seemingly unfocused account of life's volatile stream. Of course the sense of a lack of artifice was achieved through the effort of a great exertion of art: technique was employed to make it seem as if there was no technique. A similar process occurs in stage composition that is primarily horizontal. The lack of a centre emphasis may favour non-centric compositions that seem to be remote from structured qualities of equilibrium and organization, but the presence of the centre is still implicitly perceptible.

We can 'decentralize' only by recognizing the centre's power through avoiding it (with artifice); yet it is always there, loitering, patiently expecting acknowledgment. The horizontal may stress a multiplicity of centres or compositional weights that are not symmetrical but in balance, momentarily locked into each other rather than the vertical plane's allowances of a limited number of satisfying positions. They are not 'closed' in the sense of the pictorial's vertical tendencies because they wish to tumble away. It is their balance around an implicit centre rather than 'in' that centre that gives them a feeling of uncertainty and the predisposition to be perpetually re-orienting.

I have been looking at these two paradigms of stage composition as if to suggest they existed in a pure and rarefied state with only a limited, and therefore unified, vantage point from which to observe the space. Of course theatres offer the opposite of such a situation. The audience has a wide difference of viewing angles, both from side to side, and in height between the orchestra, mezzanines and balconies. At first, such a disparity might seem like an insurmountable obstacle towards creating any conceptual consistency by the director and designer, except in theatres with the most limited variation in differences of seating. Perhaps the seeming contradiction in the multiplicity of views is another example of the multivalent visual richness and ambiguity possible in the theatre? Although it would seem that a great difference in the viewing angles would diminish the intelligence of the design intent, a type of phenomenon similar to the robustness of perspective appears to intrinsically compensate for such disparities in the mind of the viewer.[14] Robustness, along with other compensatory activities such as size and colour constancy, acts to regiment and stabilize the perceptual sensibility of art that has perspective formats. It is a cognitive correcting action that our minds seem to execute intuitively. It was originally expected that viewing angles other than one in line with the perspective's observational centre of a work would suffer from varying degrees of distortion relative to how far removed the observer's point of view was from the observation point of the scene's central geometric projection. It seems the presence of the mind's perceptual mechanisms for 'correcting' for such discrepancies is why we may move about a perspective-based painting and feel no contradiction in the spatial metaphor we see.

Is it possible that in the theatre a similar corrective measure naturally takes over when we view a setting oriented towards the centre from a distance away from the intrinsic centre of observation? Furthermore, does this operational scheme for robustness act as an adjunct to the mental process, or matrix of mental processes, involved in seeing performance, thereby augmenting the intensity of the experience? We, the audience, become complicit in conceiving the space for the theatrical event, both for a specific event and in the general sense of the complex conception of space in a theatre. That conception depends on the unity of the vertical and the horizontal as a cognitive entity. We are always subconsciously aware of the two paradigms and their fluidity in our perception, just as directors and designers are in using them. The artistic team that can manipulate such an entanglement of polarities enhances the innate potential of the theatre to mirror life's dialectical tensions. The theatre's space-demands are negotiated by the multiple facets of our experience as part of the theatre's experience.

Robustness seems to depend on the 'awareness of the illusion'; in painting we need to be able to see the surface of the canvas, otherwise the effect is of a visual 'delusion' that may fail if its conditions are not met. Certainly, on stage, such 'awareness' is fulfilled by the clear placement of the parts of a design and their position on the floor plane, because illusionism exists virtually in the picture plane. It is another example of how the floor plane and the picture plane are intertwined in mutual elucidation through the contrast of their simultaneous presence.

It is true that director and designer are habitually concerned with a great variety of issues in the normal course of planning the implementation of a performance. These issues take the form of practical matters, such as the placement of entrances and exits, as well as conceptual questions like the period of the setting and the content of the stage's imagery. The director and designer can bridge the given auditorium and the invented stage setting by focusing on the manipulation of visual perceptions, as I have emphasized here.

I began this discussion by stating my own feelings on the importance of the ambiguity of art and how that phenomenon reflects the ambiguity that is part of everyday-life experience. No matter whether we contrast the 'Real' and the 'Ideal', sensual and intellectual, mind and body, rational and emotional, Apollonian and Dionysiac, eternal or transitory, conservative or liberal, observed and intuited, or objective and subjective, when we frame our experience in this way we seem to emulate the native imagery of day and night, winter and summer, and death and life, that must have occupied our thoughts since we began that uniquely-human process of negotiating between the observations of our natural senses, the rationale of our thinking, and the emotions of our beliefs. The contrast of architectural, horizontal, and pictorial, vertical, planes of composition is another such pair of dualistic concepts (polarities and antitheses) that capture the same sense of a basic process. It is by the very negotiation of that mental process, the cognition of ambiguous paradigms of understanding, that the theatre makes the experience of performance so deeply moving. Regardless of whether or not designers and directors are consciously aware of such processes (which I think not), or they intuitively use them (because they are perceptive visual artists), or a mixture of both, these processes are a life-sustaining force that needs to be better understood and celebrated. At their best, directors and designers working in the theatre are the 'painters of modern life', submerged in the experiential turmoil of their own time. Careening back and forth between fragmentary images of the multiple states that convey the experience of cognition, and the empathy created by that experience for the passing of time creates an event that makes theatre the great symbolic form of life. Toward a better understanding of that end I have concentrated this small effort.

Notes

1. Baudelaire, C., *The Painter of Modern Life*, London: Phaidon Press, 1995, pp. 3, & 12–13.
2. Cahill, T., *Sailing the Wine-Dark Sea: Why the Greeks Matter*, New York, London, Toronto, Sydney, Auckland: Nan A. Talese/Doubleday, 2003, pp. 146–149.
3. Hernstein Smith, B., *Belief and Resistance: Dynamics of Contemporary Intellectual Controversy*, Cambridge, Massachusetts: Harvard University Press, London, England, 1997, p. 41.
4. Ibid., xvii.
5. Ibid., xxiii, p. 39.
6. Feiner, H., 'The Real and the Ideal in Theatrical Space: Towards a Critical Methodology of Theatrical Design' in *Tradition and Innovation in Theatre Design*, Cracow: Jagiellonian University, Poland, 2001, pp. 109–117.
7. Kubovy, M., *The Psychology of Perspective and Renaissance Art*, New York: Cambridge University Press, , 1986, pp. 41–42.
8. Wolfflin, H., *Principles of Art History*, New York: Dover Publications, 1929, pp. 124–126.

9. Gordon, I.E., *Theories Of Visual Perception*, Chichester, New York, Brisbane, Toronto, Singapore: John Wiley & Sons, 1989, pp. 50–56.
10. Arnheim, R., *The Power of the Center: A Study of Composition in the Visual Arts*, Berkely and Los Angeles, California; London, England: University of California Press, 1988, pp. 42–43.
11. Ibid., p. 13, p. 19, p. 31, pp. 34–35.
12. Ibid., pp. 21–24.
13. Nochlin, L., *The Body in Pieces: Fragments as a Metaphor for Modernity*, New York: Thames and Hudson, 1994, pp. 24–26.
14. Kubovy, pp. 52–62.

Chapter 15

Design as Action: Jean Cocteau and the Ballets Russes

Gregory Sporton

The theatre depends on live presence. It is a one-off experience; it needs to tell us something about our time and to do so in a single sitting. These principles: experience, immediacy, instantiation and totality, differentiate the theatre from other cultural forms. Nowhere in theatre practice can this be more true than dance, where articulation refers not to words but bodies, and the role of design becomes integral to what we might call an audience's 'understanding', but often refers to its endurance or willingness to allow an unfolding of abstract concepts in human form. In this chapter, I want to suggest that, in the hands of a skilled practitioner, the design concepts become the action of the performance. This integration is at the heart of scenographic practice, and I want to explore these ideas through the work of Jean Cocteau.

Whilst most cultural historians credit Jean Cocteau's writings, sketches and films as the important aspects of his output, it is his example as a creator of performance that is explored here. A Ballets Russes production was a marriage between painting, music and choreography, in Diaghilev's famous aphorism, demanding a conceptual basis that was uncompromising, innovative, charged with uncertainty and visually challenging. Cocteau was crucial in developing the relationships between ex-imperial Russian theatre staff and Paris salon sophisticates, in finding an audience for the work and in providing a model of scenographic practice.

In Diaghilev's colourful and quotable life some moments stand repeating for their inspirational potential. In the context of this chapter, I want to deal with what Diaghilev thought the theatre was for and how that affected the artists he gathered around him. This is not solely for its historical merit, or even for its entertainment value, though it possesses both. It is because through it we can find some sort of guide for how we approach a scenographic task: a theatrical proposition beyond creating decor. In particular, Diaghilev's example and the performances of the Ballets Russes provide an argument about how to think about the theatre and what special attention should be shown to the experiences that flow from our attendances there. Whilst this contribution deals with historical events and people, it is not about history. There is something more interesting in how we perceive an historical moment, and it will be used here to support an argument about what the theatre, or at least a particular kind of theatre, is about.

I will return to the historicizing in a moment, but I wish to argue about the theatre as a cultural form, and then to work backwards towards Diaghilev, to the Ballets Russes and most of all to Jean Cocteau and the strange position he occupies in the history of dance and modernism. This history is about how design and action combine in a specific time and place to make theatre, about how meaning is made there and why this should remain of critical importance to our perception of the theatre at a time when it seems increasingly desirable to ascribe to directors or choreographers the authorship of a production as if we were reading a text. The focus on action is deliberate, and the role of the body in the performing space is one to which we will return, as it is a crucial part of the design process in this context.

The theatre is a particularly interesting site for cultural production. There are more detached forms of creativity, like books, music recordings or films, but performance in the theatre usually requires an expectant audience and a performer to draw us into the action. This is a distinction made in Western Theatre initially by Aristotle, who commands us in the *Poetics* not to write tragedies like epic poems, to respect that the whole work needs to be complete in the concentration span of an evening and to appreciate the difference between a narrator and an actor. The particularity of theatre practice is created by more than its 'live' element, though the liveliness is crucial to the tension. The shared experience of the audience, as the performance grows and they are drawn by the events on stage into developing a single response, is an unusual social phenomenon, and quite different from sport, where the spectators can clearly be partisan. Whilst other forms of cultural production can have the opportunity of the absence of their creators and the critical reception can be garnered over time, with reputations ebbing and flowing in relation to long-term shifts in taste, in the theatre the performers are usually in little doubt about the views of the public. This is especially true, say, in comedy, but also in drama, where the profundity of the silence indicates a public fully immersed in the action. As part of a justification for choosing my subject matter, I would simply compare the difficulties of staging Shakespeare with looking at art or architecture. In Shakespeare's case, the major creator is clearly absent, but it befalls any cast to make something new of him for the assembled public four hundred years after the first performances. Compare what this takes, say, to appreciating a Titian or looking at a building by Christopher Wren. In each of these cases there are problematics created by time, disputes over aspects of the authenticity of the experience, but no serious attempt to make of the works a modern statement, to draw out aspects of contemporary life, or to relate the experience of the past to the current audience and their perspectives on modern art-making.

These examples are not chosen haphazardly. At the National Gallery in London in 2003, the Titian Exhibition absolutely attempted to locate and contextualize his practice historically by recreating the room in which some of the pictures had been hung together in the distant past.[1] In a secondary way were the aesthetic values of the picture considered of interest to the modern public. This may indicate more about the modern trend to curatorial authority in major exhibition spaces, but the lesson was evident: historical faithfulness in gathering the pictures together was more important than the opportunity to contemplate them as works of art, and any contemplation of them in such a way needed to draw on the historical for authority. Likewise, in the case of Wren, when some demolition of buildings around St. Pauls in London gave the opportunity in 2001 to behold the church in ways not available for two hundred years.[2] What followed was a masterclass in appreciating the historical for its value as history, bringing to our notice again that which always existed as a quality of the building. There is little in either of these prominent examples that directly ask a contemporary audience to understand itself or its time by apprehension of the past, or through a direct invitation to re-interpret the past in a modern context. Whilst I am aware of attempts to do just that in theatre, and that this is also a popular approach to music that has an historical pedigree, part of the liveness of the theatre is the expectation that it will tell us something about ourselves and it will do so today, regardless of the age of the script or the reliability of the choreography.

I have thus far suggested two things about the theatre as an experience. The first is that it works in relation to a public, and the second is, regardless of the subject matter, there is an expectation that it will tell us something about the here and now. I want to add a third idea, one that most of us take for granted, but, especially in the cases discussed later, has particularly deep implications. The theatre has its opportunity to throw up a different experience every time, to be instantiated, about one instance and nothing else. This should not be confused with a unique experience: most professional performers will attest that being in long runs is very hard on the concentration after a few weeks. However, all that time in rehearsal is invested for re-creating a sense of spontaneity so that the watching public can think this is all happening before their eyes for the first time. There are cult shows, like the *The Rocky Horror Show*, that trade on repetition, and there are certainly theatrical conventions that it is assumed everybody in the audience knows, but a decent audience member tries to pretend that this is the first time they have been told this particular story, to entertain the version or form of the story that they are seeing, and this disposition is more popular, the older or better known the story happens to be. The public has to get it at a single viewing. They are happy, by and large, to enter into the theatre with an open mind, even if they emerge with a closed one, and this is not just because they are overtaken by a spirit of leisure, but also by a spirit of intrigue, conjoined with a preparedness to go some of the way with the production. Most people will have to form their views from a single performance. This, I might remind my fellow scholars in this field, is not a mistake or a problem. It means that the form of production itself defies a determination to create textual analogues about which we could have a reliable argument. Performances are slippery customers to deal with as historical events because acting styles, directorial intentions, casts, choreography and companies are subject to change, sometimes rapid change; our best faith in knowing what happened can sometimes be placed in the contemporary response to a performance. To treat it in this way revives the sense of theatre that made the action important in the first place. This is a more impressionistic account of the theatre as a scholarly subject makes some different demands.

The basic premise of this argument can be summarized in this way. The theatre depends on live presence, it is a one-off experience, it needs to tell us something about our time and it needs to do so in a single sitting. This can mean that those painstaking decors laden with symbolic purpose or metaphorical power in terms of their relationship to the text may have little or no impact on the drama where they do not help create it. This is not a call to a better understanding between designers and those overrated ersatz-generals referred to as directors (though this would be handy, and good theatre design rarely proceeds productively without it), but a search for an acknowledgement of the prominence of the experience of the theatre, the feel for the totality and potential of those shared occasions that transcend directorial decisions, and is often the result of an audience and the performers reaching an understanding about the meaning of the occasion.

To do justice to this argument about the significance of experience, immediacy, instantiation and totality, I want to look now at my historical subject, Jean Cocteau. There is no way to make an argument to suggest he understood dance in the same way as Diaghilev or Nijinsky, and indeed he depended on such people and on others to develop content. However, he certainly showed substantial technique as a developer of theatrical propositions and in his management of his productions. More significantly, he proceeded exclusively from design concepts, and this is exactly why he should interest us. He created imagery from the body, often by distorting it, and mixed that with the technical possibilities of the day. Importantly, he contributed more than a specialism: he saw the collaborative possibilities and took responsibility for them, though in different and interesting ways, as we shall see. He presumed to present what might be called 'abstract' dance, sometimes counter-intuitively to notions of dance based in the ballroom or the nightclub. He eschewed stories unless those stories themselves could be distorted, assumed, parodied or were intentionally transcendental, giving free play to the design ideas and the use of the body. For, whatever may be said about the roles of others in his work for the Ballets Russes, he emerges from the ballets as authoritative without possessing authorship, allowing the production to be guided by images, rather than language.

Jean Cocteau first met Diaghilev in 1909. Whilst most cultural historians credit his writings, sketches and films as the important aspects of his output, it is as a creator or animateur of dance that I wish to deal with him here. His association with the Ballets Russes gave it poetry, irony and fantasy at the fullest apogee of its creative importance. He claimed later to have been inspired in his career by a famous confrontation with an exhausted Diaghilev. According to Cocteau, he had been pestering the great man after a performance for advice, support and acknowledgement. They had walked together to the Place de la Concorde, and Diaghilev, finally wearying of the young man's ambitions, turned to him and uttered one of the most famous admonitions in the history of the theatre: 'Astound me!' he said. 'I'll wait for you to astound me.'[3] It was a challenge of tremendous force that, according to Cocteau, saved him from a career of decadence and pretentiousness, and focused him on the aims and purposes of creating a production.[4] This is more than a little ironic, given that he was charged by the Surrealists as being 'a craven opportunist and inconsistent stylist',[5] and detested by old Ballets Russes hands like Benois,[6] but for all his readiness to rise to the challenge, Cocteau said he only understood what was being commanded after seeing *Le Sacre du Printemps* (1913) the following year, when ballet's most famous riot broke out over the combination of Stravinsky's challenging score and Nijinsky's complex, rhythmic choreography.

Cocteau was born in 1889 into a respectable family, whose fortunes took a turn for the worse with his father's suicide when Cocteau was only ten. His semi-autobiographical novels, littered with casual suicides, hint that the cause may have been his father's self-torment with regard to his sexuality. This was not a condition Cocteau was to suffer from, and from the outset he made plain his sexual proclivities. He was a precocious figure, publishing poetry at the age of 16, writing scenarios for Diaghilev at 20. There are two of his projects I would like to briefly mention here, his first an early one, *Le Dieu Bleu*, (1912) and the other his most famous ballet collaboration, *Parade* (1917).

At the time of the discussion with Diaghilev in Paris, the young Cocteau had just provided the libretto for the *Le Dieu Bleu* (1912), collaborating with Leon Bakst, the composer Reynaldo Hahn and the choreographer Michel Fokine, whose wooden choreography historically gets the blame for the production's short run. *Le Dieu Bleu* was an extension of a trend in the Ballets Russes repertoire to present exotica in the guise of ballet. Other works of this type, often also designed by Bakst, were dances like *Thamar* (1912), *Sheherazade* (1907) or *Polovtzian Dances* (1909). It was clear in *Le Dieu Bleu* that, whatever the essences of a Ballets Russes production, the marriage between painting, music and choreography (in itself a famous aphorism of Diaghilev's), the conceptual basis needed to be uncompromising, innovative, charged with uncertainty and visually challenging. This is especially true of the Ballets Russes style in pre-War Paris, where extraordinary creative work was developing in the relationships between Russian émigré ex-imperial theatre staff and the Paris salon sophisticates, of whom Cocteau was one. In some ways, and partly due to the success of *Sheherezade* (1910) and the limitations of the choreographer Fokine, the Russians capitalized on the perception of Russia as a land of primitive mysteries and overt physicality, (quite ironic, considering that in Russia the ballet represented the best of Francophile civility). *Le Dieu Bleu*, at the end of this period, and soon to be overtaken by popularity of the developing neo-classicism style in *Les Sylphides* (1907) and *La Spectre de la Rose* (1911), presented Nijinsky as an exotic, cloud-dwelling deity, and Karsarvina as his sexy astral maiden. Cocteau's scenario effectively provided a pretext for the exploration, through dance and design, of a particular primitivist aesthetic. The ballet was an exploration of the opportunity, through the codes of dance, to exploit Nijinsky's exotic looks. By painting him blue, and presenting an erotic love story punctuated by ersatz ritual dances, Cocteau took full advantage of Nijinsky's ambivalent sexuality by locating it in the realm of Eastern spirituality. The ballet also marks a preoccupation that Cocteau's work repeatedly returned to: fables of the gods as a metaphor for modern man. *Le Dieu Bleu* elevated Nijinsky to god-like status, and it is clear that this was precisely the intention of the work from a temporal point of view. This play of content with temporal life typifies what we might now call postmodernism, but for Cocteau and the Ballets Russes the project was an extension of an existing policy with regard to Nijinsky himself and the public's perception of a company that could present sexual narratives in an aesthetic form. This was a policy that would provoke outrage later that season when Nijinsky would finish *L'Après-midi d'un Faune* (1912) by masturbating on a nymph's fallen scarf. Cocteau was perfectly aware of this kind of exploitation; it was consistent with his own sexual licentiousness and thus seemed, in a curious way, understated: 'We knew exactly how far to push things'.[7] Cocteau's own fetishistic descriptions of Nijinsky like a boxer, and his famous sketch of the dancer in the wings after a performance, with an attendant crowd dominated by the concerned eye of Diaghilev, conjure up the atmosphere of glamour, excitement and artistic vision encapsulated in a too tiny a space for the outsize talents that inhabit it.[8]

Parade (1917) was a different matter, and indicates the speed at which Cocteau's (and Diaghilev's) tastes could move in a short period of time. The aesthetics of *Parade* owe much to emerging futurism, but there is something strange and challenging about its cubist disposition. Why make ballet, where the costumes themselves restrict the possibilities of the choreography, a problem of restriction, which would later be tackled by dance artists Schlemmer and Nikolais. According to Garafola, Cocteau's genius lay in his ability to appropriate high culture to make populist art.[9] The ideas of *Parade* Garafola sources from 1913, though considering this is also the year of the riot over *Le Sacre du Printemps* (1913), such a radical stagework would possibly have received the same kind of scant contemporary attention. Diaghilev operated on the maxim that ballets needed to reach their audiences today and not tomorrow,[10] and Cocteau, with a gift for understanding the aesthetics of popular culture, incorporated circus and the cinema in his work. This combination would become a staple of ballet: even an aesthete like Balanchine has a *Slaughter on Tenth Avenue* (1936) to his name, or alternatively, Ashton's *Façade* (1931) stands out as an example of a genre developed in *Parade*.

Notwithstanding such comfortable revisionism, there is no doubt that Picasso's designs were, 'the most radical expression of cubism (yet) realized on the stage'.[11] Cocteau's persuasiveness in acquiring the services of Picasso was a source of great pride to him, conjoining the regular subject matter of Picasso's earlier pictures: dancers, acrobats, clowns, with the situation of a performance. In doing so, it provided another example of Cocteau's reflexivity, actively exploiting a connection with the visual arts to reach an audience that might have missed the value of the original pictures ten years before. That Cocteau and Picasso disagreed over aspects of the production is well known, including the composer Satie's personal smugness about the tensions between the two men, though in this kind of collaboration it seems highly contentious to ascribe triumph to one or the other.[12]

The front curtain is a famous image itself. A winged ballerina balances on a white horse being watched by a circus troupe at rest. The accoutrements of the performance process: a drum; a ladder; a ball; are scattered across the wooden floor, where the troupe's animals are also making themselves comfortable. Swathes of theatrical curtain frame the foreground and through the opening a landscape is seen of an open grass area in front of an aqueduct. The revelling theatricals are animated and lively, hinting at the satisfactions of a life beyond the conventional. The costumes, some created as enormous superstructures that made the dancers resemble large puppets, imply references to a way of enjoying popular culture differently, the notion of the carnival distorted and abstracted for use in the theatre. The complications the costumes provided for the dancers and Massine's choreography focus the work on the interplay between the narrative and the design, with the music seeking a relationship with both. Apollinaire's programme notes state: 'This new union, for so far the decors and costumes on the one hand, the choreography on the other have been linked only superficially, give *Parade* a semblance of surrealism, in which I see the beginnings [that] cannot fail to tempt the elect, or radically change the arts and customs of humanity...' However, *Parade*, rather than ushering a new age of development in Ballets Russes performances, 'came at the end rather than at the beginning of an extraordinary revolution initiated by Diaghilev in late 1914.'[13] For Kirstein, for example, this was the point in the Ballets Russes where the design components dominated pedestrian choreography, subservient as it became to the demands of such astonishing décor.[14]

A world like the ballet would clearly suit someone like Cocteau, fascinated as he was by the changing world of spontaneity and the flux of dance performances that explored the tensions of the moment. His gift, as suggested by Kirstein and Garafola, was in appropriating the commonplace and making it into art. Ballet suited his style; it was glamorous, aesthetic, fussy but also practical and pragmatic. More than all these things, it was transient. This allowed a modish young man of flexible mind and promiscuous visual tastes to use the theatre space as a temporary canvas, rather than making an historical statement about artistic practice. As a form to work through and work out ideas, it suited him perfectly. It was Cocteau's ability to see the short lives of the dances as an opportunity to experiment that made him the perfect foil for Diaghilev's creative project.

Stylistically, it is difficult to be definitive about a person whose work spans the whole of the modern era in art, whose output is located in many different forms, but this is precisely the temperament that I want to explore and encourage here: a sense of the outrageous, the immediate, the necessary and, occasionally, the astounding. Cocteau's own estimation of modernism, in *An Indirect Critique* (1932), we see something of that flavour. He dated the 'modern' era as between 1912, coinciding with his production *Le Dieu Bleu*, and 1930, when he began his first film. More interesting for us is what comes later in his account. For Cocteau, because 'Modernism' can be confined to an historical time period, it follows that the meaning of the word 'modern' had also changed. For Cocteau, this indicated a specific aesthetic as well as a process; modernism, the stuff of which had made him famous, had become obsolete. Here you may begin to detect my admiration of the artist, prepared to make and remake himself in the same way performances are made and remade, and to recognize, to be ruthless in recognizing, when the moment has passed.

At the beginning of this chapter I made some basic arguments about the nature of the theatre, and made note of some of the implications for a theatre practice. Rather than concentrating on those, I have chosen to look closely at how design could be invoked in another way, partly by leaving behind the world of drama and text, and partly by fusing it to practice in the theatre that attempts, as a basic principle, to present visual imagery. The boldness of the strategies discussed leaves us dazzled by their audacity, but also humbled by their discipline and effect. Creating a body of work in a practice of bodies provides us with another way of seeing our practice of theatre. The interesting question is this: occupying as we do a 'post-skill age', the technical means to produce effects leaves at our disposal new ways of presenting our visions. The concept of the designer, who designs either as the extension of the director's will or to create an environment that draws attention to his brilliance, is no longer dealing in temporal theatre. Just as *Parade* has become symbolic of the possibilities of collaboration, and also a point of decline for the Ballets Russes, the balance between possibilities and intention becomes a question of taste, as taste itself becomes a question of restraint. As the visual practice of theatre-makers extends, so should the ambitions of the practitioner. The scenographic project is one that attempts to extend the area of design into the performance as part of its time and space, for the very reasons discussed above. The challenge for visual practice in the theatre is to see itself as an integrated process with theatre-making, when theatre can be a visionary statement of its own time, and effective in the shaping of the people who make and share in it. As Diaghilev knew, mediocre theatre was hardly theatre at all. 'Astound me!' he said, and we should remember why.

Notes

1. Titian Exhibition at London's National Gallery, 19 February–18 May 2003, included an attempt to recreate the 'camerino d'alabastro' of Alfonso d'Este at Ferrara.
2. Glancey, J., 'London's Glory: See it whilst you can', *The Guardian,* 3 February, 2002, London: Guardian Newspapers Ltd.
3. Beaumont, C. W., *The Diaghilev Ballet in London,* London: Adam & Charles Black, 1940, p. 190.
4. Kochno, B., *Diaghilev & the Ballets Russes,* New York: Harper & Row, 1970, p. 176.
5. Mauries, P., *Jean Cocteau,* London: Thames & Hudson, 1998, p. 15.
6. Beaumont, p. 378.
7. Mauries, p. 54.
8. Buckle, R., *Nijinsky,* London: Orion Books, 1991, p. 258
9. Garafola, L., *Diaghilev's Ballet Russes,* New York; Oxford: Oxford University Press, 1989.
10. Nijinska, B., *Early Memories,* London: Faber & Faber, 1981, p. 473.
11. Hansen, R. C., *Scenic and Costume Design for the Ballet Russes,* Ann Arbor, Michigan: UMI Research Press, 1985, p. 59.
12. Indeed, it was revisions to Satie's score that caused a serious rift between Diaghilev and Cocteau in 1917.
13. Garafola, L., *Diaghilev's Ballet Russes,* New York; Oxford: Oxford University Press, 1989, p. 76.
14. Kirstein, L., *By, With, To & From,* New York: Farrar, Straus, Giroux, 1991, p. 114–115.

Part IV

Postscript to the Director

Lastly, in the postscript to the director, Lilja Blumenfeld explores the theoretical writings of philosophy, their relevance and resonance for the director and designer relationship.

Chapter 16

From *Hamlet* with Love: A Letter to the Other

Lilja Blumenfeld

I started to write this chapter as a letter, a letter to my friend, a director. After twenty years of partnership there should be a lot to say, and saying has, for various reasons, often been difficult or impossible. To write an academic text in the form of a letter is yet another challenge. Here the subject would become the object of research. As if I positioned myself on a platform, then stepped aside, and witnessed. While trying to write a letter, several questions arose and the writing process turned out to be surprisingly difficult. Even worse, it turned out to be completely confusing. If I would write this letter to a friend, it should be a letter to a friend and have all the necessary components that are normally included in a letter like this. If it was a letter from a designer to a director, a certain formality would enter the communication, merely because one of us is identifying himself as a director and the other as a designer. Then what would I want to say? Is saying necessary? And is there anything to be said at all?

We are used to thinking that theatre is communication, but what do we mean? This chapter has not so much to do with *Hamlet*, the latest production completed in cooperation, as it does have with identity, language and communication. It is dealing with the human language director and designer would speak within the production process, using a letter as the agent of speech. There is no single theory to be applied to the discourse of scenography. As I am currently undertaking research in the field of psychoanalysis and phenomenology, this chapter would be an attempt to apply the notions of 'self', 'ego' and 'other' to the director/designer relationship, as well as to scenography. These notions are reflected, of course, in a wide range of texts, of which I would only refer to a few: Bakhtin, Levinas, Sartre, Lacan, and Žižek.

In this chapter I argue that, instead of the 'monologue of a director', which for a surprisingly long time has been considered to be the essence of the director-centred production, the concept of production is worked out through a 'dialogue' between the director and the designer in the first place. Behind the central 'Father figure' of the director there is always the other, the scenographer who becomes invisible, 'transparent', within the production process, but is hidden in scenography, which itself is a certain language, a speech within the rhetoric of theatre.

Any form of speech is always a dialogue while it consists of a speaker, a listener, and the relation between them. Letter writing assumes a sender, a receiver and a letter as agent between them. Imaginary or real, it is always addressed to a receiver; a letter that has an addressee can never be a monologue. It is never just compiled of the utterances of a single individual, however self-sufficient and demanding these can be in their absolute one-sidedness.

Letter writing has attracted many thinkers, artists and writers. Franz Kafka alone left behind over 3,000 pages of letters. In his letter to Milena Jesénska he has written the following:

The easy possibility of writing a letter has perhaps…shaken the world in a most appalling way. Writing a letter is talking to the ghosts and not only to the ghost of the recipient, but also your own ghost, developing under one's own hand through the lines of a letter one is writing, or even the series of letters, one confirming the other and referring to it as witness. How on earth did anyone get the idea that people might be able to communicate through letters! You can think of a distant person and touch the one who is close to you, and what is left, is beyond humanity. But writing a letter however means to reveal oneself in front of the ghosts, who are waiting greedily. The written kisses never arrive; they are exhausted by ghosts on their way. With the help of this rich nourishment they multiply enormously.[1]

In the world of faxes, e-mails and voice-mail, Kafka's words strike us with their prophecy. The number of messages that are sent out in the world is frightening. The seduction of pressing the button will seize us, as well as the shame for giving up too easily to our darkest desires. The letters are sent and received; the messages tend to be 'too late' and sometimes 'too early'. We cannot claim the letters back, as they have already been caught by the 'ghosts' Kafka was writing about. A portion of shame is always included with personal expression. If the letter will be read in public, the intimacy is destroyed and the naked truth revealed. The multiple co-receivers hungrily witness the message coming up in their mailbox, as if sitting around the same boiling cauldron.

Through the letters we can please or harm, and have equal pleasure of both; and through Internet we can do all this anonymously. Letters to the dead, dead letters, ghost letters, and love letters embody the same desire. Talk to the letter is talk to the void; it is this way we are reaching out our grasping hand to the other.

In *Hamlet*, as in many other Shakespeare plays, the letters carry the information of the events that had taken place somewhere else, witnessed by someone else and are, thus, represented to the audience in order to make them aware as well as to trigger the action. Polonius is happy to have found, 'the very cause of Hamlet's lunacy' and reveals the content of his love letters to Ophelia: 'This in obedience, hath my daughter shown me; and more above, hath his solicitings, as they fell out by time, by means, and place, all given to mine ear'.[2] From Hamlet we learn that the content of the letter, which sentenced him to death, was carefully replaced with the death sentence of Rosencrantz and Guildenstern: 'Folded the writ up in the form of th' other; subscrib'd it, gave't th' impression, plac'd it safely, the changeling never known.'[3] The letter from Hamlet strikes Claudius as if the message had been sent by some ghost from otherness: 'From Hamlet! Who brought them?'[4] Lady Macbeth, Edmund, and even Orlando, (who attaches love letters of poetry to a tree in the Forest of Arden), are acting as if under the spell of desire for one another.

In *The Purloined Letter*, a story by Edgar Allan Poe, a letter is stolen from the Queen by the Minister under her very eyes and replaced by another. The letter is obviously containing some information which might endanger the reputation of the Queen in front of her husband, the King. In order to discover under the microscope the infinitesimal gaping of the slightest abyss, the thorough searching has secretly taken place for more than eighteen months, but the police prefect has found nothing. Despite all efforts, the letter is still hidden in the apartment, in an open place, but stays invisible under the conventional 'imbecile' gaze. Jacques Lacan's comments on what is hidden are relevant here: 'For it can literally be said that something is missing from its place only of what can change it: the symbolic. For the real…is always in its place, it carries it glued to its heel.'[5] Monsieur Dupin, who hears the story from the police officer, calls the Minister and discovers the letter at the Minister's place, snatches it and replaces with the other, getting a nice fee for the job. The original letter is thus finally returned to the actual addressee, the Queen, but has lost its significance on the way. We will never learn what was written in the letter, and who the author was will remain an enigma to the end. The missing letter is continuously replaced within the narrative:

> The signifier is a unit in its very uniqueness, being by nature a symbol only of an absence.
>
> Which is why we cannot say of the purloined letter that, like other objects, it must be or must not be in a particular place, but that unlike them it will be and not be where it is, wherever it goes.[6]

Lacan argues that between letter and the place there exist relations which are odd or rather bizarre, and what is said is to be understood to the letter, or a letter waits you at the post office, or you are acquainted with letters, but there is never a letter that is anywhere, whatever the context may be. Finally, Lacan states that the sender will in the end receive his own message from the receiver, but in reverse form. Thus, the symbolic chain becomes a circle of displacements, and the story of the purloined letter tells us that a letter will always arrive at its destination. Sending, uttering out to the unknown, we trust that some hope of arrival is included. However, there must be a possibility that a letter would go astray. If Romeo had received the letter from Lorenzo, the tragedy would have not taken place. Yet the letter addressed to Romeo got him anyway, though in a 'reverse form' and 'too late.' A very similar case was a letter which carried the death sentence to Rosencrantz and Guildenstern, a letter which Hamlet had turned over for his own sake, to defer his imminent death, and to keep it at a distance.

Scenography is a created 'otherness'. The place and the characters of the fictional reality of theatre do not derive from the continuum of spectators; they are the 'other'. The paradox of the theatre is embedded in the fact that through the otherness of place and characters, a credible reality is created. The non-human objects within the performance space could be defined as 'other' to the human characters within the same space. The space framing the objects/characters and the humans/characters can itself become a character, working as the

Other towards objects and humans; together they create a certain 'rhetoric' of drama, the character of which depends on how distanced or engaged its audiences are. The 'otherness' of theatre is defined by what happens in the spectators' mind in their own personal little theatres. In the production process the Designer is always the other towards the Director. But what does the other mean in this case, other or Other?

In his book *Time and the Other,* Emmanuel Levinas argues that the face of the other is always the servant; the different. This also brings to mind the Hegelian story of master and servant, of superior and inferior, of God and human. There is always this certain divine quality applied to the notion 'director', as the agent of absolute knowledge. Levinas argues that:

> The other as Other is not only an alter ego: the Other is what I myself am not. The Other is this, not because of the Other's character, or physiognomy, or psychology, but because of the Other's very alterity. The Other is, for example, the weak, the poor, 'the widow and the orphan,' whereas I am the rich or the powerful.[7]

Yet, as a single human being, the designer looks at the director as he/she would look at the other. Thus, the perspectives always remain twofold. As Levinas continues,

> ...if the relationship with the other involves more than relationships with mystery, it is because one has accosted the other in everyday life where the solitude and fundamental alterity of the other are already veiled by decency. One is for the other what the other is for oneself; there is no exceptional place for the subject. The other is known through sympathy, as another (my) self, as the alter ego. The exteriority of the other is not simply due to the space that separates what remains identical through the concept, nor is it due to any difference the concept would manifest through spatial exteriority. The relationship with alterity is neither spatial nor conceptual.[8]

He argues that the subject is always provided with two objects: the ego and the other, the latter with lowercase 'o'.

We tend to think that we know about someone we think we know, their life, their life story, their personality, their feelings and emotions. In production process the designer and the director maintain their own, and accept each other's, alterity. As humans, they will have to cope with the other and the Other. The game between designer and director includes at least four players in juxtaposition. Just like anyone else, the designer and the director are camouflaged with their egos, which allow them to enter the commerce of everyday life without tearing each other apart because they are civilized and decent people, but not only that – it is because they have become to appreciate each other's alterity.

There seems to be no language between the one and the other, yet the transmitted message, the letter, belongs to the 'dimension of language'; it is only through language that this communication could be made possible. The human condition itself is essentially a language, which distinguishes human societies from natural ones. As Lacan has put it: 'there is no speech without language', and language is, 'an order constituted by laws', about which we could 'at least learn what they exclude'.[9] In *God, Death and Time,* Levinas makes a distinction between Saying and Said. What is said depends on another sort of absence, which Levinas calls the signifier, meaning that the one who speaks, commands ethically, putting the other's ego under question. There is always ethics included in what could be said or what should be said, and how. On the other hand it is impossible to escape saying if saying itself is inevitable. The sign that we give to the other is the sign of, 'the impossibility of keeping silent', which Levinas calls the 'whole scandal of sincerity'.

> It is inseparable from giving, for it is sincerity which opens our reserves. The hand that gives exhausts its reserves without being able to dissimulate anything. Sincerity would thus be a Saying without Said, 'a speaking of nothing in particular', it is like the transparency of avowal, the recognition of debt, an indictment of oneself.[10]

According to Levinas, Saying is never present in the Said, as Said is always 'too late or too early, is already caught.'[11] In his book *Totality and Infinity* he states that:

> it belongs to the very essence of language, which consists in continually undoing its phrase by the foreword or exegesis, in unsaying the said, in attempting to restate without ceremonies what has already been ill understood in the inevitable ceremonial in which the said delights.[12]

The production process itself is a continuous saying, unsaying and resaying of the said. Some of what is said is dropped in the middle of the game; some of it gets lost and is never recalled. The sincerity of saying is the attribute of a designer and, in its transparency, it is also a scandal; we can call it, 'a scandal of scenography'. Theatre is created in a continuous dialogue between the designer and the director. Without their 'saying' and their 'said' there will be no theatre. I have deliberately left out the actors from this argument, as the importance of their presence in performance is not in question here.

The director/designer relationship is a binary opposition, which is equivalent as well as private – the two being linked onomatopoetically and synaesthetically at the same time. For the conventional eye the director is 'white' and the designer is 'black', the designer is the 'non-director', and the director is the 'non-designer'. The director directs, just as the bird sings and the dog barks. The director is 'theaterizing' the theatre. We think 'theatre' and mean 'director', or vice versa we think 'director' and mean 'theatre'. Through theatre practice we certainly know that this is not the case, and the designer is hidden behind the director, just like the signified is hidden behind the signifier; it is absent from its place, yet this absence itself becomes meaningful. Mikhail Bakhtin has looked at the dialogue in a dialectical relationship between the 'self' and the 'other', in which 'self' occupies the central position. The notion of 'dialogue' is opposed to the 'monologue', the kind of speech in which language suppresses the voice of the other. Bakhtin uses the notion of 'heteroglossia' to describe the inscription of multiple voices engaged in a dialogue within the same text, by utterances, itself a thought with a voice:

> The authentic environment of an utterance, the environment in which it lives and takes shape, is a 'dialogised heteroglossia', anonymous and social as language, but simultaneously concrete, filled with specific content and accented as individual utterance.[13]

In theatre the 'heteroglossia' of performance is formed by multiple voices, it is not just the monologue of the director.

According to traditional thinking, the director is the mirror, a *speculum superius* of heavenly illumination. *Lumen* of his genius casts a shaft of celestial light upon the designer and the rest of the company involved in theatre making. A designer, a *speculum inferius*, is reflecting back *lux* of a human. As if looking at the solar eclipse through the darkest of glasses, the designer looks back to the Director in fascination and awe. The director is the Creator and the designer is the created. The director is the Container and the designer is contained. The director is Signifier and the designer is signified, the S and the s, corresponding to the barrier between them, the mirror. Thus, the director looks at the designer as if looking into the mirror. As if placed between two parallel mirrors, they see each other to reflect indefinitely, seeing their image repeated; one sees himself through the eyes of another while looking at himself, and without the other, he would not see himself seeing himself.

Then what makes us so dependent on this specular image? The signification of the image according to Lacan is that it, 'links all the objects' of my, designer's, desires to the other's, director's, desire, 'more closely than to the desire they arouse in me.' The mirror image applies to the ego of course, and the ego is a means of the speech delivered to the other from the unconscious, a weapon for resisting its recognition. The ego is thought to be fragmented when it conveys speech, and a whole when it does not hear it. Lacan has stated:

> Men are far from confirming the expression that says, they see no further than the end of their nose; on the contrary, their misfortune is such that their world begins at the end of their nose, and they can apprehend their desire only by means of the same thing that allows them to see their nose itself: a mirror. But no sooner has this nose been discerned than they fall in love with it, and this is the first signification by which narcissism envelops the forms of desire.[14]

Looking at the Other is the matter of gaze, depending on modes of looking. Slavoj Žižek in his book *Looking Awry* has made a distinction between looking at the object straight on and matter of factly, on which condition we see it 'as it really is', and looking at it with a gaze puzzled by our desires and anxieties, which would give us a 'distorted', a 'blurred' image. The object (a) can be perceived only by a gaze already 'distorted' by desire, an object that does not exist for an 'objective' gaze. In other words, the object (a) is always perceived in a distorted way, because outside this distortion, 'in itself,' it does not exist, since it is nothing but the embodiment, the materialization of this very distortion or confusion introduced by desire into so-called 'objective reality.' This object is 'objectively' nothing, but viewed from a certain perspective it assumes the shape of 'something.'[15] The otherness of 'director' and 'designer' is just the matter of gaze and does not exist in objective reality. According to Levinas, 'being' is not just an empty notion, it has its own dialectic. 'Solitude' and 'collectivity' belong to this dialectic and are not merely psychological notions, like the need one can have for the Other. Within the production process, the notion of 'collectivity' becomes real. There is nothing to be done alone in theatre. The multiplicity of languages is inscribed to the very essence of theatre, which itself is a form of collectively-created otherness. 'We are surrounded by beings and things with which we maintain the relationships. Through sight, touch, sympathy and cooperative work, we are with the others. All these relationships are transitive: I touch an object, I see the other.'[16]

And yet Levinas continues:

> But I *am* not the other. I am all alone. It is thus *being* in me, the fact that I exist, my existing, that constitutes the absolutely intransitive element, something without intentionality or relationship. One can exchange everything between beings except existing. In this sense, to be is to be isolated by existing. In as much as I am, I am a monad. It is by existing that I am without windows and doors, and not by some content in me that would be incommunicable. If it is incommunicable, it is because it is rooted in my being, which is what is most private in me. In this way every enlargement of my knowledge or my means of self-expression remains without effect on my relationship with existing, the interior relationship par excellence.[17]

In the director/designer relationship, just like in any other human relationship, everything is exchangeable; everything is communicable except the very essence of the two humans. Solitude is a category of being which, in the phenomenon of death, finds itself bordering on the edge of a mystery. The idea of stepping into the territory of the unknown and doing it alone is frightening. The process of creating scenography is very much like that – stepping into the unknown. Despite the collective nature of theatre-making in the production, the designer is a solitary being. He/she works out the scenographic universe seated at the desk gazing at the scale model; the otherness is creating itself with the help of his/her own hands and is growing under his/her own eyes. To look at the model of the fictional universe is to look at the yawning abyss. The gaze of the designer is that of the creator, but the creator with the lowercase 'c' facing his/her own absence.

It is a shame to be a designer and not the director. It is the shame of a designer facing the director and the undisclosed recipient of the message of this shame. Through shame I have discovered I am a designer. I am deeply ashamed of myself as a designer, under the very eyes of the director, spectators, critics who are witnessing this shame.

Jean-Paul Sartre in his *Being and Nothingness* is looking at the notion of 'shame' in relation to the other:

> I am ashamed of what I am. Shame therefore realizes an intimate relation of myself to myself. Through shame I have discovered an aspect of my being…In fact no matter what results one can obtain in solitude by the religious *practice* of shame, it is in its primary structure shame *before somebody*.[18]

We can never meet with anything but the consciousness, which is ours. Thus the other, who witnesses our shame, is the indispensable mediator between us and ourselves: 'I am ashamed of myself *as* I *appear* to the other.'[19] For the Other I appear as an object. Yet this object is not just an empty image. Sartre has noted that shame is by nature 'recognition'; he has stated that, 'shame is an immediate shudder, which runs through me from head to foot without any discursive preparation.'[20]

An image of a designer appears to a director as an object, but the object which is unsurpassable, inevitable and disposable. The image of the designer is usually an image of a slave or a servant, the profession of the designer thus often becomes frighteningly similar to that of a prostitute. It is though, more often, that he/she is treated like a friend or a partner. However, we know that friends and partners ought to be equal, and we also know that it is not always the case. I recognize myself as a designer, and thus this recognition gives me a shudder of shame; and as a designer I will have to cope with this shudder and live with this shame. The other not only reveals to me who and what I am, but establishes me as an entirely new type of being and, before the appearance of the other, this new being was not potentially there. Without ever meeting the director, I would have never become a designer; I would have never known the shame. The shame of the designer towards the director is the shame of the created towards the Creator. The director becomes a certain 'Father-character'. And this of course immediately brings to mind the Freudian name of the Father, the murder and the guilt, which has been included ever since. At the same time the shame is needed by the other, as without the notion of 'shame' the relationship would have not been complete. Without the shame of the designer the director could not exist. This is a relationship in which original sin is included.

Hamlet is a play about the triumph of death. The ghost of Hamlet's father returning from Hell himself becomes an embodied Death. He instructs Hamlet to avenge his murder and introduces the desire for the Other; in a way, with his very presence he contaminates the living. From now on Hamlet would not look otherwise but 'awry' at life and the rest of the humans. Death will soon after take over from the living, picking out the characters one by one. 'Ultimately Death is the only one to sit down at the table, to feast on the living.'[21] Hamlet becomes a murderer, but as a dramatic character he still manages to make himself a lovable hero. With his dying breath he asks Horatio to tell *his* story, but what he actually wants is essentially human, he is, like anyone else, craving for love above all in this life and beyond.

Love and death are both phenomena which cannot be defined properly; both assume the step towards the other side. In the phenomenon of death, solitude finds itself bordering on the edge of a mystery. Within the mystery of the production process, the designer is always masked; the designer is a performer, but a veiled performer of backstage. Just as 'Death unmasks the face of the Other', the opening of the production reveals the empty face of a designer. We may say that going through a number of productions a designer 'dies' a number of 'deaths' and Hamlet's lines: 'You cannot, sir, take from me anything that I will more willingly part withal, except my life, except my life, except my life'[22] become disturbingly relevant.

The existence of someone willing to go through this symbolic chain of 'deaths' is lacking common sense; is totally irrational. If someone is intentionally trying to erase oneself from the picture, we may well ask why anyone would want to do it in the first place. If one has a desire, it is normal to seek an object that will gratify and erase it; the desire to die is best enacted when death is kept at a distance. Love and death are both realms which cannot be defined properly; both assume the step towards the other side, from which there is no turning back. The death drive of a scenographer drags him/her to look for jouissance in a 'scenographic act'. Thus, we can compare his/her act of self erasure with a 'suicide', which immediately becomes an act of love. Referring to his mentor Jacques Lacan, Stuart Schneidermann in his book *Jacques Lacan: The Death of an Intellectual Hero* writes the following:

> Suicide does not represent a desire for death, but rather a love of death. Love is far more impatient than desire; love demands love unconditionally and instantaneously. People, who commit suicide, are lovers of death, and suicide thus becomes an act of love.[23]

The otherness created by a designer is facing him/her like an empty grave waiting for a dead body, reminiscent of the Lacanian signifier of absence as well as the scene in *Hamlet*, in which two clowns shovel earth from the freshly dug grave, which stays open to accept Ophelia's body. Polonius and Ophelia were buried without prescribed rituals; the designer in the production process will never be 'buried' properly. The absence of the designer becomes as significant as the empty grave waiting for a body.

As Lacan has put it, 'we think that we can negotiate with the living, but the dead, existing in otherness, are far more difficult to handle.' The return of the dead itself is, 'a sign of a disturbance in the symbolic rite.' The dead return, 'as collectors of some unpaid symbolic debt'.[24] The return of the 'living dead' then materializes a certain symbolic debt persisting, 'beyond physical expiration.'[25] Hamlet's father returns from the Hell with the message for his son. He is upset because, being killed in an instant, he remained in a state of sin and 'was left to face his Maker unshriven.'[26] Like the ghost of Hamlet's father, the ghost of the designer keeps coming back to the place in which the 'crime' (scenography) has taken place. In this way the designer would die a 'second death', acting like Hamlet or Antigone, as pointed out by Žižek. The Scenographer knows what he/she is up to; he/she is the one who has the knowledge of the Gods. Within the performance process the 'ghostly' designer becomes somewhat 'transparent.' Thus the designer, the scenographer is always present, yet hidden in scenography.

We can hardly say anything about the world we are trapped in. We may well ask: how could it be possible to say anything about the other, if we can say so little about our own deepest abysses? Letters become words and words become letters. I made a research on letters and messages, language and speech, but actually nothing could make me write this letter to my friend. Just like the purloined letter, the unwritten letter to the Other becomes a signifier, the meaning of which lies in its pure absence. What is not said is Said anyway. Scenography represents to us something not immediately present and is valuable for what it does not reveal. The letter by a scenographer is written and re-writing itself in scenography. According to Lacan: 'the unconscious is the discourse of the Other.'[27] Referring to Heidegger, Lacan states that we ought, 'to rediscover a secret to which truth has always initiated her lovers and that 'it is in hiding that she [truth] offers herself to them most truly.'[28]

The presence of a scenographer within scenography is so obvious that we are left to wonder about the imbecile conventional gaze which does not notice what should be noticed in the first place. Lacan's comment on the moral of *The Purloined Letter* by Poe reads as follows: 'Eat your *Dasein*!', and we wonder what did he actually mean.[29] Levinas comments on the Heideggerian notion of '*Dasein*': the human existence, the being in the world is 'an adventure that is the stage upon which being plays.'[30] Through scenography the (transparent) scenographer offers a clapping hand to the otherness he/she is creating. In the production process, the scenographer (the subject) totally absorbs scenography (the object), be it *Hamlet* or any other play does not make any difference here, as well as becoming totally absorbed by scenography, being overwhelmed and fascinated, and fascinated by this fascination.

*

If this is not Love, it must be a Disease.

Notes

1. Kafka, F., *Letters to Milena*, Vintage, 1992, p. 210, translation by the author.
2. William Shakespeare, *Hamlet*, Act II, scene 2.
3. Ibid., Act V, scene 2.
4. Ibid., Act I, scene 7.
5. Lacan, J., *Seminar on 'The Purloined Letter'*, Les Presse du Reel, 2005, p. 66.
6. Ibid., p. 63.
7. Levinas, E., *Time and the Other*, Pittsburgh: Duquesne University Press, 1987, p. 83.
8. Ibid., p. 82–83.
9. Lacan, J., *Écrits*, London: Routledge, 2001, p. 118.
10. Levinas, E., *God, Death and Time*, Stanford Ca: Stanford University Press, 2000, p. 192.
11. Ibid.

12. Levinas, E., *Totality and Infinity*, Pittsburgh: Duquesne University Press, 1999, p. 30.
13. Bakhtin, M., Original lectures given at University of Copenhagen. *Discourse in the Novel*, in *The Dialogic Imagination*, M. Holquist, (Ed.) Austin: University of Texas Press, 1994, p. 272. See also Bruhn & Lundquist, *The Novelness of Bakhtin*, Oxford, New York: Oxford University Press, 2000.
14. Lacan, J., *Écrits*, New York: W.W. Norton, 2007, p. 129.
15. Žižek, S., *Looking Awry*, Cambridge, Mass: MIT Press, 1992, pp. 11–12.
16. Levinas, *Time and the Other*, p. 42.
17. Ibid., p. 42 (Emphasis in original).
18. Sartre, J.P., *Being and Nothingness*, London: Routledge, 2003, p. 245.
19. Ibid., p. 246.
20. Ibid., p. 246.
21. Schneidermann, S., *Jacques Lacan: The Death of an Intellectual Hero*, Harvard: Harvard University Press, 1984, p. 153.
22. William Shakespeare, *Hamlet* Act II, scene 2.
23. Stuart Schneidermann, *Jacques Lacan: Death of an Intellectual Hero*, Harvard: Harvard University Press, 1994, p. 24.
24. Žižek, p. 23.
25. Ibid.
26. Ibid., p. 27.
27. Jacques Lacan, *Seminar on 'The Purloined Letter,'* p. 28.
28. Ibid., p. 53.
29. Ibid., p. 139.
30. Emmanuel Levinas, *God, Death and Time*, p. 30.

Bibliography

Abel, L., *Metatheatre: A New View of Dramatic Form*, New York: Hill & Wang, 1963.

Ardrey, R., *African Genesis*, New York: Antheneum, 1973.

Aristotle, *The Ethics*, Harmondsworth: Penguin Books, 1976.

Arnheim, R., *The Power of the Center: A Study of Composition in the Visual Arts*, Berkeley & Los Angeles, CA; London, England: University of California Press, 1988.

Austin, J.L., *How to do Things with Words*, Cambridge: Harvard University Press, 1962.

Bachelard, G., *The Poetics of Space: The Classic look at How we Experience Intimate Places*, New York: Orion Press, 1964.

Balanchine, G., *Choreography*, New York: Eakins Press Foundation, 1983.

Baudelaire, C., *The Painter of Modern Life*, London: Phaidon Press Limited, 1995.

Baugh, C., *Theatre Performance and Technology: The Development Of Scenography In The Twentieth Century*, London: Palgrave Macmillan, 2005.

Beacham, R., *Adolphe Appia:Artist and Visionary of the Theatre*, London: Routledge, 1993.

Beaumont, C. W., *The Diaghilev Ballet in London*, London: Adam & Charles Black, 1940.

Bennett, S., *Theatre Audiences A theory of production and reception*, London: Routledge, 1994.

Benois, A., *Reminiscence of the Russian Ballet*, London: Wyman & Sons, 1947.

Bergman, G., *Lighting in the Theatre*, Stockholm:Almqvist & Wiksell, 1977.

Butler, J., *Bodies that Matter, On the Discursive Limits of Sex*, New York: Routledge, 1993.

Buckle, R., *Diaghilev*, London: Weidenfield & Nicholson, 1979.

Buckle, R., *Nijinsky*, London: Orion Books, 1991.

Callow, S., *Being an Actor*, New York: Vintage, 2004.

Carner, M., *Puccini A Critical Biography*, London: Gerald Duckworth, 1958.

Chaudhuri, U., *Staging Place: the Geography of Modern Drama*, Ann Arbor: University of Michigan Press, 1997.

Certeau, M. de, *The Practice of Everyday Life*. Berkekey, CA: University of California Press, 1984.

Craig, E.G., *On the Art of the Theatre*, London: Heinnemann, 1911; reprint Mercury Books, 1962.

Devlin, A.J., (Ed.) *Conversations with Tennessee Williams*, Jackson: University Press of Mississippi, 1986.

Diamond, E., (Ed.) *Performance and Cultural Politics*, London: Routledge, 1996.

Elam, K., *The Semiotics of Theatre and Drama*, London New York: Methuen, 1980.

Elsom, J., *Post-War British Theatre Criticism*, London: Routledge & Kegan Paul, 1980.

Esslin, M., *The Field of Drama: How The Signs of Drama Create Meaning on Stage*, London: Methuen, 1988.

Filipowicz, H., *A Laboratory of Impure Forms: the Plays of Tadeusz Różewicz*, New York, London: Greenwood Press, 1991.

Fitzball, E., *35 years of a Dramatic Authors Life*, London: W. Kent, 1859.

Garafola, L., *Diaghilev's Ballet Russes*, New York; Oxford: Oxford University Press, 1989.

Giannachi, G., & Luckhurst, M., (Eds.), *On Directing*, London: Faber & Faber, 1999.

Goldstein, M., *The Political Stage: American Drama and the Theatre of the Great Depression*, New York: Oxford University Press, 1974.

Gordon, I.E., *Theories Of Visual Perception*, Chichester, West Sussex: John Wiley & Sons, 1989.

Gorelik, M., *Toward a Larger Theatre*, Landrum, MD: University Press of America, 1988.

Gropius, W., & Wensinger, A.S., *Theatre of the Bauhaus*, Baltimore: John Hopkins University Press, 1961.

Hamblin, J., *The Artistic Approach of the Grieve Family to Selected Problems of Nineteenth Century Scene Painting*, Diss: Ohio State U, 1966.

Hansen, R.C., *Scenic and Costume Design for the Ballet Russes*, Ann Arbor, Michigan: UMI Research Press, 1985.

Haskell, A. L., *Balletomania*, London & Southampton: Camelot Press, 1946.

Hayman, R., *Tennessee Williams: Everyone Else is an Audience*, New Haven: Yale University Press, 1993.

Henderson, M., *Mielziner: Master of Modern Stage Design*, New York: Back Stage Books, 2001.

Hernstein Smith, B., *Belief and Resistance: Dynamics of Contemporary Intellectual Controversy*, Cambridge, MA; London: Harvard University Press, 1997.

Holquist, M., (Ed.) *The Dialogic Imagination*, Austin: University of Texas Press, 1994.

Hornby, R., *Drama, Metadrama, and Perception*, London & Toronto: Associated University Presses, 1986.

Howard, P., *What is Scenography?* London, New York: Routledge, 2002.

Husserl, E., *The Crisis of European Sciences and Transcendental Phenomenology*, Evanston, IL: Northwestern University Press, 1938/1954.

Kaye, N., *Site-specific Art: Performance, Place and Documentation*, London: Routledge, 2000.

Kazan, E., *A Life*, New York: Knopf, 1988.

Kenny, Shirley, S., *British Theatre and the Other Arts, 1660–1800*, Washington: Folger Press, 1984.

Kirstein, L., *By, With, To & From*, New York: Farrar, Straus & Giroux, 1991.

Kluver, B., *A Day with Picasso*, Cambridge, MA: MIT Press, 1997.

Kochno, B., *Diaghilev & the Ballets Russes*, New York: Harper & Row, 1970.

Koegler, H., *The Concise Oxford Dictionary of Ballet*, Oxford; New York: Oxford University Press, 1987.

Kubovy, M., *The Psychology of Perspective and Renaissance Art*, New York: Cambridge University Press, 1986.

Kwon, M., *One Place After Another: Sitespecific Art and Locational Identity*, Cambridge, MA. & London: MIT Press, 2002.

Lacy, S., (Ed.) *Mapping the Terrain: New Genre Public Art*, Seattle: Bay Press, 1995.

Lacan, J., *Écrits*, London: Routledge, 2001.

Lacan, J., *Seminar on 'The Purloined Letter'*, Les Presse du Reel, 2005.

Levinas, E., *Time and the Other*, Pittsburgh: Duquesne University Press, 1987.

Levinas, E., *God, Death and Time*, California: Stanford University Press, 2000.

MacCabe, C., (Ed.), *High Theory/Low Culture*, Manchester Manchester University Press, 1986.

Mackintosh, I., *Architecture, Actor and Audience*, London, New York: Routledge, 1992.

Macksey, R. & Donato, E., (Eds.) *The Structuralist Controversy: the Languages of Criticism and the Sciences of Man*, Baltimore & London: John Hopkins UP, 1975.

Manfull, H., *Taking Stage, Women Directors on Directing*, London, Methuen Drama, 1999.

Marranca, B., (Ed.) *The Theatre of Images*, New York: Drama Book Specialists, 1977.

Mauries, P., *Jean Cocteau,* London: Thames & Hudson, 1998.

Meisel, M., *Realizations: Narrative, Pictorial and Theatrical Arts in Nineteenth Century England,* Princeton NJ: Princeton University Press, 1983.

Mielziner, J., *Designing for the Theatre: A Memoir and a Portfolio,* New York: Bramhall House, 1965.

Morphos, E., (Ed.) *A Dream of Passion: The Development of the Method,* New York: Penguin Books, 1988.

Murphy, B., *Tennessee Williams and Elia Kazan: A Collaboration in the Theatre.* Cambridge: Cambridge University Press, 1992.

Nelson, R.J., *Play within a Play: The Dramatist's Conception of his Art: Shakespeare to Anouilh,* New Haven: Yale University Press, 1958.

Nijinska, B., *Early Memories,* London: Faber & Faber, 1981.

Nochlin, L., *The Body in Pieces: Fragments as a Metaphor for Modernity,* New York: Thames & Hudson, 1994.

Oddey, A., *Devising Theatre,* London: Routledge, 1994, 1996.

Oddey, A., *Performing Women,* Basingstoke: Palgrave Macmillan. 2005.

Oddey, A., *Re-Framing the Theatrical: Interdisciplinary Landscapes for Performance,* Basingstoke: Palgrave Basingstoke: Macmillan, 2007.

Orgel S. & Strong, R., *The Theatre of the Stuart Court,* volume 1, Sotheby Park Bernet: University of California Press, 1973.

Pearson, M. & Shanks, M., *Theatre/Archaeology,* London: Routledge, 2001.

Rabkin, G., *Drama and Commitment,* Bloomington, IN: Indiana University Press, 1964.

Reid, L.A., *Meaning in the Arts,* London: Allen & Unwin, 1969.

Rosenberg B. & White, D., (Eds.) *Mass Culture,* Glencoe: Free Press, 1957.

Rothschild, D. M., *Picasso's Parade,* London: Phillip Wilson Publications, 1991.

Rudnitsky, K., *Russian and Soviet Theatre,* London: Thames & Hudson, 1988.

Sartre, J.P., *Being and Nothingness,* London: Routledge, 2003.

Schlueter, J., *Metafictional Characters in Modern Drama,* New York: Columbia University Press, 1979.

Schneidermann, S., *Jacques Lacan: The Death of an Intellectual Hero,* Cambridge, MA: Harvard University Press, 1984.

Shank, T., *Contemporary British Theatre,* London: Macmillan, 1994.

Shead, R., *Ballets Russes,* London: Greenwich Editions, 1989.

Shevtsova, M., *Dodin and the Maly Theatre,* London: Routledge, 2004.

Smith, W., *Real Life Drama:The Group Theatre and America* 1931–1940, New York: Alfred A. Knopf, 1990.

Smiley, S., *The Drama of Attack: Didactic Plays of the American Depression,* Columbia, MO: University of Missouri Press, 1972.

Spiegelburg, H., *Doing Phenomenology: Essays on and in Phenomenology,* The Hague: Martinus Nijhoff, 1975.

Strinati, D., *An Introduction to Theories of Popular Culture,* London: Routledge, 1995.

Volbach, W.R., *Adolphe Appia, Prophet of the Modern Theatre : A Profile,* edited and translated by Richard C. Beacham, Wesleyan University Press, 1968.

Volbach, W.R., *Adolphe Appia, Essays, Scenarios, and Designs,* edited Richard C. Beacham, UMI Research Press, 1989.

Walton, Michael, J. (Ed) *Craig on Theatre.* London: Metheuen, 1983.

Wright, E., *Post-Modern Brecht: a representation,* London: Routledge, 1989.

Wolfflin, H., *Principles of Art History,* New York: Dover Publications, 1929.

Žižek, S., *Looking Awry,* Cambridge, MA: MIT Press, 1992.

Notes on Contributors

Christine A. White, Nottingham Trent University, UK

Christine White is Head of Narrative and Interactive Arts at Nottingham Trent University School of Art & Design. She has been a designer and lecturer in Higher Education for twenty years. She was the Convenor for the Scenography Research Group for the International Federation for Theatre Research from 1994–2002. She is Convenor for the Research Group Digital Visualisations and New Media in Performance and has pioneered scenography research in the UK. She is editor for *Scenography International* www.scenography-international.com. Her books include *Technical Theatre*, (Hodder Arnold, 2001) *Computer Visualisations 3D Modelling for Theatre Designers*, (with Gavin Carver, Focal Press, 2003) *The Potential of Spaces* (with Alison Oddey, Intellect, 2006) and *Modes of Spectating*, (with Alison Oddey, Intellect, 2009). She has written papers on lighting and sound in performance and she is a member of the Arts and Humanities Research Council Peer Review College for Scenography, Performance and New Media. She is manager for the Nottingham Media Academy, a Skillset partner, www.ntu.ac.uk/academy.

Charles Erven, Loyola Marymount University, USA

Charles A. Erven is Associate Professor of Theatre Arts. His BA and MFA are from the University of Wisconsin-Madison. Erven teaches courses in theatre technology and design. He is a professional scenographer and member of the United Scenic Artists of America. His work has been seen at the Milwaukee Repertory Theatre, the Milwaukee Chamber Theatre and First Stage Milwaukee as well as the Madison Repertory Theatre and Racine Theatre Guild in Wisconsin. He has also designed for theatres in Chicago, California, Colorado, the Virgin Islands, New York, Tblisi, Georgia, and Tashkent, Uzbekistan. Erven has organized international student production tours to Russia, Kazakhstan, Uzbekistan, the Czech Republic, Ireland and Wales. In 1997 and 2001, Erven designed and/or directed productions that performed at Podium, a biennial international festival in Moscow. His design work has been included in exhibitions at the Milwaukee Art Museum, the Milwaukee Institute for Art and Design, the USITT Biennial Scenography Exposition and the Central States Exhibition of Scene Design. In March 2001, he presented a paper, 'Collaboration on the Global Stage: A Scenographic Approach to Undergraduate Theatre Productions,' at the

Mid America Theatre Conference in Chicago. Since 1990, his research has focused on the integration of American and Eastern European approaches to scenography. Erven recently designed scenery for LMU's productions of *J.B.* and *The Seagull*.

Anne Fletcher, Southern Illinois University, Carbondale, USA

Anne Fletcher is Assistant Professor. She teaches courses in Theatre History including an undergraduate survey course and graduate classes in American Political Theatre and Contemporary Developments. She received her PhD from Tufts University where her dissertation was on Group Theatre designer Mordecai Gorelik. She followed adjunct teaching in Boston and a voyage teaching for Semester at Sea with several years at Winthrop University in South Carolina. Her work has appeared in The New England Theatre Journal, Theatre Journal, and Theatre Symposium. She has presented at ATHE, ASTR, the SETC Theatre History Symposium and other professional conferences.

Kathleen Irwin, University of Regina, Canada

Kathleen Irwin is Associate Professor in the Theatre Department, University of Regina. Her current research focuses on community-based, interdisciplinary site-specific performance and installation. In 2002, she completed *The Weyburn Project*, a performance located in an abandoned wing of the Mental Hospital in Weyburn, SK and is currently developing a performance at Claybank Brick Factory in 2006 in partnership with Common Weal Community Arts Inc. In two site-specific performance/installations, *The Bus Project* (June 2003) and *We – the City* (August 2003), her work animated sites of everyday activity (bus depots and an Anglican Bishop's residence) to unlock memory and reassign meaning. Her research focuses, as well, on aspects of intentionality and chance in collaboration/community-based work. She is completing her doctorate at the University of Art and Design, Helsinki.

Věra Velemanova, Theatre Institute Prague, Czech Republic

Věra Velemanová has worked for the Theatre Institute in Prague since 1996. Her exhibitions, focusing on Russian emigrants in Czechoslovakia and on Theatre of Czechoslovakian Legionnaires in Russia during World War I, were exhibited at the Embassy of the Czech Republic in Russia, at the Vinohrady Theatre in Prague and in the Slavic Library in Prague. Since 2000, she has been employed at the Theatre Institute as a theatre historian, working on the *Bibliographical Dictionary of Czech Theatre* in the Department of Czech Theatre Studies. Her specialization is Czech scenography and the theatre of Russian emigrants. She has published various studies and reviews in the *Divadelní revue (Theatre Review)* and in the *Divadelní noviny (Theatre News)* and Exhibition catalogues. She was co-author of *Libor Fára 1925-1988* (Praha, 1999); author of the Who´s Who of Czech scenographers (*Allgemeine Künst- lerlexikon*, Saur, Leipzig-München); co-author of *Le Théâtre d'Art de Moscou*; *Ramifications, voyages* (Paris, 2005); co-author of *Libor Fára/dílo* (Praha, 2006) and editor of *František Tröster: Artist of Light and Space* (Praha, 2007).

Alison Oddey, University of Northampton, UK
Alison Oddey is Professor of Contemporary Visual Culture and Performance at the University of Northampton and initiated the Research Seminar series 'Different Directions' which began with Scenography and Performance. She is a performer, writer, broadcaster and teacher. Her books include *Devising Theatre*, (Routledge, 1994,1996), *Performing Women*, (Palgrave Macmillan, 1999, 2005), *The Potentials of Spaces*, (with Christine White, Intellect, 2006), *Re-Framing the Theatrical*, (Palgrave Macmillan, 2007) and *Modes of Spectating*, (with Christine White, Intellect, 2009). She has interviewed directors and designers discussing with them their ways of working and creative practice. She has been involved in research in the performing arts and cross-disciplinary landscapes of art and culture. She has guest lectured at the universities of Amsterdam and Utrecht, Holland; Antwerp, Belgium and Zurich, Switzerland. Her previous work, discussing spirituality and performance in the context of the meditative, has developed into her current research project, which links her work in art and urban spaces with new partnerships in alternative health.

Ewa Wąchocka, University of Silesia, Katowice, Poland
Ewa Wąchocka (Ph.D) is Head of the Department of Theatre Studies at the University of Silesia. She was theatre critic and now she is occupied in modern drama and theory of drama. Her publications include books *Między sztuką a filozofią: O teorii krytyki artystycznej Stanisława Ignacego Witkiewicza*, (University of Silesia, 1992), *Od symbolizmu do post-teatru* and *Autor i dramat* (Katowice, 1996) as well as articles in collective works, and in Polish and German journals. 'Un-presented Reality: On Polish Society's Self-Identification in Drama since 1989', *Toroto Slavic Quarterly* no. 9.

Scott Dahl, University of Michigan-Flint, USA
Scott Dahl is a designer and lecturer in Theatre.

Harry Feiner, Queens College City University of New York, USA
Harry Feiner is a designer and lighting designer and a member of United Scenic Artists. He has designed for the Pearl Theatre Company, The Pittsburgh Public Theatre, The Philadelphia Drama Guild, The McCarter Theatre, George Street Playhouse, Studio Arena Theatre, The Pennsylvania Stage GeVa, Syracuse Stage, Actors' Studio, Two River Theatre Company, Raw Space, and The North Carolina, New Jersey and Colorado Shakespeare Festivals. Opera designs for Central City Opera, The Philadelphia Opera Theatre, Syracuse Opera, Opera Theatre of Rochester, Boston Lyric Opera, The Bronx Opera, The Orchestra of St. Luke's, Chatauqua Opera, and The Manhattan School of Music. Dance designs for North Carolina Dance Theatre and The Pascal Rioult Dance Theatre. Resident designer for the Missouri Repertory Theatre (1980–84). Principal designer for the Lake George Opera Festival (1995–97). He teaches theatre design at Queen's College, City University New York. He is a member of the International Federation for Theatre Research group for Scenography and has presented at international conferences.

Julia Listengarten, Florida State University, USA

Julia Listengarten is currently Associate Professor of Theatre and Director of Graduate Studies at UCF. After receiving her master's degree from the Russian Academy of Performing Arts in Moscow, she graduated from the University of Michigan with a PhD in Theatre Studies. Previously, she has taught at St. John's University and Purdue and worked professionally in NYC as a dramaturg and director. Her translation of the Russian absurdist play *Christmas at the Ivanovs'* premiered Off-Broadway at Classic Stage Company and was included in the anthology *Theater of the Avant-Garde, 1890–1950*. Her book *Russian Tragifarce* was published by Associated University Presses (2000), and her most recent articles 'Translating Politics and Performing Absurdity' and 'Jewish Comedy and the Art of Affirmation' are included in *Translation in Perspectives* and *Blackwell Companion to Twentieth century American Drama*, respectively. Among Julia's directing credits are *What the Butler Saw, Nora, Picnic, The Dining Room, Bus Stop*, and *Three Sisters*. She is currently working on an anthology entitled *Theater of the Avant-Garde: 1950-2000*.

Gregory Sporton, University of Central England, UK

Gregory is Head of Research for the Department of Visual Communication at the Birmingham Institute of Art & Design, University of Central England. Dr. Sporton studied at the Victorian College of the Arts in Melbourne, Australia, prior to a career dancing for various small contemporary dance companies around the world. He has an MA from the University of Warwick and a PhD from the University of Sheffield. His interests focus mainly on the cultural positioning of dance, and he has recently been doing fieldwork in Russia.

Lilja Blumenfeld, Estonian Academy of the Arts, Estonia, and University of Art & Design Helsinki, Finland

Lilja Blumenfeld was the Head of Scenography at the Estonian Academy of Arts from 1999–2005. She has designed extensively in Estonia and more recently in the UK. She has published articles and written essays on scenography. Her work in the School of Motion Picture, Television and Production Design involves her in the vocational training of designers and the historical and theoretical debate of that practice. She has designed more than 40 productions in different theatres in Estonia and recently designed a production of *Yerma* at Arcola Theatre, London. She has won domestic and international awards for her artwork. Her and her students' work has been exhibited in Prague several times; in WSD (World Stage Design) 2005 she presented her scenography for *Hamlet* (Drama 2005, Festival Award). Since 1998 she has been an active member of OISTAT (International Organization of Scenographers, Theatre Architects and Technicians) Education Commission, and in 2006 she was elected an interim chair for the History and Theory Commission.

Index

A Midsummer Night's Dream, 146, 176
A Streetcar Named Desire, 30, 104, 106–8, 110, 114
A Woman in Black, 168
Abel, Lionel, 182
Absurdism, 193
Action Design, 33
'Action scenography', 84
Actor(s), the, 25, 33, 186, 194, 198, 201, 205, 213, 226
   role of, 143
Actor-manager, 14, 144–45
Adelphi Theatre, London, 146
Adler, Luther, 44, 204
Adler, Stella, 38, 43, 198
Adobe Photoshop, 151–52
Aida, 170
Alexander, Eric, 11, 17
Alfreds, Mike, 167
All God's Chillum Got Wings, 129
An Indirect Critique, 239
An Inspector Calls, 174
Apollinaire, 239
Appia, Adolphe, 17, 23, 27, 116, 137–38, 143–44
Arabian Nights, 167–68
Architectonic forms, 139
Ardrey, Robert, 40, 191–93, 195–96, 198, 201–2, 205–6
Aristotle, 211, 234
Arnott, Brian, 139
Aronson, Boris, 193–94, 197
Arrabal, Fernando, 139, 142
Art and citizenship, 121
Artaud, Antonin, 67
Artist(s)

citizen, 121
   dance, 238
   role of the, 121
   theatre, 121
   visual, 213
Artistic partnership, 103, 110
Ashton, Frederick, 238
Assyria, 142
Audiences, 24–25, 27, 32, 38, 60, 112, 121, 133, 139, 143–44, 168, 170, 173, 186–87, 194, 201, 205, 218–19, 228
   as a viewer, 144
   reception, 45, 144, 175
Ayers, Lemuel, 114

Bachelard, Gaston, 63–64
Bakhtin, Mikhail, 249
Bakst, Leon, 237
Balanchine, George, 238
Ballets Russes, 233, 236–37, 239–240
Bangham, Jerry, 17
Barker, Howard, 56
Baugh, Christopher, 14
Bennett, Susan, 133
Big Night, 45
Billington, Michael, 92
Birth Rate, 184
Body(ies), 233
   imagery from, 236
   practice of, 239
   role of, 234
Bohnen, Roman, 204
Bond, Edward, 56
Bonnie and Clyde, 76

Brecht, Bertolt, 74, 121, 137, 193, 195, 197
Britten, Benjamin, 89–90, 98–99
Brook, Peter, 67, 145–46
Butler, Judith, 68–69

Cabaret, 24–25
Camino Real, 114
Carnovsky, Morris, 204
Caryl Churchill, 29
Casey Jones, 196, 198, 200–2, 205
Cat on a Hot Tin Roof, 104, 112–14
Catt, Christopher, 24–25
Chaudhuri, Una, 63–67
Cheesemond, Robert, 12, 17
Chekhov, Anton, 17, 78–79, 82
Chitty, Alison, 145–46, 175
Choreography, 235, 238
Clurman, Harold, 39–40, 42, 47–48, 192, 195–96,
    198, 202, 204–5
Cobb, Lee J., 204
Cocteau, Jean, 233, 236–39
Collaborative
    models, 103
    relationships, 110
    team, 89, 99, 114
Commedia dell'arte, 186
Communism, 42
Community, 60–61, 121
    agendas, 60
    groups, 60
    of voices, 60
Complicite, 95
Computer, 151–52
    aesthetic, 97
    psychology of, 156
Constable, Paule, 94
Constructivism, 121, 124, 126, 133
Copeland, Aaron, 205
Costume design, 124
    digital, 158
Costume designer, 26, 81, 83, 94, 151, 156
Craig, Edward Gordon, 17, 23, 30, 116, 139,
    143–44
Creative collaboration, 55, 61, 104
Crossfiring, 60
Cubofuturism, 121–22, 124, 133
    costume and stage designs, 122

Cultural assumptions, 124, 129, 133
Cyrano de Bergerac, 74
Dalcroze, Jacques, 27
Dance, 163, 233, 236
Day and Night, 129
de Certeau, Michel, 62, 68
Death of a Salesman, 110–12
Derrida, Jacques, 182
Design
    and action, 233
    concept, 108, 110, 233
    decisions, 92
    power of, 106
    principles, 110
    process, 93–94, 151–52
    role of, 24, 233
    scenic, 96, 139, 142
    symbolic, 139
    theory, 37
    vision, 108, 112, 116
Designing opera, 98
Designing space, 163, 168
Designer, the, 17, 23, 29, 31, 50, 89, 146, 240, 253
    European, 197
    methodological practice, 163
    role of the, 116
    vocabulary of the, 30
Desire Under the Elms, 129
Devised
    texts, 55–56
    work, 55
Devising, 167
Dexter, John, 145
Diaghilev, Sergei, 233, 236–40
Digital
    media, 158
    platform, 151, 156, 158
    techniques, 152
Director, the, 17, 23, 30–32, 93
    as map reader, 96
    as a painter, 96
    as a referee, 96
    as sole 'auteur', 137, 139
    as a weather forecaster, 96
    of the visual images, 138
    Oxbridge trained, 145
    role of, 137–38, 143–44, 173, 222

Director-auteur, 16
Directorial
  concept, 26
  vision, 110, 137, 144–45, 156
Directors & Designers, 11, 27, 30, 33, 55
  as a theatre artist, 116
  choices, 91
  collaboration, 31, 94, 110
  creative relationships of, 11
  creative team of, 58–59
  otherness of, 251
  relationships of, 16, 23, 27, 89, 94–95, 99, 103,
    163, 193, 245, 249, 251
Dodin, Lev, 17
Dominant ideology, 121
Donmar Studio, 91, 93
Donnellan, Declan, 17
Dorst, Tankred, 75, 78–79
Dr. Faustus, 25–26
Drama, Metadrama, and Perception, 182
Drier, Martin, 17
Dusek, Jan, 33

Easy Rider, 76
Edgar, David, 167, 172
Eliade, Mircea, 74
Elsom, John, 175
Expressionism, 193
Exter, Alexandra, 122–24

Façade, 238

Famira Kifared, 122–23
Far Away, 29
Farmer, Frances, 204
Farnes, Richard, 99
Fernando Krapp Wrote Me a Letter, 75, 78, 84
Fiesta, 49
Film, 98
  and theatre, 98
  directing, 206
  silent, 79, 84
Fine Arts, 14–15
Fisher, Rick, 141
Fitzball, Edward, 142
Flatz, Roswitha, 17
Fokine, Michel, 237

Foreman, Richard, 116
Found space, 55, 63
  in performance, 61
Freud
  gestalt psychology, 195
Frejka, Jiří, 80

Futurism, 238

Garcia, Victor, 139–40
Geddes, Norman Bel, 201
Genet, Jean, 76–78
Gentlewoman, 37, 42–43, 45–49
Geopathology, 64
Gestalt
  paradigm, 215
  theory, 215
Ghost Road Theater Ensemble, 30
Giroflé-Girofla, 126–27, 130

Gloriana, 90–91
God, Death and Time, 249
Gogol, Nikolai, 80
Golden Boy, 195–96, 198
Gordon, Michael, 202
Gorelik, Mordecai, 37–38, 40, 42, 44–45, 47–50,
    163, 191–98, 201–3, 205–6
Government Inspector, 80
Greenwood, Judith, 139
Grieves family, 14
Grotowski, Jerzy, 67
Group Theatre, the, 38, 40–46, 48, 110, 191–98,
    202, 204–6
Guys and Dolls, 31

Habima National Theatre, Tel Aviv, 74
Hahn, Reynaldo, 237
Hall, Peter, 145–46
Hamlet, 245–46, 252, 254
Heidegger, Martin, 254
Helburn, Theresa, 49
Herbert, Jocelyn, 175
Hersey, David, 139, 141
Hornby, Richard, 182
Houston, Andrew, 55
Howard, Sidney, 42
Husserl, Edmund, 13

Ideology (ies)
political, 173
Ilkhom Drama Theatre, 30
Image(s), 15, 29, 32, 139, 142, 151, 156, 194, 252
analogue, 152
digital, 15
electronic, 15
expressive, 26
of New York, 206
of society crushing the individual, 129
production, 196
reading of, 95
role of, 116
scenographic, 145–46
theatre of, 116
visceral, 33
visual and spatial, 32, 139–40, 142, 239
Interactive web site, 57, 59–60
International Federation for Theatre Research, 11
Internet, the, 96, 246
Ionesco, Eugene, 17
Irresistible Rise of Arturo Ui, 74
Irving, Henry, 14
Irwin, Kathleen, 55
Italian Renaissance Theatre, 31
Ivanov, 82

Jones, Inigo, 14–16, 173
Jones, Robert Edmund, 23, 197
Jonson, Ben, 14–16

Kafka, Franz, 74, 246
Kalman, Jean, 141
Kazan, Elia, 103, 108, 110, 112, 116, 163, 191–98, 202, 205–7
Kellam, William, 199, 203
Kinetic forms, 142
Kinetic stage, 142
King Lear, 56
Kingsley, Sidney, 38
Kircher, Athenasius, 142
Klimt, Gustav, 75
Korogodsky, Danila, 27, 29

L'Après-midi d'un Faune, 237
La Ronde, 152, 154–56
La Spectre de la Rose, 237

Labyrinth Theatre, Prague, 74–75
Lacan, Jacques, 247, 249, 253–254
Launay, Michel, 139
Lawson, John Howard, 37–38, 40–43, 45–50, 195
Le Dieu Bleu, 237–38
Le Sacre du Printemps, 236, 238
Lear, 56
Lébl, Petr, 73–84

Lecocq, Charles, 126, 129
Leijon, Jan Erik, 17
Les Miserables, 167
Les Sylphides, 237
Levin, David, 74
Levinas, Emmanuel, 248–49, 251
Lewis, Bobby, 196, 205
Lighting, 223
aesthetic of, 143
composition, 23
design, 137, 139, 143
designer, 94, 138–43, 145, 202
dimmers, 138
directing of, 139
equipment, 139
evocative nature of, 143
moving lights, 139
operators, 140
power of, 138
rig, 137
score, 79
Lloyd, Phyllida, 89–90, 92, 94–95, 98–99
Loosova, Lucie, 25–27
Louden, Andrew, 156
Lyceum, 15
Lyth, Claire, 152

Marek, Jan, 83
Marxism, 42
Mary Barton, 156–57
Mary Stuart, 89–91, 94–95, 98–99
Mass culture, 171–72
theory, 171–72
McBurney, Simon, 89, 95–98
McCallum, Heather, 17
McTeer, Janet, 93, 99
Measure for Measure, 89, 95–98
Mecklenburgisches Staatsheater, 74

Meisel, Martin, 14
Men in White, 38–39, 44, 195, 198
Mendes, Sam, 145–46
Metamorphosis, 74
Metaphor, 163, 174–75, 197–98, 201–2
   spatial, 228
Metatheatre, 182, 186
'Method' acting, 43
Methodology
   archaeological, 66
Meyerhold, Vsevolod, E., 80, 122, 126, 133, 198
Mielziner, Jo, 103–4, 106, 108, 110, 112, 114, 116
Miller, Arthur, 48, 110
Mise-en-scène, 24, 27, 110, 122, 144, 192–93, 201, 212
Mnemonic, 95
Model box, 99
Modernism, 239
Modleski, Tania, 173
Molthen, David, 32
Mood boards, 151–53, 156, 158
Morgan, Abi, 151
Morrison, Paul, 203
Moscow Art Theatre, 38
Moscow Kamerny Theatre, 121–22, 124, 130, 133
   production, 129
My Heart's In The Highlands, 205

Natalya Tarpova, 129
National Theatre, Prague, 74
Naturalism, 146, 187, 195
Nelson, Ruth, 194, 204
New media, 142
Nicholas Nickleby, 167
Nijinsky, Vaslav, 236–38
Nikolais, Alwin, 238
Noon, Katharine, 30
Nowák, William, 73, 75, 78, 82–84
Nunn, Trevor, 145

Oddey, Alison, 17
Odets, Clifford, 42, 48, 195
Odyssey Theatre, 28
Oenslager, Donald, 23, 197
On the Art of the Theatre, 23
O'Neill, Eugene, 129
Opera North, 95, 99

Optimistic Tragedy, 130, 132
Oral history, 57
Ortel, Sven, 95, 97
Ostrovsky, Aleksandr, 129
Ostuud, Erik, 17
Outcry, 104

Parade, 237–40
Pearson, Mike, 58, 61, 65
Pericles, 92
Performance
   community-based, 56, 60
   creator of, 233
   devised, 65
   postmodern, 65
   site-oriented, 55
   site-specific, 56–58, 61, 63
   text, 146
   theory of, 138
Period of Adjustment, 104
Peter Grimes, 89–91, 94, 99
Phèdre, 124–25
Phenomenology, 13, 58–59, 61–63, 245
   experience of place, 69
   of space, 64
Physical Theatre, 13
Picasso, 238
Pictorial, the, 213, 221, 223, 229
Pile, Steve, 67–68
Pirandello, Luigi, 182, 184
Piscator, Erwin, 195
Platform Event, 17
Polovtzian Dances, 237
Pons, Helena, 203
Popova, Lyubov, 126
Popular culture, 172
   feminist analysis of, 172
Postmodernism, 237
Postmodern aesthetic, 167
Post-War British Theatre Criticism, 175
Priestley, J.B., 175
Process(es)
   aesthetic, 103
   collaborative, 38, 60, 95, 104, 114
   creative, 197
   democratic, 137
   filmic, 96

of production design, 34, 37
of theatrical negotiations, 116
of theatre production, 137, 140
playing, 96
production, 167, 171, 174, 245, 248–49, 251, 253–54
rehearsal, 92, 97, 99
'theatre/archaeology', 61
visual, 169
Production sketches, 110
Psychoanalysis, 61, 63, 245
Puccini, Giacomo, 170
Pushkin Theatre, 133
Pye, Tom, 89–90, 95–96, 98

Quiet City, 196, 205–6

Racine, Jean, 124
Realism, 163, 183
Reeves, Emma, 156
Rehearsal room, 89–90, 94–96, 98, 145
  organics of the, 98–99
Reid, Francis, 17
Rhinoceros, 31
Rice, Elmer, 28
Richard III, 141–42
Ring Cycle, 92, 94
Rivera, Octavio, 17
Rocky Horror Show, 235
Role of the designer, 14
Romeo and Juliet, 122
Rostand, Edmond, 74
Royal National Theatre (RNT), 17, 89, 92, 97, 141, 146
Royal Shakespeare Company (RSC), 146
Royal Opera House, 98
Różewicz, Tadeusz, 182–83
Ryndin, Vadim, 130, 132–33

Salomé, 122–23
Saroyan, William, 205
Satie, Erik, 238
Scenic
  artists, 14, 147
  design, 106
  environment, 80

movements, 98
solution, 28
Scenographer, 58
Scenographic
  aesthetic, 142,
  components, 173, 176
  context of productions, 142
  dialogue, 30
  elements, 140, 173
  evolution, 133
  experimentations, 12
  image, 140
  impulse, 65
  practice, 233
  presentation, 174
  problems, 32
  solutions, 26
  strategies, 58
  success, 32
  task, 233
  team, 16–17, 137, 141, 144–47, 174–75
  technique, 27
  treatment, 29
  vision, 26
Scenography, 11–15, 17, 33, 58, 63, 104, 137–40, 143–44, 146–47, 163, 174, 193, 227, 247, 251, 254
  aesthetics of, 12, 133
  as stage setting, 12
  as costume, 12
  as lighting design, 12
  as sound design, 12
  as masks, 12
  as puppets, 12
  choreography of, 12
  cubofuturist, 124
  discourse of, 245
  model of, 222
  poetic of, 174
  politics of, 12
  study of, 11
Scenography International, 12
Schaeffer, Boguslaw, 182, 185–87
Schechner, Richard, 38, 67
Schiller, Friedrich, 89–90, 92
Schlemmer, Oskar, 238

Schnitzler, Arthur, 152
Semiotics, 13
Semyonov, Sergei, 130
Set designer, 73, 83
Seven Lears, 56
Shakespeare, William, 56, 89, 92, 95, 146, 234, 246
Shanks, Michael, 58, 65
Shared Experience, 141, 168
Shaw, Fiona, 89
Shaw, George Bernard, 129
Shaw, Irwin, 205
Sheherazade, 237
Shutt, Christopher, 95
Simonson, Lee, 194
Site–specific
    event, 66
    installation, 55
    practice, 65
Six Characters in Search of an Author, 184
Slapstick, 74
Slaughter on Tenth Avenue, 238
Smetana, Bedřich, 74
Smith, Art, 204
Smith, Wendy, 40
Smoláková, Vlasta, 78
Snake, 74
Socialist realism, 129
Something for Cordelia, 56
Sormova, Eva, 11
Sossi, Ron, 28–29
Soviet totalitarian government, 129
Sound designer, 95
'Spatial performativity', 59
Spatial relationship, 62
Spectacle, 14, 58, 163, 173, 186
    effect of, 168
    use of, 171
Spectacle theatre, 15, 169
Spectator(s), 17, 60, 141, 167–70, 173–75, 234, 251
St. Joan, 129
Stage designer, 24–25
Stage pictures, 99
Staging Space, 63
Stalin, Joseph, 126
Stanislavski, Constantin, 37–38, 194
    based-acting, 11
Štefková, Kateřina, 81, 83

Stenberg brothers, the, Georgii and Vladimir, 126, 129–31, 133
Stepanova, Varvara, 126
Strasberg, Lee, 37–39, 41–44, 48–49, 191–93, 205
Stravinsky, Igor, 236
Strinati, Dominic, 172
Structural realism, 121, 129–30, 133
Stuart Masques, 14
Success Story, 37–44, 46, 48
Summer and Smoke, 104, 106, 108–10, 114
Sunset Boulevard, 146
Surrealism, 193, 236
Svoboda, Josef, 73, 142
Sweet Bird of Youth, 104, 114–15
Symbolism, 187

Tairov, Alexander, 121–22, 124, 126, 129–130, 133, 206
Tarelkin's Death, 126
Tartuffe, 31
Technology, 15, 95, 129, 138, 145, 169–71
    digital, 139
    innovative, 140
    lighting, 138, 141–42
    of cameras, 95
    of change and transformation, 173
    of microphones, 95
    of video projectors, 95
    playing with, 96
    tool of, 94
    use of, 137, 140, 167, 174–75
    video, 95
Tender, 151, 153, 156
Thamar, 237
Tharp, Twyla, 138
Thatcher, Margaret, 92
The Actor, 185
The Adding Machine, 28
The Architect and the Emperor of Assyria, 139
The Art of the Theatre, 143
The Bacchae, 141–142
The Balcony, 76
The Blacks, 76
The Brandenbergers in Bohemia, 74
The Chairs, 17
The Claybank Project: Crossfiring, 57–58
The Dionysian Lear, 56, 59

The Gentle People, 205–6
The Glass Menagerie, 104–6, 110, 114
The Hairy Ape, 129–131
The Inspector Calls, 175
The Interrupted Act, 184
The Maids, 76–79, 82–84
The Man Who Was Thursday, 126, 128, 130
The Milk Train Does Not Stop Here Anymore, 104
The Old Vic, 175
The Poetics of Space, 63
The Powerbook, 89, 96–97
The Practice of Everyday Life, 62
The Pure in Heart!, 40, 42, 45, 47–48, 50
The Rose Tatoo, 145
The Seagull, 76–80, 82–84
The Seven Descents of Myrtle, 104
The Thunderstorm, 129
The Turn of the Screw, 98
The Weyburn Project, 55, 59–60
Theatre, 170, 181–82, 186–87, 201, 249
  Broadway, 197
  composition in, 226
  cultural form, 233
  epic, 195
  experience of, 236
  liveness of, 235
  of the Absurd, 182
  physical, 167–68
  popular, 171, 173
  relationship with Time, 223
  scenographic, 167
  site for cultural production, 234
  socialist realist, 133
  spatial composition in, 212
  spectacle-based, 122, 167
  temporal, 240
  'theatricality' of, 167
  West End, 167, 171
Theatre Audiences, 133
Theatre on the Balustrades, 76, 82–83
Theory/theories of
  design, 195
  plasticity, 143

semiotics, 138
  the market place, 143
Thompson, Mark, 92
Three-dimensional scenery, 23
Throckmorton, Cleon, 197
Thunder Rock, 40, 196, 198, 202, 204–5
Time and the Other, 248
Tobiáš, Egon, 74
Topoanalysis, 64
Total Theatre, 13
Totalitarianism, 133
Tröster, František, 73, 80
Turkel, Stud, 32
Tutam, 185
Twelfth Night, 152

Uncle Vanya, 17, 76, 82
Ure, Joan, 56

Vaghtangov, Yevgeny, 37
Vanstone, Hugh, 94
Vesnin, Alexander, 124–26, 128–30
Visconti, Luchino, 75
Vishnevsky, Vsevolod, 130
Vojcev, 74, 84
Vonnegut, Kurt, 74

Wagner, Richard, 30, 92
Walters, Harriet, 93, 99
Ward, Anthony, 89–92, 94–95, 99
Warner, Deborah, 89, 96, 98
Weil, Mark, 30–31
Wesele, 74, 80–81, 83
Williams, Tennessee, 103–4, 106, 108, 110, 112, 114, 116
Wilson, Robert, 116
Winterson, Jeanette, 89
Witkiewicz, Stanislaw, 182
Working, 32
Wyspiański, Stanislaw, 74, 80

Yakulov, Georgii, 126–27